TRAM ATLAS N
No

Trondheim
16

Sverige

Suomi

Norge

Tampere
96

Bergen
8

Turku
99

Helsinki
100

Oslo
20

Uppsala
95

Stockholm
76

Tallinn
118

Eesti

Norrköping
72

RU

Göteborg
64

Rīga
124

Landskrona
63

Liepāja
133

Latvija

Daugavpils
136

Aarhus
36

Danmark

Lund
58

Lietuva

Odense
42

Kaunas
140

København
44

Vilnius
142

D

RU

PL

BY

2021

AARHUS: Letbanen @ Vandtärnet (Ringvejen)

TRAM ATLAS Nordeuropa
Northern Europe

Robert Schwandl Verlag
Hektorstraße 3
D-10711 Berlin

Tel. 030 - 3759 1284 (0049 - 30 - 3759 1284)
Fax 030 - 3759 1285 (0049 - 30 - 3759 1285)

www.robert-schwandl.de
books@robert-schwandl.de

Ein großes Dankeschön an Aarne Alameri, Bernhard Kußmagk, Brendan Fox, Christoph Aders, Felix Thoma, John Hansen, Jörg Häseler, Jussi Iltanen, Kent Lindahl, Lauri Kangas, Per Gunnar Andersson, Rikard Ågren, Thomas de Laine, Thomas Johansson, Vadims Falkovs, Willy Forström and everybody who has sent me updates over the years, thanks!

Wir möchten Sie einladen, uns etwaige Fehler bzw. Veränderungen mitzuteilen, denn hoffentlich wird es in einigen Jahren eine neue, aktualisierte Ausgabe dieses Atlasses geben.
We'd like to encourage you to report any errors or updates, because hopefully in a few years, there will be a new, updated edition of this atlas.

2. Auflage 2021

Text & Netzpläne | Text & Network Maps © Robert Schwandl
    English Text by Robert Schwandl & Mark Davies
Fotos ohne Vermerk | Unlabelled photos © Robert Schwandl

Alle Angaben über Fahrpreise (2020) ohne Gewähr!
All fares listed are for 2020 and subject to change!

Druck: Königsdruck, Berlin
ISBN 978-3-936573-63-3

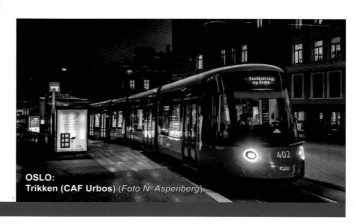

OSLO:
Trikken (CAF Urbos) *(Foto N. Aspenberg)*

STOCKHOLM: Tunnelbana (C30) @ Gärdet > Ropsten (Foto Thomas Johansson)

● VORWORT

Knapp 8 Jahre nach der ersten Ausgabe liegt nun die zweite unseres „Tram Atlas Nordeuropa" vor Ihnen. Sie ist etwas dicker geraten, obwohl wir beim Thema Obus bereits stark gestrafft haben – bei zukünftigen Ausgaben dieser Reihe (vor allem in Hinblick auf den „Tram Atlas Südosteuropa") werden wir auf Obusse überhaupt weitgehend verzichten und uns auf das eigentliche Thema, nämlich Straßenbahnen und U-Bahnen konzentrieren. Und davon gibt es in Nordeuropa immer mehr, denn mit Aarhus, Odense, Lund und Tampere kamen bzw. kommen demnächst vier neue hinzu. Auch der Ausbau der bestehenden U-Bahn- und Straßenbahn-Netze schreitet in vielen Städten rasch voran, wobei sich Helsinki mit einer Vielzahl an Projekten als die heimliche Boomtown herausgestellt hat. Im Baltikum geht es hingegen gemächlicher zu, aber auch da bringen wir Sie auf den neuesten Stand.

Trotz gründlichster Recherche mit Hilfe von Karten, Satellitenbildern, Google-Streetview und was das moderne Zeitalter noch so zu bieten hat, trotz eines erneuten Besuchs der meisten Städte in Norwegen, Dänemark und Schweden im Laufe des Corona-Jahres 2020 und Helsinki bereits 2018 und trotz der engagierten Unterstützung vieler Straßenbahnfreunde sowie einzelner Mitarbeiter der verschiedenen Verkehrsbetriebe hat sich bestimmt wieder der eine oder andere Fehler eingeschlichen. Im Hinblick auf eine dritte Ausgabe sind wir natürlich für jeden Hinweis dankbar! Wir wünschen eine gute Fahrt mit diesem Reisebegleiter!

Berlin, im Januar 2021

Robert Schwandl

STOCKHOLM: Lidingöbanan

DAUGAVPILS: Tramvajs (Foto W. Wellige)

● *FOREWORD*

About 8 years after the first edition of our 'Tram Atlas Northern Europe', you now have the completely revised second edition in your hands. It is slightly thicker than the previous edition, even though we have dedicated much less space to trolleybuses – for future editions of this series (and particularly in view of the forthcoming 'Tram Atlas Southeastern Europe') we have decided to no longer cover trolleybus systems, but instead to concentrate on our core subject, which is metros and trams. And Northern Europe has an increasing number of them, with four new systems having opened or being opened soon in Aarhus, Odense, Lund and Tampere. Many of the existing metro and tram systems are being expanded, and Helsinki with its numerous projects has turned out to be a real urban rail boomtown! The pace in the Baltic States is somewhat slower, but we will also bring you up-to-date in that region.

Despite the most thorough research with the aid of maps, satellite images, Google Street View and everything the modern era has to offer, despite personally revisiting most cities in Norway, Denmark and Sweden during the Corona year of 2020 and Helsinki already back in 2018, and despite the great support received from so many tramway enthusiasts and some tram operators, there may still be some mistakes – so in view of a future third edition, your feedback will be very much appreciated! We wish you a pleasant journey with your new travel companion!

Berlin, January 2021

Robert Schwandl

LUND: Sparväg

TALLINN: Urbos #507 @ Lennujaam > Ülemiste linnak (Foto Christopher Hecht)

HELSINKI: Artic #447 @ Mannerheimintie/Kaivokatu (Rautatieasema)

GÖTEBORG: Flexity #490 @ Saltholmen   *(Foto A. Forsberg)*

KØBENHAVN: Metro M4 @ Nordhavn

Benutzerhinweise | *User Instructions*

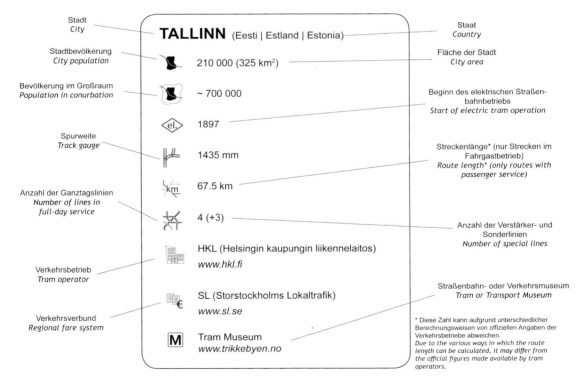

Stadt
City

Stadtbevölkerung
City population

Bevölkerung im Großraum
Population in conurbation

Spurweite
Track gauge

Anzahl der Ganztagslinien
*Number of lines in
full-day service*

Verkehrsbetrieb
Tram operator

Verkehrsverbund
Regional fare system

TALLINN (Eesti | Estland | Estonia)

210 000 (325 km²)

~ 700 000

1897

1435 mm

67.5 km

4 (+3)

HKL (Helsingin kaupungin liikennelaitos)
www.hkl.fi

SL (Storstockholms Lokaltrafik)
www.sl.se

[M] Tram Museum
www.trikkebyen.no

Staat
Country

Fläche der Stadt
City area

Beginn des elektrischen Straßen-
bahnbetriebs
Start of electric tram operation

Streckenlänge* (nur Strecken im
Fahrgastbetrieb)
Route length (only routes with
passenger service)*

Anzahl der Verstärker- und
Sonderlinien
Number of special lines

Straßenbahn- oder Verkehrsmuseum
Tram or Transport Museum

* Diese Zahl kann aufgrund unterschiedlicher
Berechnungsweisen von offiziellen Angaben der
Verkehrsbetriebe abweichen.
*Due to the various ways in which the route
length can be calculated, it may differ from
the official figures made available by tram
operators.*

Beachten Sie, dass ...

... das Zeichen **>** in den knappen Bildbeschreibungen stets
die Blickrichtung und nicht die Fahrtrichtung anzeigt.

... in Fahrzeugtabellen Ein- und Zweirichtungsfahrzeuge
durch => und <=> unterschieden werden.

... in Linienübersichten nur der Takt außerhalb der Hauptverkehrszeiten, z.B. (7-8'), angegeben wird.

Please note that ...

*.... the > sign in the short photo captions denotes the
direction of view and not the direction of travel of the
vehicle shown!*
*... in rolling stock lists, single and double-ended vehicles
are distinguished by => / <=>!*

*... in the list of lines, only the off-peak headway, e.g.
(7-8') is shown!*

LUND: Spårväg @ LTH > Universitetssjukhuset   (Foto Per Gunnar Andersson)

SKANDINAVIEN – Einleitung

Aus nordischer Sicht gehören zu Skandinavien nur die Länder Norwegen, Dänemark und Schweden, aus mitteleuropäischer Sicht rechnet man landläufig auch Finnland mit dazu. Allerdings sind die vier Länder ohnehin kein homogenes Gebilde, sondern unterscheiden sich in vielen Dingen voneinander. Norwegen, Dänemark und Schweden verbinden vor allem die sehr ähnlichen Sprachen, die gegenseitig weitgehend verstanden werden können. Deshalb reicht es auch für Besucher, Basiskenntnisse einer dieser Sprachen zu erwerben, um vor allem schriftliche Informationen leichter verstehen zu können. Finnisch ist hingegen keine germanische Sprache und deshalb auch für die übrigen Nordeuropäer unverständlich. Da hilft es manchmal, dass Finnland aufgrund seiner früheren Zugehörigkeit zu Schweden in vielen Bereichen zweisprachig ist und offizielle Informationen auch auf Schwedisch veröffentlicht werden. Als Besucher kommt man aber sonst mit Englisch überall mühelos zurecht.

Entsprechend dem allgemein höheren Preisniveau in Skandinavien ist aus mitteleuropäischer Sicht auch der überall gut ausgebaute öffentliche Nahverkehr etwas teurer, auch in Norwegen, dem einzigen Nicht-EU-Land der Region (es gehört jedoch zum Schengen-Raum). Den Euro findet man nur in Finnland, die drei anderen Länder nutzen weiterhin jeweils ihre eigene „Krone", natürlich überall mit einem anderen Wechselkurs. Allerdings ist in Nordeuropa bargeldloses Bezahlen im Vergleich zu Deutschland wesentlich weiter verbreitet und mancherorts kann nur mit Karte oder Smartphone bezahlt werden! Auch Fahrscheine sind zunehmend nur noch über Apps erhältlich!

SCANDINAVIA – Introduction

From a Nordic perspective, Scandinavia only includes Norway, Denmark and Sweden, but from a Central European perspective, Finland is generally considered a part of it, too. The four countries are not a homogeneous region, however, but differ from one another in many ways. Norway, Denmark and Sweden have very similar languages, which can be mutually understood without much effort. It is therefore sufficient for visitors to acquire some basic knowledge of one of these languages to understand, in particular, written information. Finnish, however, is not a Germanic language, and is therefore impossible to understand for other northern Europeans, too. Finland was a part of Sweden for many centuries, and as a result, is officially bilingual. For many visitors, it will therefore be helpful that a lot of official information is also published in Swedish. But generally, getting by with English is not a problem anywhere.

In accordance with the generally higher price levels in Scandinavia, from a Central European perspective, using the rather good public transport systems is slightly more expensive, also in Norway, the only non-EU country in the region (though a member of the Schengen Area). The Euro is only found in Finland, while each of the other three countries continues to use its own 'crown', with a different exchange rate in each country, of course. Cashless payment, however, is far more common in Northern Europe than in Germany for example, and in some places, only card and mobile phone payment is accepted. Increasingly, even tickets for urban transport are only available via apps.

HELSINKI: Metro @ Keilaniemi Kägeludden

Der Ausbau des städtischen Schienennahverkehrs schreitet in Nordeuropa stetig voran. Seit der ersten Auflage dieses Tram-Atlasses im Jahr 2013 ging 2017 die Stadtbahn in Aarhus in Betrieb, kürzlich – im Dezember 2020 – folgte die Straßenbahn in Lund und noch 2021 sollen auch die Straßenbahnen im dänischen Odense und im finnischen Tampere ihren Betrieb aufnehmen. Die Erweiterung der Bybane in Bergen geht kontinuierlich voran und in Oslo beginnt demnächst der Bau der Fornebubane. Kopenhagen vollendete 2019 „Cityringen", während ein Ast für die M4 sowie im Westen des Großraums die tangentiale „Letbane" im Bau sind. Stockholm eröffnete 2017 „Citybanan", das Herzstück des S-Bahn-Netzes, und beschloss außerdem den Ausbau des Tunnelbana-Netzes mit diversen Projekten. In Helsinki wurde 2017 der erste Abschnitt der „Länsimetro" abgeschlossen, der zweite befindet sich im Bau; dazu kommt die Umsetzung der tangentialen „Jokeri"-Stadtbahn sowie mehrerer Straßenbahnprojekte in den Hafengebieten. Während in Turku und Uppsala weiter konkret an neuen Straßenbahnen geplant wird, sind andere der in der ersten Auflage vorgestellten Projekte wieder in den Schubladen verschwunden, so in Aalborg, Stavanger oder Malmö.

Seit dem Ende der Zugverladung auf der Strecke über Puttgarden nach Rødby im Dezember 2019 führt eine Bahnreise nach Skandinavien stets von Hamburg über Flensburg nach Dänemark, wobei es direkte Verbindungen sowohl nach Aarhus als auch nach Kopenhagen gibt. Von Kopenhagen kommt man seit dem Jahr 2000 schnell über die Öresund-Brücke nach Malmö, von wo aus man die anderen Städte in Schweden und Norwegen auf längeren Zugfahrten erreicht, Hinweise dazu gibt es in den einzelnen Kapiteln (oder unter *www.bahn.de*).

The expansion of urban rail transport is progressing steadily in Northern Europe. Since the first edition of this tram atlas in 2013, a light rail system has been opened in Aarhus in 2017, and more recently – in December 2020 – trams started running in Lund. Still in 2021, the first trams will also start operating in Odense (Denmark) and Tampere (Finland). The expansion of the Bybane network in Bergen is continuing and in Oslo the construction of the Fornebubane is about to start. Copenhagen completed its 'Cityringen' in 2019, while a branch for line M4 as well as the tangential 'Letbane' in the west of the conurbation are under construction. In 2017, Stockholm opened 'Citybanan', the heart of the S-Bahn network, and decided to expand the Tunnelbana network with various projects. In Helsinki, the first section of the 'Länsimetro' was brought into service in 2017, while the second section is under construction; in addition, the implementation of the tangential 'Jokeri' light rail line and several tram projects in the port areas are underway. While new tram systems are being planned in Turku and Uppsala, a number of other projects presented in the first edition of this atlas have been shelved, for example in Aalborg, Stavanger and Malmö.

Since the end of the train ferry between Puttgarden and Rødby in December 2019, all train journeys to Scandinavia have run from Hamburg via Flensburg to Denmark, with direct services to Aarhus and Copenhagen. On the Öresund Bridge, which opened in 2000, it is just a quick hop from Copenhagen to Malmö in Sweden, from where other cities in Sweden and Norway can be reached on longer train journeys; information on this can be found in each chapter of this book (or check train times at www.bahn.de).

Variobahn #201 @ Birkelandsskiftet

BERGEN

Bergen ist Norwegens zweitgrößte Stadt und liegt im äußersten Westen des Landes. Rund viermal täglich kommt man mit den Zügen der norwegischen Staatsbahn Vy (vormals NSB) von Oslo nach Bergen (484 km, ca. 7 Stunden). Auf der kurzen Strecke zwischen Bergen und Arna pendelt 2-3 Mal pro Stunde ein *Lokaltog* durch den 7,7 km langen Ulrikentunnel (seit Dezember 2020 im Skyss-Verbundtarif!). Dazu kommen etwa stündlich Regionalzüge nach Voss, einige davon fahren weiter bis Myrdal, wo man zur bekannten *Flåmsbana* umsteigen kann.

Der Nahverkehr im ehemaligen *Fylke* (Bezirk) Hordaland (jetzt Teil von Vestland) wird von *Skyss* organisiert. Für Besucher bieten sich eine 24-Stunden-Karte (*24-timarsbillett*) für 100 NOK (10 €) oder 90 Minuten gültige Einzelfahrscheine für 39 NOK (60 NOK beim Busfahrer) an, beide sind an Automaten als elektronische Einweg-Tickets erhältlich und müssen in der Stadtbahn entwertet werden. Für andere Fahrscheine braucht man eine *Skysskortet* (z.B. eine 7-Tage-Karte für nur 250 NOK), diese ist jedoch für Besucher nicht unmittelbar erhältlich. Alle Tickets gibt es natürlich auch über die App „Skyss Billett". Diese Preise gelten 2020 für die *Sone A* (ganz Bergen), in der die gesamte Stadtbahnstrecke (auch nach Erweiterung nach Fyllingsdalen und später nach Åsane) liegt.

Bergen, located in the extreme west of the country, is Norway's second largest city. National rail operator Vy (formerly known as NSB) runs about four trains a day between Oslo and Bergen (484 km, 7 hours). The short stretch between Bergen and Arna has 2-3 'Lokaltog' services per hour through the 7.7 km Ulrikentunnel (since Dec 2020, part of the Skyss fare system!). There are also hourly regional trains to Voss, with some continuing to Myrdal, where transfer to the famous Flåmsbana is provided.

Public transport in the former Fylke (county) of Hordaland (now part of Vestland) is administered by 'Skyss'. For visitors, a 24-hour pass (24-timarsbillett) sells for 100 NOK (€10), while single tickets valid for 90 minutes cost 39 NOK (60 NOK from the bus driver). Both types of tickets are sold as single-use electronic tickets from vending machines and have to be activated inside the vehicles. Other tickets (like a 7-day ticket for just 250 NOK) require a rechargeable Skysskortet, which visitors cannot acquire on the spot. All tickets are available via the 'Skyss Billett' app, of course. The prices shown are valid in 2020 for 'Sone A', which inludes all of Bergen municipality and thus the entire light rail line (even after the system's expansion to Fyllingsdalen and Åsane).

Variobahn #205 @ Rastølen

Bybanen – Stadtbahn

Am 22. Juni 2010 kehrte ein städtisches schienengebundenes Verkehrsmittel in Form einer modernen Stadtbahn nach Bergen zurück. Von 1897 bis 1965 gab es in Bergen bereits ein elektrisches Straßenbahnnetz, das allerdings kaum über den inneren Stadtbereich hinausreichte. Die neue Stadtbahn verkehrt in der Innenstadt wie eine Straßenbahn, teils wird die Trasse von Bussen mitgenutzt, nur kurze Abschnitte dürfen vom Individualverkehr befahren werden.

Bybanen – Light Rail

On 22 June 2010, urban rail transport returned to Bergen in the form of a modern light rail system. From 1897 to 1965, Bergen had already had an electric tram network, but it was limited to the inner city. The new Bybanen [city railway] runs like a tramway in the inner city, with parts of its route being shared with buses, while only some short sections may be used by private motor vehicles, too. Most of the route from about Nygård

BERGEN (Norge | Norwegen | Norway)

 285 000 (445 km²)

 ~ 350 000

 Tram – 2010; Trolleybus – 1950

 1435 mm

 Tram – 20.4 km; Trolleybus – 7.2 km

 Tram – 1; Trolleybus – 1

 Bybanen – www.bybanen.no

 Skyss – www.skyss.no

 Tram Museum – www.bergenstekniskemuseum.no

NSB Lokaltog @ Bergen

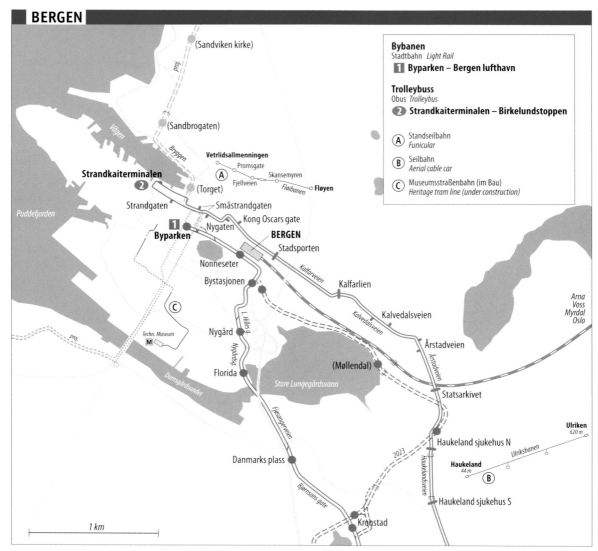

Bybanen
Stadtbahn *Light Rail*
1 **Byparken – Bergen lufthavn**

Trolleybuss
Obus *Trolleybus*
2 **Strandkaiterminalen – Birkelundstoppen**

(A) Standseilbahn
Funicular

(B) Seilbahn
Aerial cable car

(C) Museumsstraßenbahn (im Bau)
Heritage tram line (under construction)

Der größte Teil der Strecke, südwärts ab etwa Nygård, ist vom Autoverkehr getrennt, allerdings gibt es zahlreiche niveaugleiche Kreuzungen, an denen die Stadtbahn jedoch in der Regel durch Ampelbeeinflussung Vorfahrt genießt. Die Fahrgäste überqueren die Gleise an allen Haltestellen.

southwards is separated from road traffic, although there are numerous level crossings where trains are given priority through direct traffic light control. Passengers have to cross the tracks at each station.

Variobahn #208 © Bergen lufthavn

Variobahn #213 @ Inndalsveien (Wergeland > Brann stadion)

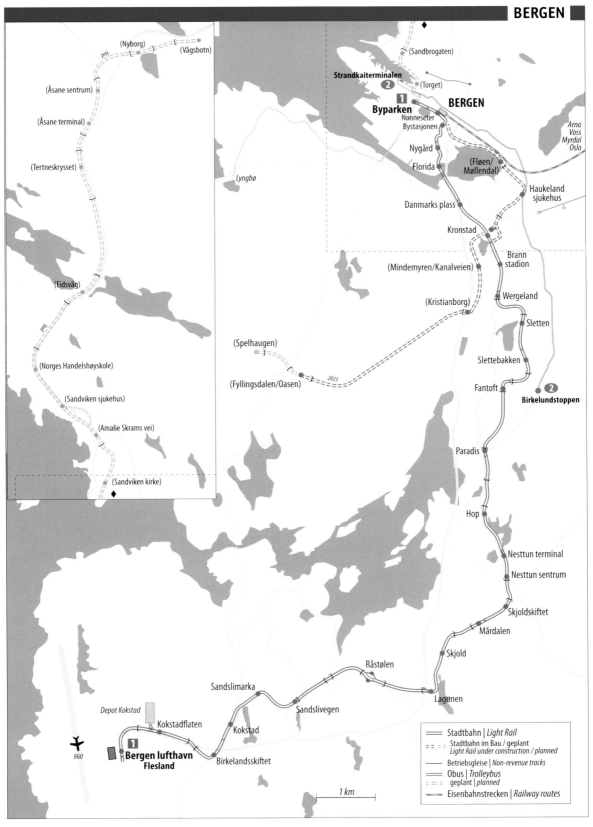

(Nyborg)
(Vågsbotn)
proj.
(Åsane sentrum)
(Åsane terminal)
(Tertneskrysset)
Lyngbø
(Eidsvåg)
proj.
(Norges Handelshøyskole)
(Sandviken sjukehus)
(Amalie Skrams vei)
(Sandviken kirke)

(Sandbrogaten)
Strandkaiterminalen
2
1
Byparken
BERGEN
(Torget)
Nonneseter
Bystasjonen
Nygård
Florida
(Fløen/ Møllendal)
Arna
Voss
Myrdal
Oslo
Haukeland sjukehus
Danmarks plass
Kronstad
Brann stadion
(Mindemyren/Kanalveien)
Wergeland
(Kristianborg)
Sletten
(Spelhaugen)
Slettebakken
(Fyllingsdalen/Oasen)
2023
Fantoft
2
Birkelundstoppen
Paradis
Hop
Nesttun terminal
Nesttun sentrum
Skjoldskiftet
Mårdalen
Skjold
Råstølen
Lagunen
Sandslimarka
Sandslivegen
Depot Kokstad
Kokstadflaten
Kokstad
1
Bergen lufthavn Flesland
BGO
Birkelandsskiftet

	Stadtbahn | Light Rail
	Stadtbahn im Bau / geplant Light Rail under construction / planned
	Betriebsgleise | Non-revenue tracks
	Obus | Trolleybus
	geplant | planned
	Eisenbahnstrecken | Railway routes

1 km

Variobahn #202 @ Nesttun terminal

Auf der aktuellen 20,4 km langen Strecke liegen insgesamt elf signalgesteuerte Tunnelabschnitte. Mit 1110 m ist der Fantofttunnel der längste. Die Stadtbahn wurde teilweise durch eine City-Maut finanziert. Für den Betrieb ist *Keolis Norge AS* zuständig.

Die ursprüngliche Strecke Byparken – Nesttun (9,8 km) wurde am 22. Juni 2013 bis Lagunen (3,4 km) und am 15. August 2016 bis Birkelandsskiftet (4,8 km) verlängert, bevor sie schließlich am 22. April 2017 den Flughafen in Flesland (2,4 km) erreichte. Darauf sollte eine Verlängerung von der Innenstadt nach Norden bis Åsane folgen, jedoch wurde dann der Bau der Strecke nach Fyllingsdalen vorgezogen, während die Detailplanung der Nordstrecke fortgesetzt wird.

Die zweite Linie zweigt am Busbahnhof von der Bestandsstrecke ab, führt dann am Nordufer des Store

Along the currently 20.4 km line there are 11 tunnel sections with railway signals. At 1110 m, the Fantofttunnel is the longest. The light rail line was partially funded by the city's congestion charge. Keolis Norge AS is responsible for the day-to-day operation.

The original route from Byparken to Nesttun (9.8 km) was extended to Lagunen on 22 June 2013 (3.4 km) and to Birkelandsskiftet (4.8 km) on 15 August 2016 before reaching the airport at Flesland on 22 April 2017 (2.4 km). After that, a northern extension to Åsane was supposed to follow, but the route to Fyllingsdalen was then given priority, while detailed planning for the northern route continues.

The second line diverges from the existing line at the bus station, running along the north bank of the Store

Variobahn #208 @ Nygård (> Bystasjonen)

Variobahn #201 & 213 @ Bergen lufthavn

Variobahn #218 @ Sandslivegen

Lungegårdsvann entlang, um dann unterirdisch das Krankenhaus Haukeland zu erschließen. Im Bereich des ursprünglichen Betriebshofs Kronstad kreuzt sie die Linie 1 eine Ebene tiefer auf einer ehemaligen Güterbahntrasse und führt dann entlang des Kanalveien nach Süden zur Haltestelle Kristiansborg. Von hier folgt ein rund 3 km langer Tunnel durch den Berg Løvstakken, parallel dazu wird ein Rad-/Fußgängertunnel errichtet. Die Strecke endet vorerst kurz nach der Tunnelausfahrt am Einkaufszentrum Oasen, nachdem eine Weiterführung bis Spelhaugen aus Kostengründen zurückgestellt wurde.

Auf der Bybanen sind Zweirichtungs-Variobahnen von Stadler Pankow unterwegs. Die 100%-niederflurigen Fahrzeuge haben eine Fußbodenhöhe von 350 mm, im Türbereich 315 mm. Die ersten 20 Fahrzeuge waren ursprünglich fünfteilig und wurden 2017 mit zwei Mittelmodulen verlängert, während die letzten acht bereits als siebenteilige Variobahnen geliefert wurden.

Lungegårdsvann before serving the Haukeland Hospital with an underground station. In the area of the original Kronstad depot, line 2 intersects with line 1, with the new line running on the lower level on a former freight railway alignment. It then turns south along Kanalveien to the Kristiansborg stop, from where it enters a 3 km tunnel through the Løvstakken mountain, parallel to which a cycle/pedestrian tunnel is also being built. The route ends shortly after the tunnel exit at the Oasen shopping centre, with an extension to Spelhaugen having been shelved for financial reasons.

Bybanen is operated with bi-directional Variobahn vehicles from Stadler Pankow. The 100% low-floor vehicles feature a floor height of 350 mm above the rail and 315 mm at the doors. The initial 20 vehicles had five sections, but they were extended in 2017 with two additional centre modules, while the last eight vehicles were delivered as seven-section trams.

Variobahn

Bybanen > Fahrzeuge | *Rolling Stock* (750 V DC)

Nummer *Number*	Anzahl *Quantity*	Hersteller *Manufacturer*	Typ *Class*	Länge *Length*	Breite *Width*	Ausgeliefert *Delivered*
201-220*	20	Stadler	Variobahn <=>	42.0 m*	2.65 m	2009-2013
221-228	8	Stadler	Variobahn <=>	42.0 m	2.65 m	2016

* ursprünglich 32 m, 2017 verlängert auf 42 m | *initially 32 m, extended to 42 m in 2017*

Im ehemaligen Straßenbahndepot in Møhlenpris ist *Bergens Tekniske Museum* mit seiner ***Trikkebyen*** [Tramstadt] untergebracht, von wo auf einer kurzen Strecke zeitweise Fahrten mit den Wagen BS 10 und 47 (ex Oslo 74) sowie Reko-Wagen aus Berlin durchgeführt werden. Der Weiterbau ins Stadtzentrum wird seit längerer Zeit von Freiwilligen vorangetrieben, an mehreren Stellen liegt bereits ein Gleis in der Straße.

Reko-Wagen #62 (ex Berlin)

The 'Bergen Tekniske Museum' is housed in the former tram depot at Møhlenpris with its ***Trikkebyen*** [tramway city]. From there, Reko cars from Berlin as well as BS 10 and 47 (ex Oslo 74) cars offer heritage journeys on a short line. For a long time, volunteers have been working to bring the line into the city centre, and in several places a track can already be seen in the roadway.

(Foto Bernhard Kußmagk)

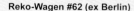

MAN Trolleybus #8196 @ Østre Murallmenningen (Strandkaiterminalen)

Obus

Bis zur Inbetriebnahme der Obuslinie im schwedischen Landskrona war der Obusbetrieb in Bergen lange Zeit der einzige in Skandinavien. In Norwegen fuhr dieses Verkehrsmittel erstmals bereits 1909 in Drammen (bis 1967), später auch in Oslo (1940-1968) und Stavanger (1947-1963).

Die in Bergen im Jahr 1950 in Betrieb genommene Obuslinie 5 wurde 1994 auf Dieselbetrieb umgestellt, so dass heute als einzige Obuslinie die Linie 2 verbleibt, welche 1957 die ehemalige Straßenbahnlinie 2 nach Fridalen ersetzte. Für die knapp über 7 km lange Strecke standen zuletzt nur noch einzelne Niederflur-Gelenkbusse vom Typ N6221 von MAN/Neoplan mit einer elektrischen Ausrüstung von Kiepe zur Verfügung, doch 2020 wurden zehn Trollino-18-Busse von Solaris ausgeliefert. Diese sind mit Batterien ausgestattet, womit eine Verlängerung der Linie auch ohne Oberleitung möglich ist, etwa über Møhlenpris nach Lyngbø (Laksevåg).

Trolleybus

Until the opening of the trolleybus line in Landskrona, Sweden, Bergen had for a long time been the only city in Scandinavia to retain this means of transport. In Norway, trolleybuses first ran in Drammen (1909-1967), arriving later in Oslo (1940-1968) and Stavanger (1947-1963).

In 1950, line 5 became Bergen's first trolleybus route, but its conversion to diesel operation in 1994 left line 2, which had been introduced later, as the only remaining one. It was launched in 1957, when it replaced the old tram line 2 to Fridalen. For the single route, which is just over 7 km long, only a few low-floor articulated buses of type N6221 from MAN/Neoplan with electric equipment from Kiepe were available until 2020, when ten Trollino 18 vehicles ordered from Solaris arrived. These are equipped with batteries to allow extensions of the line without overhead wires, for example via Møhlenpris to Lyngbø (Laksevåg).

Fløibanen – Blick von der Bergstation | *View from the upper terminus*

Fløibanen

Die Fløibane führt vom Stadtzentrum auf den 320 m hohen Hausberg Fløyen. Dabei handelt es sich um eine konventionelle eingleisige Standseilbahn mit Ausweiche in der Mitte. Sie wurde 1918 in Betrieb genommen und erfüllt mit ihren drei, nicht symmetrisch angeordneten Zwischenstationen auch eine städtische Verkehrsfunktion, ist jedoch nicht ins Tarifsystem von *Skyss* integriert. Ihre Hauptaufgabe liegt darin, Touristen schnell und bequem auf den Berg zu bringen, von wo sie die großartige Aussicht über die Stadt und Umgebung genießen können. Die Bahn wurde 2002 grundlegend saniert, aus dieser Zeit stammen auch die aktuellen Fahrzeuge. 2021 kostet eine Berg- und Talfahrt 100 NOK.

The Fløibane runs from the city centre up to the 320 m high Fløyen Mountain. It is a conventional single-track cable-hauled funicular with a passing loop in the middle. It was brought into operation in 1918, and with its three, asymmetrically located intermediate stations, it also fulfils an urban transport function, although it is not integrated into the Skyss fare system. Its main task, however, is to take tourists quickly and easily to the mountain top, from where they can enjoy a great view of the city and its surroundings. The railway was modernised in 2002, when the current vehicles were also purchased. At present in 2021, a return journey costs 100 NOK.

Fløibanen – Talstation | *lower terminus*

Fløibanen – Talstation | *lower terminus*

LHB #96 @ St. Olavs gate   (Foto Julian Ryf)

TRONDHEIM

Norwegens drittgrößte Stadt liegt etwa 500 km nördlich von Oslo im *Fylke* Trøndelag. Eine Bahnfahrt (viermal pro Tag, 551,3 km) dauert fast sieben Stunden. Diese Fahrten werden seit Juni 2020 von der Bahngesellschaft NORD (Teil der schwedischen SJ) durchgeführt, welche nach Ausschreibung des norwegischen Bahnverkehrs auch in der Region Trondheim als „Trønderbane" etwa stündlich Regionalzüge betreibt, auf der Nordstrecke über den Flughafen Værnes bis Steinkjer, auf der Südstrecke bis Melhus Skysstasjon, Lundamo oder Støren. In den kommenden Jahren soll dieser Korridor abschnittsweise zweigleisig ausgebaut und elektrifiziert werden. Drei Züge täglich fahren in den hohen Norden nach Mo i Rana, zwei davon weiter bis Bodø. Zweimal täglich kommt man auch an den Grenzbahnhof Storlien, wo Anschluss ins schwedische Östersund und weiter nach Sundsvall besteht.

Für den Bus- und Straßenbahnverkehr in Trøndelag ist *AtB* verantwortlich. Für die *Sone A* (Trondheim und einzelne Nachbargemeinden) gelten 2020 folgende Fahrpreise: Einzelfahrscheine (90 Minuten) - 40 NOK; 24-Stunden-Karte - 120 NOK, erhältlich in Kiosken oder im Kundencenter. Für andere Zeitkarten (z.B. eine 7-Tage-Karte für 280 NOK) benötigt man die elektronische *t:kort* oder die App „AtB Mobillett".

Norway's third largest city is located about 500 km north of Oslo in the Fylke (county) of Trøndelag. The train journey from Oslo (four times a day, 551.3 km) takes almost seven hours. Since June 2020, these trains have been operated by NORD (a subsidiary of the Swedish SJ), which also runs local trains (branded 'Trønderbane') in the Trondheim region roughly every hour: on the northern line to Steinkjer with a stop at the airport at Værnes, and on the southern line to Melhus Skysstasjon, Lundamo or Støren. In the mid-term future, this corridor will become partly double-track and electrified. Three trains a day run further north to Mo i Rana, with two of them continuing to Bodø. Two trains a day also go to the border station Storlien, where connections via Östersund to Sundsvall in Sweden are available.

Bus and tram transport in Trøndelag is the responsibility of AtB. For 'Sone A' (Trondheim and some adjacent municipalities), the following fares are valid in 2020: single tickets (90 minutes) - 40 NOK; 24-hour passes - 120 NOK — these are available at kiosks and the Customer Centre. For other season tickets (e.g. a 7-day ticket for 280 NOK), the electronic 't:kort' or the 'AtB Mobillett' app is necessary.

Regionalzug | *Regional train* @ Værnes (Airport) (2013)

TS (Trondhejms Sporvei) #33 (1951) @ Sporveismuseet (Munkvoll)

TRONDHEIM (Norge | Norwegen | Norway)

- 205 000 (496 km²)
- ~ 220 000
- (1901) 1924
- 1000 mm
- 8.8 km
- 1
- Gråkallbanen/Boreal
  www.boreal.no
- AtB
  www.atb.no
- M Tram Museum
  – sporveishistoriskforening.no

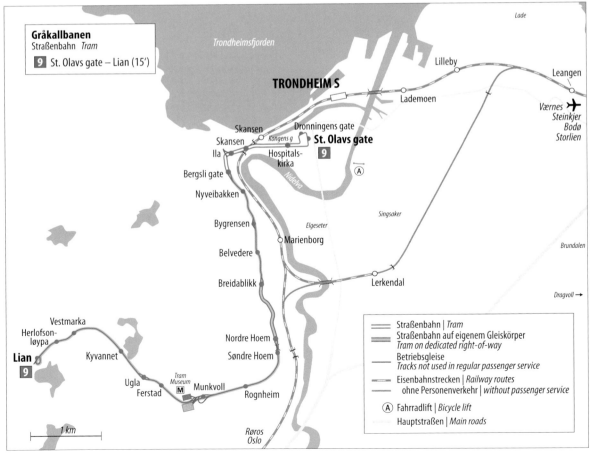

Gråkallbanen
Straßenbahn *Tram*

9 St. Olavs gate – Lian (15′)

Legend:
- Straßenbahn | *Tram*
- Straßenbahn auf eigenem Gleiskörper | *Tram on dedicated right-of-way*
- Betriebsgleise | *Tracks not used in regular passenger service*
- Eisenbahnstrecken | *Railway routes*
- ohne Personenverkehr | *without passenger service*
- Ⓐ Fahrradlift | *Bicycle lift*
- Hauptstraßen | *Main roads*

LHB #93 @ Nyveibakken *(Foto Julian Ryf)*

Gråkallbanen

Die heutige Straßenbahnstrecke von Trondheim verbindet das Stadtzentrum mit den nicht sehr dicht besiedelten Wohngebieten im Westen am Rand der Bymarka, die Strecke steigt dabei auf über 250 m über dem Meeresspiegel an. Auf dem mittleren Abschnitt kann man die schöne Aussicht über das Nidelva-Tal, die Stadt und den Fjord genießen. Die von einer privaten Gesellschaft errichtete Strecke wurde etappenweise in Betrieb genommen, am 18. Juli 1924 bis Munkvoll, 1925 bis Ugla und schließlich 1933 bis Lian, der namensgebende Berg Gråkallen etwa 4 km weiter nordwestlich wurde nie erreicht.

In Trondheim gab es allerdings bereits seit 1901 eine städtische elektrische Straßenbahn, die Linie 1 verlief von Ila über das Stadtzentrum in den östlichen Stadtteil Lademoen. Die Gleise wurden zwischen Ila und St. Olavs gate von der Gråkallbanen mitgenutzt. Später kamen noch eine Strecke vom Bahnhof nach Süden bis Elgeseter und ein Abzweig nach Singsaker hinzu. Die erste Linie wurde schließlich 1958 bis Lade verlängert. Im Laufe der 1960er Jahre erwarb die Stadt immer mehr Anteile an der Gråkallbanen, bis diese 1971 vollständig in das städtische Netz eingegliedert wurde.

Bis 1983 wurden alle Strecken außer Lian – Lade eingestellt und neue Fahrzeuge bestellt, jedoch kam wenige Jahre nach deren Anlieferung 1988 auch das Aus für diese Linie. Unter dem Druck der Bevölkerung und

Trondheim's only tram line connects the city centre with the rather sparsely populated residential areas in the west on the edge of the Bymarka, with the altitude of the line increasing from sea level to about 250 m. Along the middle section, passengers can enjoy a beautiful view of the Nidelva valley, the city and the fjord. Built by a private company, the line was put into operation in stages, on 18 July 1924 to Munkvoll, in 1925 to Ugla and finally in 1933 to Lian. The namesake mountain, Gråkallen, which lies about 4 km further northwest, was never reached.

Trondheim, however, had an urban electric tramway from as early as 1901 — line 1 from Ila via the city centre to the eastern district of Lademoen. The tracks between Ila and St. Olavs gate were shared with the Gråkallbanen. Later, a route from the railway station south to Elgeseter as well as a branch to Singsaker were added. The first line was eventually extended to Lade in 1958. During the 1960s, the city acquired more and more shares in the Gråkallbanen, until in 1971, it was fully integrated into the urban tram network.

Although by 1983, every route except Lian – Lade had been abandoned, new vehicles had still been ordered. However, in 1988, only a few years after their delivery, the remaining line was also closed down. Under popular pressure, and given the fact that the still almost new

Tram > Fahrzeuge | *Rolling Stock* (600 V DC)							
Nummer *Number*	Anzahl *Quantity*	Hersteller *Manufacturer*	Typ *Class*	Länge *Length*	Breite *Width*	Ausgeliefert *Delivered*	
93-97, 99	6	Linke-Hoffmann-Busch (LHB)	LHB GT6 =>	20.0 m	2.60 m	1984-1985	

LHB #95 @ Søndre Hoem > Nordre Hoem   (Foto Felix Thoma, 2013)

angesichts der Tatsache, dass die fast neuen Fahrzeuge mit 2,60 m Breite bei Meterspur nicht zu verkaufen waren, wurde der westliche Teil, die ursprüngliche Gråkallbanen, am 18. August 1990 wiedereröffnet. Sie wird heute von der privaten *Boreal Bane AS* als Linie 9 betrieben. Während auf dem Innenstadtabschnitt die Gleise in der Fahrbahn der Kongens gate liegen, verläuft die Strecke ab Ila (Gleisdreieck) eingleisig auf eigenem Gleiskörper abseits von Straßen mit mehreren Ausweichmöglichkeiten.

Ein kleines Museum erwartet Straßenbahnfreunde in den Sommermonaten gegenüber vom Depot in Munkvoll.

metre-gauge vehicles with an unusual width of 2.60 m were impossible to sell, the western part of the line, i.e. the original Gråkallbanen, was reopened on 18 August 1990. It is now operated as line 9 by a private company called 'Boreal Bane AS'. While in the city centre, the tracks are embedded in the roadway of Kongens gate, from Ila, where there is a track triangle, the route runs single-track on a separate right-of-way with several passing loops.

A small museum located opposite the tram depot in Munkvoll, is open for tram enthusiasts during the summer months.

LHB #96 @ Tordenskiolds gate (Hospitalskirka > St. Olavs gate)   (Foto Julian Ryf)

Trikken: Ansaldo SL95 #162 @ Bjørvika (Aug. 2020)

OSLO

Die norwegische Hauptstadt (bis 1924 Christiania bzw. Kristiania) liegt an der nördlichen Spitze des Oslofjords. Per Bahn erreicht man Oslo von Deutschland aus nur mit mehrmaligem Umsteigen, mindestens in Kopenhagen und Göteborg. Alternativ kann man auch mit der Fähre ab Kiel anreisen.

Während alle von der T-bane erschlossenen Gebiete im Osten und Südosten innerhalb der Stadtgemeinde liegen, gehören die Vororte westlich des Lysakerelva zur Gemeinde Bærum (Hauptort Sandvika), jedoch umfasst das Tarifgebiet Oslo („Sone 1") das gesamte T-bane-Netz (aber nicht alle anschließenden Buslinien!). Wie Bærum gehörten die übrigen Nachbarkommunen zum *Fylke* (Bezirk) Akershus (540.000 Einw.), welches im Zuge einer Gebietsreform zum 1. Januar 2020 im *Fylke* Viken aufging. Im Großraum von Oslo (Stor-Osloregionen), der von Drammen im Westen bis an die schwedische Grenze im Osten reicht, leben insgesamt etwa 1,5 Mio. Menschen, fast ein Drittel der Gesamtbevölkerung Norwegens.

Das Osloer Schienen-verkehrsnetz besteht aus Straßenbahn (*trikk*), U-Bahn (*T-bane*) und S-Bahn (*lokaltog*). Der kommunale

The Norwegian capital (until 1924 Christiania or Kristiania) is located at the northern tip of the Oslo Fjord. A train journey from Central Europe to Oslo is only possible with several transfers, at least in Copenhagen and Gothenburg. Another option is to take the ferry from Kiel.

While the areas in the east and southeast served by the T-bane lie within the municipal boundaries, the suburbs west of the Lysakerelva belong to the municipality of Bærum (with Sandvika as its centre), but the Oslo fare zone (sone 1) covers the entire T-bane network (though not the connecting buses!). Like Bærum, the other neighbouring municipalities used to be part of the 'fylke' (county) of Akershus (540,000 inhabitants), which was integrated into the new 'fylke' of Viken on 1 January 2020. Oslo's larger metropolitan region (Stor-Osloregionen), which extends from Drammen in the west to the Swedish border in the east, is home to some 1.5 million people, nearly a third of Norway's total population.

Oslo's urban rail network includes trams (trikk), metro (T-bane) and suburban trains (lokaltog). The municipal transport company, which was

T-banen: Siemens MX3x73 @ Frognerseteren

T-bane: Siemens MX3x19 & 3x65 @ Hauger (Kolsåsbanen)

Verkehrsbetrieb, vormals *Kollektivtransportproduksjon AS*, tritt seit 2013 als *Sporveien* auf und ist für den Betrieb sowie die Instandhaltung bzw. den Ausbau der Infrastruktur verantwortlich.

Für die Koordination des Personennahverkehrs in Oslo und im früheren Bezirk Akershus ist *Ruter* verantwortlich. Anders als in den übrigen Großstädten Norwegens wird hier ein echter Verkehrsverbund wie in Deutschland angeboten, d.h. auch die Nahverkehrszüge der staatlichen Vy (ex-NSB) sowie zahlreiche Fähren sind voll in das Zonentarifsystem

formerly known as 'Kollektivtransportproduksjon AS', was renamed 'Sporveien' in 2013. It is responsible for the operation as well as the maintenance and expansion of the infrastructure.

'Ruter' is responsible for the coordination of public transport in Oslo as well as the former 'fylke' of Akershus. Unlike in the other major cities in Norway, 'Ruter' offers a fully integrated zonal fare system, which also includes local and regional trains operated by the national railway company Vy (ex NSB) as well as numerous

OSLO (Norge | Norwegen | Norway)

 695 000 (454 km²)   ~ 1 000 000

 Tram - 1894; T-bane - 1898

 1435 mm

 Tram ~ 42 km; T-bane ~ 85 km
(Jar – Bekkestua: 2.4 km gemeinsam | shared)

 Tram - 6; T-bane - 5

 Sporveien - www.sporveien.com
   Trikken - www.trikken.no
   T-bane - www.tbanen.no

 Ruter - www.ruter.no

 Tram Museum - www.sporveismuseet.no

SL79 #140 @ Sandakerveien   (Foto Svein Fröne, 2021)

integriert, welches sich in die Zone 1 (Oslo und das östliche Gebiet von Bærum) und bis zu drei weitere Zonen in jede Himmelsrichtung unterteilt (z.B. liegt der Flughafen Gardermoen in Zone 4N). Bei längeren Fahrten werden maximal fünf Zonen berechnet.

Für Besucher bietet sich für die Zone 1 eine 24-Stunden-Karte für 114 NOK an, Einzelfahrscheine kosten 38 NOK im Vorverkauf, beim Fahrer jedoch 20 NOK mehr. Beides bekommt man in Kiosken als elektronische Einwegkarten (Automaten in U-Bahn-Stationen verschwinden Mitte 2021!). Wer länger bleibt, besorgt sich erst für 50 NOK an Kiosken oder in Kundenzentren eine aufladbare *Reisekort* und lädt diese mit einer 7-Tages-Karte für 320 NOK oder nutzt die App „RuterBillett".

[100 NOK = 9.44 €]

ferries. The region is subdivided into zone 1 (Oslo and the eastern part of Bærum) and up to three additional zones in each direction (e.g. Gardermoen Airport is in zone 4N). For trips across the region, a maximum of 5 zones is charged.

For visitors, a 24-hour pass for zone 1 for 114 NOK is recommended. Single tickets cost 38 NOK if bought in advance, and 20 NOK extra if bought from the driver. Single tickets and 24-hour passes are available from kiosks as single-use electronic cards (ticket vending machines in metro stations will disappear in mid-2021!). For longer stays, a 7-day pass for 320 NOK is a good option, but it requires a rechargeable 'Reisekort', which is sold for 50 NOK at customer service centres and in kiosks; or simply use the 'RuterBillett' app.

* dauerhaft außer Betrieb | *permanently out of service*
X vorübergehend außer Betrieb | *temporarily out of service*

OSLO

Sognsvann

Norsk Teknisk Museum

Kjelsås

Kjelsås 11 12

Kjelsåsalleen

Grefsen stadion

Kringsjå

Holstein

Grefsenplatået

Østhorn

Nydalen

Glads vei

Tåsen

Doktor Smiths vei

Berg

Nydalen

Storo

Disen

Frognerseteren

Vettakollen

Gulleråsen

Gråkammen

Slemdal

Ris

Gaustad

Vinderen

Steinerud

Borgen

Frøen

Rikshospitalet 17 18

Gaustadalleen

Forskningsparken

Ullevål stadion

Grefsenveien

Grefsen

Grefsen stasjon 17 18

Sinsenkrysset

Universitetet Blindern

Sandaker senter

Sinsen

Blindern

John Colletts plass

Torshov

Sinsenterrassen

Løren

Ullevål sykehus

proj.

Ring 2

Vestli 4

Adamstuen

Biermanns gate

Rosenhoff

Tram Museum

Stensgata

Birkelunden

Carl Berners plass

Carl Berners plass

Hasle

Majorstuen 11 12 19

Bislett

Olaf Ryes plass

Sofienberg

Vestli 5

Frogner stadion

Bogstadveien

Rosenborg

Homansbyen

Dalsbergstien

Welhavensgate

Frydenlund

Schous plass

Lakkegata skole

Tøyen

Vigelandsparken

Frognerplass

Lilleaker Bekkestua 13

Elisenberg

Briskeby

Riddervolds plass

Holbergs plass

Heimdalsgata

Helsfyr (Bergkrystallen) 1

Ellingsrudåsen 2

Mortensrud 3

Bergkrystallen 4

Nobels gate

Niels Juels gate

Lille Frogner allé

Inkognitogata

Nationaltheatret

Tullinløkka

Tinghuset

Stortinget 3

Stor-torvet

Storgata

Nybrua

Lilletorget

Tøyen

Ensjø

Skarpsno

Solli

Ruseløkka

Jernbanetorget

Grønland

Skillebekk

Aker brygge

Kontra-skjæret

Øvre Slottsgate

Dronningens gate

OSLO S

22

Bjørvika

Middelalderparken

Oslo Hospital

Ekebergparken

13 19 Ljabru

Trikk
Straßenbahnlinien *Tram lines*

11	Majorstuen – Kjelsås (10')
12	Majorstuen – Kjelsås (10')
13	Bekkestua – Lilleaker (20') – Ljabru (10')
17	Rikshospitalet – Grefsen stasjon (10')
18	Rikshospitalet – Grefsen stasjon (10')
19	Majorstuen – Ljabru (10')

Straßenbahn | *Tram*
Betriebsgleise | *Tracks without passenger service*
T-bane – U-Bahn | *Metro*
Eisenbahnstrecken | *Railway routes*

* Umleitungsstrecke über Lilletorget bis 2021
Temporary route via Lilletorget until 2021

500 m

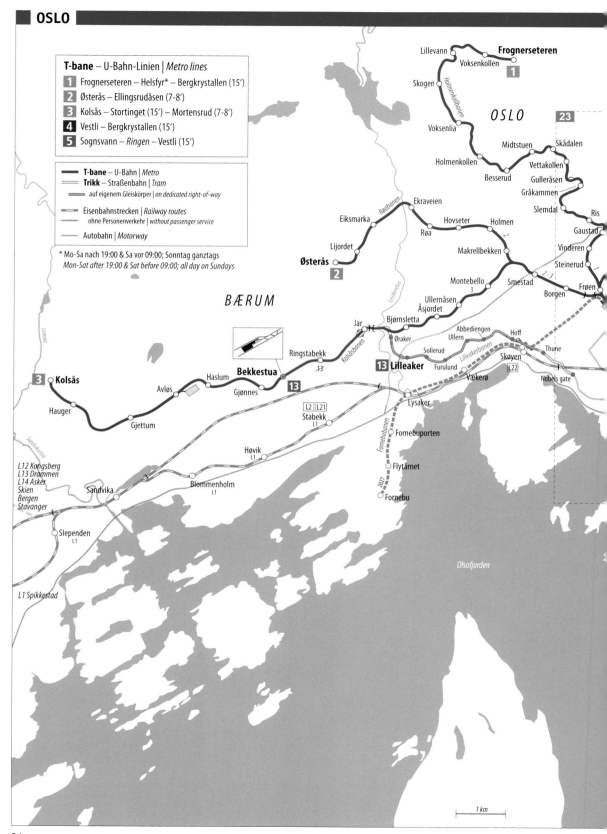

T-bane – U-Bahn-Linien | *Metro lines*

1 Frognerseteren – Helsfyr* – Bergkrystallen (15′)
2 Østerås – Ellingsrudåsen (7-8′)
3 Kolsås – Stortinget (15′) – Mortensrud (7-8′)
4 Vestli – Bergkrystallen (15′)
5 Sognsvann – *Ringen* – Vestli (15′)

T-bane – U-Bahn | *Metro*
Trikk – Straßenbahn | *Tram*
auf eigenem Gleiskörper | *on dedicated right-of-way*
Eisenbahnstrecken | *Railway routes*
ohne Personenverkehr | *without passenger service*
Autobahn | *Motorway*

* Mo-Sa nach 19:00 & Sa vor 09:00; Sonntag ganztags
  Mon-Sat after 19:00 & Sat before 09:00; all day on Sundays

B Æ R U M

O S L O

Lillevann
Voksenkollen
Frognerseteren 1
Skogen
Voksenlia
Midtstuen
Skådalen
Holmenkollen
Vettakollen
Besserud
Gulleråsen
Gråkammen
Slemdal
Ris
Ekraveien
Gaustad
Hovseter
Holmen
Eiksmarka
Røa
Vinderen
Lijordet
Makrellbekken
Steinerud
Østerås 2
Montebello
Smestad
Frøen
Borgen
Ullernåsen
Åsjordet
Jar
Bjørnsletta
Abbediengen
Hoff
Øraker
Ullern
Thune
Ringstabekk
Sollerud
Skøyen
Bekkestua 13
Furulund
13 Lilleaker
Nobels gate
Haslum
Vækerø
3 Kolsås
Avløs
Gjønnes
Lysaker
Hauger
L2 L21
Gjettum
Stabekk
Fornebuporten
Høvik
L12 Kongsberg
L13 Drammen
L14 Asker
Skien
Bergen
Stavanger
Blommenholm
Flytårnet
Sandvika
Fornebu
Slependen
Olsofjorden
L1 Spikkestad

1 km

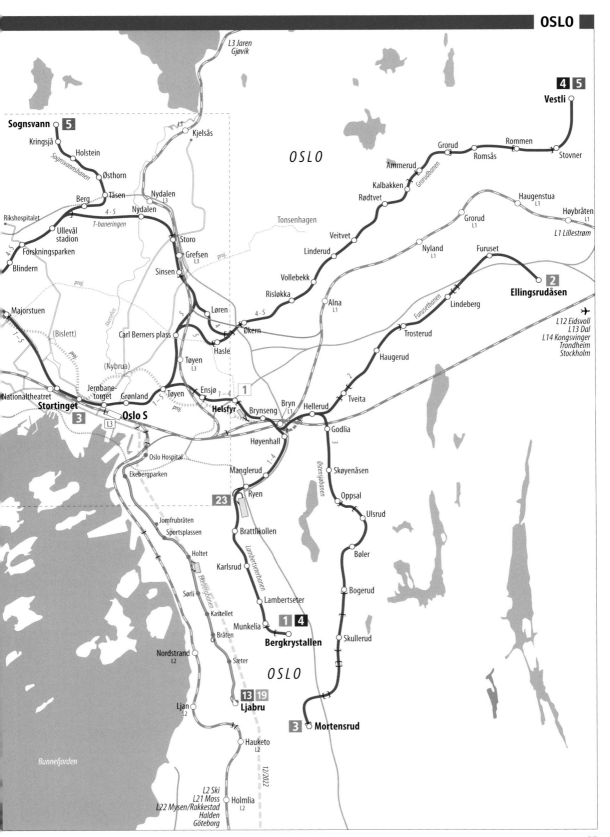

Bunnefjorden

25

Ansaldo SL95 #142 @ Ekebergparken

Trikken – Straßenbahn

Die Osloer Straßenbahn, auf Norwegisch *trikken* (kurz für *elektrikken* – „die Elektrische") genannt, erschließt große Teile der inneren Stadt, zwei Äste führen jedoch ähnlich der T-bane in die Vororte hinaus. Trotz Ausbaus der Kolsåsbane auf Metro-Standard wurde der traditionelle Mischbetrieb westlich von Jar beibehalten. Auf dem 2,7 km langen Abschnitt bis Bekkestua fährt die Tram auf Metro-Gleisen, wofür in Jar und Bekkestua eigene Niedrigbahnsteige errichtet wurden, Ringstabekk wird hingegen von der Straßenbahn ohne Halt durchfahren. Die Einfädelung östlich von Jar wurde kreuzungsfrei ausgeführt. Der Mischbetrieb

Trikken – Tram

Oslo's tramway, called 'trikken' (short for 'elektrikken' – 'the electric') in Norwegian, covers large parts of the inner city, with two branches leading out to the suburbs, similar to the T-bane. Despite the upgrading of the Kolsåsbane to metro standard, the traditional joint operation of T-bane and tram on the same tracks persists on a 2.7 km section west of Jar. At Jar and Bekkestua, the trams have their own low platforms, while they skip Ringstabekk, which is only served by the T-bane. The junction east of Jar was built with full grade-separation. The mixed operation, however, may

SL79 #113 @ Sportsplassen

SL79 #130 @ Disen

SL95 #146 @ Dronning Eufemias gate (Bjørvika)

soll jedoch 2024 mit Einführung eines neuen Signalsystems bei der T-bane enden.

Die Geschichte der Osloer Straßenbahn geht auf das Jahr 1875 zurück, als die erste Pferdebahnstrecke eröffnet wurde. Daraus wurde 1897 *Grønntrikken* (die grüne Tram). Bereits 1894 wurde allerdings Norwegens erste elektrische Straßenbahn, *Blåtrikken* (die blaue Tram) vom Stadtzentrum nach Majorstuen entlang der heutigen Linie 19 sowie entlang Drammensveien (heutige SL 13) in Betrieb genommen. Dazu kam 1899 die kommunale *Rødtrikken*, die jedoch bereits 1905 von der grünen Tram übernommen wurde. Aus den beiden privaten Gesellschaften entstand 1924 die kommunale *AS Kristiania Sporveier* (ab 1925 *AS Oslo Sporveier*). Neben einigen Stadtstrecken kamen im Laufe des 20. Jahrhunderts mehrere Vorortlinien hinzu: Ekebergbanen (1917), Lilleakerbanen (1919), Østensjøbanen (1926) und Lambertseterbanen (1957). Während die letzten beiden später ins T-bane-Netz integriert wurden, sind die beiden ersteren auch heute noch Teil des Straßenbahnnetzes. Nachdem Ende der 1950er Jahre die größte Ausdehnung erreicht worden war, beschloss man 1960, das gesamte Netz stillzulegen und nur bestimmte Strecken in das geplante U-Bahn-Netz aufzunehmen. Dazu kam es bekannterweise nicht und in den 1990er Jahren konnten schließlich sogar zwei Neubaustrecken eröffnet werden: 1995 über Aker brygge und 1999 vom John Colletts plass zum Rikshospitalet. Der Bau der lange geplanten Strecke nach Tonsenhagen ist weiterhin ungewiss, genauso wie eine immer wieder auftauchende Halbringlinie entlang des Ring 2, wo heute die Buslinie 20 verkehrt.

In jüngster Vergangenheit entstand südlich des Hauptbahnhofs eine Neubaustrecke entlang der Dronning Eufemias gate und Bispegata im Zuge eines großen städtebaulichen Projekts mit der neuen Oper, der neuen Stadtbibliothek und dem neuen Munch-Museum (Bjørvika-Viertel). Die Stichstrecke bis zur Haltestelle Bjørvika wurde bereits seit August 2017 zeitweise genutzt, bis die durchgehende Strecke über Middelalderparken schließlich am 4. Oktober 2020 die traditionelle Route der Ekebergbane durch die Schweigaards gate nördlich des Bahngeländes ersetzte.

In Vorbereitung auf die Ankunft neuer Fahrzeuge wurden in den vergangenen Jahren zahlreiche Abschnitte erneuert, dabei wurde im Zentrum die vormals eingleisige Führung durch Parallelstraßen (Tollbugata/Prinsens gate) zugunsten einer weitgehend der Tram vorbehaltenen zweigleisigen

end in 2024 with the implementation of a new signalling system on the T-bane network.

The history of Oslo's tramway dates back to the year 1875, when the first horse tramway was opened. This became 'Grønntrikken' (the green tram) in 1897. Norway's first electric tram, 'Blåtrikken' (the blue tram), however, began operating in 1894 from the city centre to Majorstuen along today's line 19 and along Drammensveien (now line 13). A third company, the municipal 'Rødtrikken' appeared in 1899, but was absorbed by the green tram in 1905. The two private companies merged in 1924 to become the municipal 'AS Kristiania Sporveier' (from 1925 'AS Oslo Sporveier'). Besides some urban routes, several suburban lines were also built during the 20th Century: Ekebergbanen (1917), Lilleakerbanen (1919), Østensjøbanen (1926) and Lambertseterbanen (1957). While the last two were later integrated into the T-bane network, the older two are still part of the tram network. With the network having reached its maximum expansion towards the end of the 1950s, it was decided in 1960 to abandon the entire system, except for certain routes which were to be integrated into the new metro network. These plans did not materialise, however, and eventually in the 1990s, two new routes were opened: via Aker Brygge in 1995, and from John Colletts plass to Rikshospitalet in 1999. The construction of the long-planned route to Tonsenhagen remains uncertain, while plans for a semi-circular route along Ring 2, which is now served by bus line 20, are resurrected from time to time.

In recent years, a new line has been built south of the main railway station along Dronning Eufemias gate and Bispegata in conjunction with a major urban redevelopment project which includes a new opera, new city library and the new Munch Museum (Bjørvika district). While an initial section up to the Bjørvika stop had been used temporarily since August 2017, the through route via Middelalderparken replaced the traditional route of the Ekebergbane through Schweigaards gate north of the railway tracks on 4 October 2020.

In view of the arrival of new vehicles, numerous sections have been upgraded in recent years; the former single-track operation through parallel streets (Tollbugata/Prinsens gate) was given up in favour of a mostly tram-only two-track route through Prinsens gate. At Majorstuen, the tram stop was moved to Bogstadveien, while a loop was built around the block, allowing trams

SL79 #133 @ Prinsens gate (Øvre Slottsgate)

CAF Urbos SL18 #401 (© CAF)

Trasse durch die Prinsens gate aufgegeben. In Majorstuen wurde die Straßenbahnhaltestelle 2020 in den Bogstadveien verlegt und gleichzeitig eine Blockschleife errichtet, so dass hier aus allen Richtungen gewendet werden kann. Für die bis mindestens 2021 andauernden Arbeiten in der Storgata wurde die Straßenbahn im September 2019 vorübergehend auf eine 700 m lange Neubaustrecke durch die Stenersgata, Christian Krohgs gate und Hausmanns gate verlegt.

Der Wagenpark der Osloer Straßenbahn bestand jahrelang aus 72 Wagen, nämlich 40 sechsachsigen, hochflurigen Gelenktriebwagen vom Typ SL79 sowie 32 achtachsigen, dreiteiligen Fahrzeugen vom Typ SL95 von Ansaldo, welche bis auf die Bereiche über den Enddrehgestellen niederflurig sind. Letztere sind Zweirichtungswagen, die auf den Linien 13, 17 und 18 benötigt werden, da am Rikshospitalet und in Bekkestua keine Wendeschleifen zur Verfügung stehen. Wegen enger Kurvenradien können sie nicht auf der Briskeby-Strecke eingesetzt werden. Aufgrund wiederholter Mängel an diesen Wagen kommt es immer wieder zu einem Fahrzeugengpass, der nun durch die Beschaffung von insgesamt 87 Straßenbahnen von CAF (mit einer Option auf 60 weitere für potenzielle Netzerweiterungen) beseitigt werden wird. Der Abteilung *Sporveien Vognmateriell AS* stehen Betriebshöfe in Grefsen und Holtet zur Verfügung.

coming from any direction to turn around there. For the modernisation of Storgata, which will take until 2021 at the earliest, since September 2019 the trams have temporarily been diverted onto a 700 m newly-built route through Stenersgata, Christian Krohgs gate and Hausmanns gate.

For many years, the tram fleet has consisted of 72 cars, namely 40 six-axle, high-floor articulated trams of type SL79 as well as 32 eight-axle, three-section vehicles of type SL95, which are low-floor except for the parts above the end bogies. The latter are double-ended cars, which are required on lines 13, 17 and 18 as there are no turning loops at Rikshospitalet and Bekkestua. They cannot be used on the Briskeby route because of its tight curves. Due to frequent technical problems with these cars, there is often a shortage of rolling stock. The delivery of a total of 87 Urbos trams from CAF may eventually solve this problem; there is an option for an additional 60 trams to cater for any possible network expansion in the future. 'Sporveien Vognmateriell AS' has two workshops and depots, one at Grefsen and the other at Holtet.

Trikken > Fahrzeuge | *Rolling Stock* (600 V DC)						
Nummer *Number*	Anzahl *Quantity*	Hersteller *Manufacturer*	Typ *Class*	Länge *Length*	Breite *Width*	Ausgeliefert *Delivered*
101-140	40	Duewag/ABB Strømmen	SL79 =>	22.3 m	2.50 m	1982; 1989
141-155, 157-172	31	Ansaldo/Firema	SL95 <=>	33.1 m	2.60 m	1998-2004
401-487	2 / 87	CAF	SL18 (Urbos) <=>	34.2 m	2.60 m	2020 (2021-2024)

Ekebergbanen # 1001 (Skabo, 1917)

Holmenkollbanen #8 (MAN/Schukert, 1897)

Sporveismuseet Vognhall 5

Das Osloer Straßenbahnmuseum ist in einer alten Wagenhalle unweit des Knotens Majorstuen beheimatet. Es wird von der *Lokaltrafikkhistorisk forening* betrieben und zeigt Osloer Fahrzeuge aus allen Epochen, darunter auch Wagen der verschiedenen Vorortbahnen. Das Museum ist ganzjährig von Samstag bis Montag, 12-15 Uhr, geöffnet. Am letzten Sonntag jedes Monats sind historische Trams auch auf den Straßen der Stadt unterwegs.

The Oslo Tramway Museum is housed in an old tram depot building near the Majorstuen hub. It is maintained by the 'Lokaltrafikkhistorisk forening', and displays Oslo's trams from every era, including cars from the different suburban lines. The museum is open year-round from Saturday to Monday, 12:00 to 15:00. On the last Sunday of every month, some old vehicles can also be seen running on the city streets.

Kristiania Elektriske Sporvei #307 (Herbrand/SS, 1913)

HkB (Holmenkollbanen) #42 (Skabo, 1917)

Løren – neueste T-bane-Station in Oslo | *newest T-bane station in Oslo*

T-banen – U-Bahn

Ähnlich wie die grüne Linie in Stockholm geht die Osloer T-bane (für *tunnelbane*) auf mehrere Vorortbahnen zurück, wodurch sie aufgrund ihrer Trassierung mit engen Radien und teils starken Steigungen sowie der einfachen Gestaltung der oberirdischen Stationen mancherorts den Eindruck einer Hochflurstadtbahn erweckt. Auf allen Linien wird ein 15-Minuten-Takt angeboten, lediglich auf der Linie 2 sowie auf dem Ostast der Linie 3 fahren die Züge tagsüber alle 7-8 Minuten, wobei jene der Linie 3 im Stadtzentrum in der

T-banen – Metro

Much like the Green Line in Stockholm, the Oslo T-bane (for 'tunnelbane') is the successor of several suburban tramway lines. It therefore often gives the impression of a high-floor light rail system, with rather tight curves and several steep sections combined with the basic design of the above-ground stations. The lines are all served every 15 minutes, except for line 2 and the eastern leg of line 3, where there is a train every 7-8 minutes during daytime service, when every other train on line 3 turns

Hovseter

Grønland

Schleife Stortinget wenden. Im Innenstadttunnel, durch den alle Linien verkehren, ist somit die Kapazitätsgrenze erreicht. Da sich die Liniennummern vor allem auf den westlichen Ästen in den vergangenen Jahren wiederholt geändert haben, werden die einzelnen Strecken meist mit ihren traditionellen Namen bezeichnet.

Die älteren westlichen Vorortbahnen (Holmenkollbanen von 1898 – ab 1928 unterirdisch von Majorstuen bis Nationaltheatret; Røabanen 1912-1972; Sognsvannbanen 1934; Kolsåsbanen 1924-1942) fuhren ursprünglich mit Oberleitung, sie wurden ab 1993 auf T-bane-Standard gebracht, ein Prozess, der auf der Kolsåsbane bis 2014 andauerte.

Im Osten der Stadt wurde die 1926 bis Oppsal gebaute Østensjøbane 1958 nach Metro-Kriterien bis Bøler verlängert, nachdem bereits ein Jahr zuvor die Lambertseterbane für die zukünftige U-Bahn errichtet worden war. 1966 begann der unterirdische Betrieb mit Stromzufuhr über seitliche Stromschiene bis Jernbanetorget (Bahnhofsplatz) im Stadtzentrum. In den folgenden Jahren kamen weitere Neubaustrecken hinzu (Østensjøbanen bis Skullerud 1967; Furusetbanen 1970-1981; Grorudbanen 1966-1975). 1977 wurden die östlichen Bahnen zwar unterirdisch bis „Sentrum" verlängert, mussten jedoch 1983 wegen Baumängel wieder zum Hauptbahnhof zurückgenommen werden. 1987 konnte schließlich der durchgehende Tunnel zwischen Jernbanetorget und Nationaltheatret mit der umgebauten viergleisigen Zwischenstation Stortinget [Parlament] in Betrieb genommen werden. Aufgrund der unterschiedlichen Stromversorgung war ein durchgehender Betrieb aber vorerst nicht möglich, weshalb die östlichen Linien am U-Bahnhof Stortinget über die heute noch bestehende Schleife, die die äußeren Gleise verbindet, wendeten. Ab 1993 wurden stufenweise durchgehende Linien geschaffen, wobei bis zum Umbau der Kolsåsbane ab 2008 und der Holmenkollbane 2009/2010 auf diesen Linien an der Station Montebello bzw. Frøen von Oberleitungs- auf Stromschienenbetrieb gewechselt wurde.

Neben den Modernisierungsmaßnahmen der bestehenden Strecken kamen in den letzten Jahrzehnten folgende Neubauabschnitte hinzu: 1998 Skullerud – Mortensrud; 2003 Ullevål stadion – Storo und 2006 Storo – Carl Berners plass (T-baneringen). Nachdem der Quasi-Neubau der Kolsåsbane Ende 2014 abgeschlossen wurde, ging 2016 die 1,6 km lange Løren-Spange zwischen Sinsen und Økern in Betrieb.

around using the loop at Stortinget. The city centre tunnel, which is shared by all the lines, has thus reached its capacity limits. As the line numbers have changed repeatedly in recent years, especially on the western part of the network, the branches are usually referred to by their traditional names.

The older western suburban lines (Holmenkollbanen from 1898 – extended underground from Majorstuen to Nationaltheatret in 1928; Røabanen 1912-1972; Sognsvannbanen 1934; and Kolsåsbanen 1924-1942) were initially operated with an overhead power supply. They have been undergoing conversion to T-bane standard since 1993, a process that took until 2014 on the Kolsåsbane.

In the eastern suburbs, the Østensjøbane, opened to Oppsal in 1926, was extended to Bøler in 1958 following metro standards, with the Lambertseterbane having been completed for the future T-bane a year earlier. Underground operation to Jernbanetorget (Station Square) in the city centre using a third-rail power supply began in 1966, and in the following years more new lines were added (Østensjøbanen to Skullerud 1967; Furusetbanen 1970-1981; and Grorudbanen 1966-1975). In 1977, the eastern lines were extended underground to Sentrum, but they had to be cut back to the railway station again in 1983 due to flaws in construction. Finally in 1987, the now lengthened tunnel between Jernbanetorget and Nationaltheatret, including a rebuilt four-track station in the city centre, now called Stortinget [Parliament], was brought into service. Due to the different power supply systems, through operation was still not possible, so trains arriving from the eastern lines reversed at Stortinget station using the loop that connects the outer tracks, which still exists. Through lines were gradually established from 1993, although until the upgrading of the Kolsåsbane (starting in 2008) and the Holmenkollbane (in 2009/2010), trains on these lines used to switch from overhead to third-rail operation at Montebello and Frøen stations, respectively.

Besides the modernisation of the existing routes, the following new sections have been added in recent decades: in 1998, Skullerud – Mortensrud; in 2003, Ullevål stadion – Storo and in 2006, Storo – Carl Berners plass (T-baneringen). While the rebuilding of the Kolsåsbane was completed in 2014, the 1.6 km Løren link between Sinsen and Økern opened in 2016.

MX3x43 @ Kolsås

Stortinget

MX3x06 & 3x83 @ Majorstuen

Trotz Ausbaumaßnahmen stellt die Holmenkollbane eine Besonderheit im T-bane-Netz dar. Während auf den anderen Strecken meist Doppeltraktionen, also 6-Wagen-Züge, im Einsatz sind, verkehren nach Frognerseteren als Linie 1 nur 3-Wagen-Züge, wobei selbst dann nur die Türen der beiden ersten Wagen geöffnet werden können, da manche Bahnsteige zu kurz sind. Eine Ausnahme bildet die Station Holmenkollen, wo bei Veranstaltungen auch 6-Wagen-Züge halten können. Trotz seitlicher Strom-schiene gibt es auf dieser Strecke weiterhin zahlreiche, mit Schranken gesicherte Bahnübergänge. Die Linie 1 erklimmt eine Höhe von 469 m über NN.

Despite all the upgrading, the Holmenkollbane remains the 'odd man out' in the T-bane network. While all the other lines are usually operated with double trainsets, i.e. 6-car trains, the Frognerseteren route (line 1) can only be served by 3-car trains, and only the doors of the first two carriages can be opened, as the platforms are too short. The only exception is Holmenkollen station, whose long platforms allow 6-car trains to be used during special events. Despite the use of a third-rail power supply, there are still many level crossings, although they are all safeguarded with barriers. Line 1 climbs from sea level to an altitude of 469 m.

Ulleval stadion

Stovner

MX3x05 @ Østhorn

Für die Anbindung des ehemaligen Flughafengeländes auf der Halbinsel Fornebu soll bis ca. 2027 eine neue, vollkommen unterirdische T-bane-Strecke von Majorstuen über Skøyen und Lysaker (8,3 km) errichtet werden. Zur Entlastung der Innenstadtstrecke ist mittelfristig eine zweite Verbindung zwischen Tøyen und Majorstuen angedacht. Im Zusammenhang mit diesen beiden Projekten soll der Bahnhof Majorstuen erweitert und in den Untergrund verlegt werden. Seit Langem ist auch geplant, die Furuset-bane von Ellingsrudåsen zum Krankenhaus in Lørenskog zu verlängern.

Der Wagenpark der T-bane wurde zwischen 2006 und 2013 komplett erneuert. Die in Wien produzierten, durchgehend begehbaren 3-Wagen-Einheiten ersetzten alle älteren Wagen. Die für U-Bahnen ungewöhnlich großzügige Wagenbreite ermöglichte eine Querbestuhlung 2+3. Die Kapazität eines 110 m langen Zuges wird mit 986 Fahrgästen angegeben. Der Fußboden liegt bei 1,12 m über Schienenoberkante. Die Hauptwerkstatt für die T-bane liegt in Ryen, weitere Wartungseinrichtungen stehen in Etterstad (Helsfyr/Brynseng) und in Avløs zur Verfügung; letztere löste 2015 jene in Majorstuen ab.

To provide a link to the area of the former airport on Fornebu Peninsula, a new T-bane line will be built from Majorstuen via Skøyen and Lysaker (8.3 km) by 2027. To relieve the existing cross-city route, a second link between Tøyen and Majorstuen is planned in the medium term. In conjunction with these two projects, Majorstuen station will have to be expanded and relocated underground. An extension of the Furusetbane from Ellingsrud-åsen to Lørenskog Hospital has long been planned.

Between 2006 and 2013, the T-bane rolling stock was completely renewed. The three-car units with gangways between carriages were produced in Vienna and replaced all the older cars. The extraordinary width allowed a transversal 2+3 seating arrangement. A double trainset is 110 m long and has a capacity of 986 passengers. The floor height is 1.12 m above the top of the rail. The T-bane's main workshops are located at Ryen, with more facilities available at Etterstad (Helsfyr/Brynseng area) and Avløs; the latter made the workshops at Majorstuen redundant in 2015.

T-bane > Fahrzeuge | *Rolling Stock* (750 V DC)						
Nummer *Number*	Anzahl *Quantity*	Hersteller *Manufacturer*	Typ *Class*	Länge *Length*	Breite *Width*	Ausgeliefert *Delivered*
3x01-3x115*	115	Siemens	MX3000	54.1 m	3.16 m	2006-2014

* x = 1, 2 oder 3, je nach Wagen in einer 3-Wagen-Einheit | *x = 1, 2 or 3 depending on the position of the car in a 3-car unit*

Ansaldo #72124 @ Nationaltheatret

Lokaltog – S-Bahn

In den letzten Jahrzehnten wurde sehr viel in die Eisen-
bahninfrastruktur in und um Oslo investiert, was auch dem
Nahverkehr zugutekommt. Seit 1980 sind die westlichen
und östlichen Strecken durch einen Innenstadttunnel
verbunden (der ehemalige Westbahnhof in der Nähe des
Rathauses beherbergt nun das Nobel Friedenszentrum),
1999 wurde der unterirdische Halt Nationaltheatret um
eine zweite zweigleisige Bahnsteighalle erweitert. Im
selben Jahr ging im Zuge der Neubaustrecke zum neuen
Flughafen Gardermoen der Romeriksporten, ein 14,6 km
langer Tunnel von Oslo bis Lillestrøm in Betrieb. 2001
bzw. 2005 folgten weitere Tunnel zwischen Lysaker und
Asker, wodurch die alte Trasse für den Nahverkehr frei

Lokaltog – Suburban Rail

*In recent decades, a lot has been invested in the railway
infrastructure in and around Oslo, which has also been
beneficial for local transport. Since 1980, the western
and eastern routes have been connected by a cross-city
tunnel (the former Western Railway Station building near
the City Hall now houses the Nobel Peace Center), and
in 1999, the underground station at Nationaltheatret
was expanded with the addition of a second two-track
platform hall. That same year, Romeriksporten, a 14.6 km
tunnel from Oslo to Lillestrøm, was opened as part of a
new route to the new airport at Gardermoen. In 2001 and
2005, new mainline tunnels followed between Lysaker
and Asker, freeing the old route for local trains. Similar*

Strømmens Værksted #69685 @ Hauketo (2013)

FLIRT #75526
(in gemischtem Anstrich | *in mixed livery*) @ Skøyen

Stadler FLIRT #75573 (in neuem Anstrich | *in new livery*) @ **Skøyen**

wurde. Ähnliche Verbesserungen sind im Südosten auf der Østfoldbane Richtung Ski zu erwarten, wenn Ende 2022 der fast 20 km lange Tunnel der Follobane eröffnet wird.

Seit 2012 sind die Linien des Lokaltog im Østland mit Nummern versehen, wobei die einstelligen Linien als S-Bahn an allen Stationen (davon 21 in Zone 1) halten:

L1 Spikkestad (30') – Asker – Lillestrøm (15') - 82 km
L2 Stabekk – Ski (30') - 33 km
L3 Oslo S – Jaren (~1x/h) - 72 km

Linien mit zweistelligen Nummern (L12, L13, L14, L21, L22) benutzen hingegen im Oslo-nahen Bereich die Ferngleise und bedienen die Region stündlich. Weiter entfernt liegende Orte werden durch die Linien R10 usw. auch etwa stündlich angebunden. Einige Strecken liegen außerhalb des *Ruter*-Tarifgebiets. Alle Linien werden derzeit von der staatlichen Bahngesellschaft Vy (vormals NSB) betrieben. Der alle 10 Minuten verkehrende Flughafen-Express *Flytoget* hat einen eigenen Tarif (von Oslo 198 NOK), aber zum Flughafen Gardermoen kommt man auch mit Vy-Zügen dreimal pro Stunde, genau so schnell und für nur 110 NOK.

Auf dem Lokaltog-Netz verkehren vierteilige Triebwagen (85,7 m) der NSB-Baureihe 72 von Ansaldobreda aus dem Jahr 2002 sowie eine für Norwegen leicht abgeänderte, fünfteilige Version (105,5 m) des populären FLIRT von Stadler, der hier als NSB-Baureihe 74/75 ab 2012 vorerst vor allem auf den längeren Regionalbahnstrecken zum Einsatz kam. Die BR 75 mit mehr Sitzplätzen wird auf den S-Bahn-artigen Strecken eingesetzt. Zeitweise sind auch noch ältere modernisierte Triebwagen der NSB-Baureihe 69, die von Strømmens Værksted (später EB Strømmen) bis 1993 geliefert wurden, zu sehen.

improvements can be expected in the southeast on the Østfoldbane to Ski when the almost 20 km long Follobane mainline tunnel opens in late 2022.

In 2012, the Lokaltog lines in Østland were assigned line numbers, with the single-digit lines providing an S-Bahn/RER-style service calling at all stations (with 21 stations lying within zone 1):

L1 Spikkestad (30') — Asker — Lillestrøm (15') - 82 km
L2 Skøyen — Ski (30') - 33 km
L3 Oslo S — Jaren (~ 1 tph) - 72 km

Lines with two-digit numbers (L12, L13, L14, L21, L22), however, use the mainline tracks in the area near Oslo and serve the outer region hourly. More distant locations are also connected roughly every hour by lines R10 etc. Some sections lie outside the 'Ruter' fare system. All the lines are currently operated by the national railway company Vy (formerly NSB). The frequent Airport Express 'Flytoget' (every 10 minutes) requires a special fare (from Oslo 198 NOK), but Gardermoen Airport can also be reached three times an hour on Vy trains, which are just as fast and cost a mere 110 NOK.

The Lokaltog system is operated with 85.7 m long four-section EMUs (electric multiple units) of NSB class 72 delivered by Ansaldobreda in 2002 as well as EMUs of a slightly modified Norwegian version of the popular FLIRT (here NSB class 74/75; 105.5 m) from Stadler of Switzerland that began running on longer regional services in 2012; class 75 trains, which have more seats, are used on local services. Occasionally, modernised EMUs of NSB class 69, delivered until 1993 by Strømmens Værksted (later Strømmen EB), can still be seen.

Lystrup – L2 Variobahn #1110 & L1 Tango #2108; rechts das Gleis Richtung Grenaa | *on the right, the track to Grenaa*

AARHUS

Nachdem die Bauarbeiten im Sommer 2013 begonnen hatten, startete in Dänemarks zweitgrößter Stadt am 21. Dezember 2017 zwischen Hauptbahnhof und Universitetshospitalet (6,3 km) die erste moderne Straßenbahn (*Letbane*) des Landes. Das Gesamtprojekt umfasste eine etwa 12 km lange Neubaustrecke von Nørreport nach Norden entlang der Achse Nørrebrogade/Randersvej. Nördlich des Universitätsklinikums in Skejby verläuft die Trasse weitgehend durch unbebautes Gebiet, hier sollen in den nächsten Jahren neue Wohngebiete entstehen. Neben dem städtischen Neubauabschnitt, dessen Standard dem moderner europäischer Straßenbahnen entspricht, wurden die bestehenden Lokalbahnstrecken nach Odder im Süden (etwa 30 km) sowie nach Grenaa im Osten (etwa 70 km) ausgebaut und elektrifiziert. Der Betrieb auf der Bahnstrecke nach Odder wurde am 25. August 2018 aufgenommen, als auch die ursprüngliche Strecke bis Lisbjergskolen (3,6 km) verlängert wurde. Mit Eröffnung der Verbindung Lisbjerg – Lystrup (3,8 km) und der Aufnahme des elektrischen Stadtbahnbetriebs bis Grenaa am 30. April 2019 konnte die erste Phase der Letbane abgeschlossen werden. Am 14. September 2020 wurde auf bestehender Strecke der Halt Risskov Strandpark eröffnet.

Es werden heute zwei Linien betrieben, allerdings je nach Abschnitt mit sehr unterschiedlichen Takten, von einem 6/9-Minuten-Takt auf dem städtischen Abschnitt der L2 bis zu einem Stundentakt auf dem äußeren Abschnitt der L1. In Lystrup besteht alle 30 Minuten ein Anschluss in alle drei Richtungen. Auf den Überlandstrecken, vor allem auf der L1, werden die Tango-Fahrzeuge mit ihren Drehgestellen eingesetzt, während auf dem städtischen

With construction having started in the summer of 2013, Denmark's second largest city opened the country's first modern tramway (Letbane) on 21 December 2017, running from the railway station to Universitetshospitalet (6.3 km). The overall project included a new approximately 12 km route from Nørreport north along the Nørrebrogade/Randersvej corridor. North of the University Hospital in Skejby, the route runs through largely undeveloped land, where new housing estates will be built in the next few years. Besides the urban section, which features the typical standard of a modern European tramway, the Letbane project also included the upgrading and electrification of two existing local railways running south to Odder (approx. 30 km) and east to Grenaa (approx. 70 km), which were upgraded and electrified. Light rail service on the Odder line was launched on 25 August 2018, the same day the initial tram segment was extended to Lisbjergskolen (3.6 km). The opening of the link between Lisbjerg and Lystrup (3.8 km) together with the start of electric service all the way to Grenaa completed the first stage of the Letbane project on 30 April 2019. On 14 September 2020, a stop called Risskov Strandpark was added to the existing line.

Currently two lines are operated, but depending on the section, with very different headways, from a tram every 6/9 minutes on the urban section of line L2 to an hourly service on the outer section of line L1. In Lystrup, interchange is provided every 30 minutes in all three directions. On the interurban routes but especially on line L1, the Tango vehicles, which have bogies, are in service, while the urban section, but partly also the line to Odder,

Dokk1 – L2 Variobahn #1105 ▶ Aarhus H

Abschnitt, aber teils auch nach Odder, durchgehend niederflurige Variobahnen, wie man sie bereits aus Bergen kennt, unterwegs sind. Der Betriebshof liegt westlich des Hauptbahnhofs auf einem vormals von der dänischen Staatsbahn genutzten Gelände. Die Stadtbahn ist zu je 50% Eigentum der Stadt Aarhus und der Region Midtjylland (Mitteljütland), der Betrieb wurde an Keolis vergeben.

Die Stadtbahn ist in das Tarifsystem von Midttrafik integriert: Für Aarhus (Zonen 301-313) wird ein *Tourist Ticket* für 24, 48 oder 72 Stunden angeboten (80, 120 bzw. 160 DKK), zum Erkunden der gesamten Überlandstrecken empfiehlt sich ein *Tourist Ticket* für die gesamte Region Midtjylland für 162, 242 bzw. 322 DKK. [100 DKK = 13.44 €]

is operated with Variobahn vehicles; these feature a 100% low-floor layout and are similar to the trams used in Bergen. The depot is located to the west of the main railway station on a site previously occupied by the Danish State Railways. The Letbane is jointly owned by the City of Aarhus and the Midtjylland (Central Jutland) Region, while the day-to-day operation is outsourced to Keolis.

The light rail system is integrated into the Midttrafik fare system: a 'Tourist Ticket' for Aarhus (zones 301-313) is available for 24, 48 or 72 hours and costs 80, 120 or 160 DKK, respectively. To explore the entire Letbane network, a pass for the entire Midtjylland region is an option (162, 242 and 322 DKK, respectively).

AARHUS (Danmark | Dänemark | Denmark)

 350 000 (468 km²)

 ~ 450 000

 2017

 1435 mm

 107.7 km
(Tram 14.1 km + Tram-Train 93.3 km)

 2

 Aarhus Letbane – *www.letbanen.dk*

 Midttrafik – *www.midttrafik.dk*

Østbanetorvet – L1 Tango #2104 ▶ Aarhus H

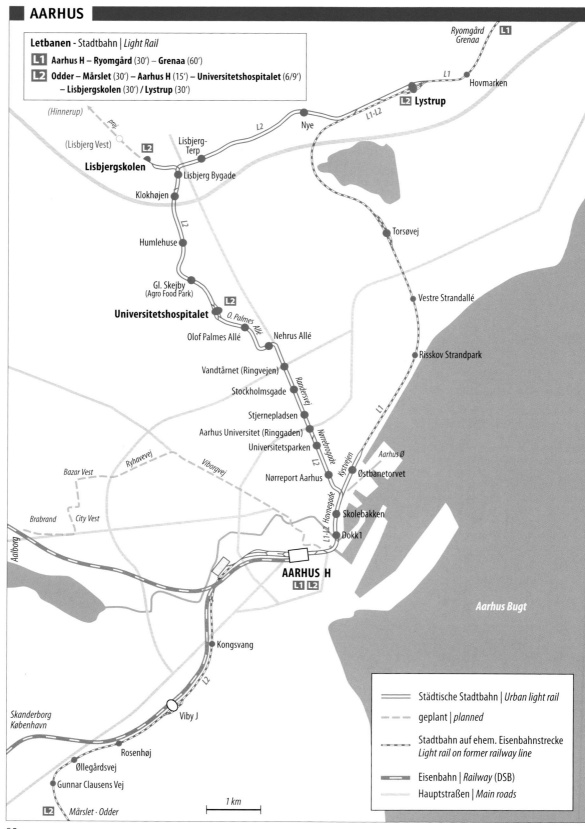

AARHUS

Letbanen - Stadtbahn | *Light Rail*

L1 **Aarhus H – Ryomgård** (30′) – **Grenaa** (60′)
L2 **Odder – Mårslet** (30′) – **Aarhus H** (15′) – **Universitetshospitalet** (6/9′)
– **Lisbjergskolen** (30′) / **Lystrup** (30′)

Ryomgård
Grenaa **L1**

L1

Hovmarken

L2 **Lystrup**

(Hinnerup)

proj.

(Lisbjerg Vest)

L2

Lisbjergskolen

Nye

L2

L1·L2

Lisbjerg-
Terp

Lisbjerg Bygade

Klokhøjen

L2

Torsøvej

Humlehuse

L2

Gl. Skejby
(Agro Food Park)

Vestre Strandallé

L2

Universitetshospitalet

O. Palmes Allé

Olof Palmes Allé

Nehrus Allé

Risskov Strandpark

Vandtårnet (Ringvejen)

Randersvej

Stockholmsgade

L1

Stjernepladsen

Aarhus Universitet (Ringgaden)

Nørrebrogade

Universitetsparken

Aarhus Ø

L2

Nørreport Aarhus

Kystvejen

Østbanetorvet

Havnegade

Bazar Vest

Ryhavevej

Viborgvej

L1·L1

Skolebakken

Brabrand

City Vest

Dokk1

Aalborg

AARHUS H

L1 **L2**

Aarhus Bugt

Kongsvang

L2

Skanderborg
København

Viby J

Rosenhøj

Øllegårdsvej

Gunnar Clausens Vej

1 km

L2 Mårslet · Odder

════	Städtische Stadtbahn | *Urban light rail*
─ ─ ─	geplant | *planned*
╪╪╪╪	Stadtbahn auf ehem. Eisenbahnstrecke *Light rail on former railway line*
══	Eisenbahn | *Railway* (DSB)
───	Hauptstraßen | *Main roads*

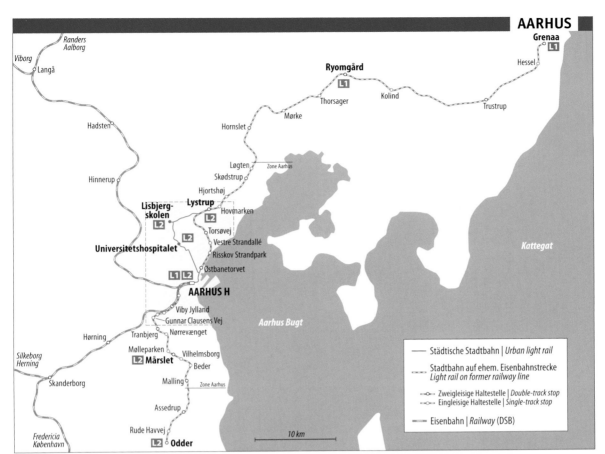

	———	Städtische Stadtbahn | *Urban light rail*				
	┅┅┅	Stadtbahn auf ehem. Eisenbahnstrecke *Light rail on former railway line*				
	┅o┅	Zweigleisige Haltestelle | *Double-track stop*				
	┅o┅	Eingleisige Haltestelle | *Single-track stop*				
	══	Eisenbahn | *Railway* (DSB)				

Variobahn

Tango

In einer nächsten Phase ist im Norden eine Verlängerung von Lisbjerg nach Hinnerup geplant, außerdem eine städtische Linie, die einerseits das Entwicklungsgebiet im Hafen (Aarhus Ø), andererseits den Westen der Stadt bis Brabrand erschließen soll. Die Umsetzung eines richtigen *Tram-Train* (Stadtbahn nach dem „Karlsruher Modell") auf bestehenden Eisenbahnstrecken wurde einst auch in Betracht gezogen.

In the next phase, an extension north from Lisbjerg to Hinnerup is planned, as well as an urban line that would, on the one hand, serve the redevelopment area in the port (Aarhus Ø), and on the other hand, link the city centre to the western neighbourhoods, with a terminus envisaged at Brabrand. In the past, the implementation of a proper tram-train on existing mainline railway tracks had also been proposed.

Letbane > Fahrzeuge | *Rolling Stock* (750 V DC)

Nummer *Number*	Anzahl *Quantity*	Hersteller *Manufacturer*	Typ *Class*	Länge *Length*	Breite *Width*	Ausgeliefert *Delivered*
1101-1114*	14	Stadler	Variobahn <=>	32.4 m	2.65 m	2016-2017
2101-2112*	12	Stadler	Tango <=>	39.2 m	2.65 m	2016-2017

* Nummerierung am anderen Wagenende 1201-1214 bzw. 2201-2212 | *Number shown at opposite end as 1201-1214 and 2201-2212*

Ryomgard – L1 Tango #2103 ▸ Aarhus H

Grenaa – L1 Tango #2111 ▸ Aarhus H

Aarhus H – L2 Variobahn #1114 ▸ Lystrup

Dokk1 > Skolebakken – L2 Variobahn #1111 ▸ Aarhus H

Humlehuse – L2 Variobahn #1113 ▶ Odder

Aarhus Universitetshospitalet – L2 Variobahn #1105

Lisbjerg Bygade > Lisbjergskolen – L2 Tango #2110 ▶ Mårslet

Nehrus Allé – L2 Variobahn #1102 ▶ Aarhus H

Hestehaven – Testfahrt im Juni 2020 | *testing in June 2020* (Foto: John Hansen)

ODENSE

Während das in der ersten Auflage dieses Atlasses vorgestellte *Letbane*-Projekt für Aalborg in Nordjütland im Jahr 2015 aufgegeben wurde, schritten die Planungen in Odense auf der Insel Fünen voran, so dass Ende 2021 die erste Linie eröffnet werden soll. Diese führt von West nach Ost am Bahnhof vorbei durch die Innenstadt und erschließt dann im Südosten Gewerbegebiete, den Campus der Süddänischen Universität sowie das neu errichtete Universitätskrankenhaus (OUH). Die Strecke endet im Süden direkt an der eingleisigen Bahnhaltestelle Hjallese, wo man am selben Bahnsteig in die Regionalzüge nach Ringe und umgekehrt umsteigen kann. Der Ausbaustandard der Letbane entspricht dem von modernen Straßenbahnen, durchgehend mit eigenem Gleiskörper und abschnittsweise mit Rasengleis. Für spätere Erweiterungen wurden bereits zwei Gleisdreiecke eingebaut.

Die Letbane wird wochentags tagsüber alle 7½ Minuten verkehren, frühmorgens und abends alle 15 Minuten. Mit dem Betrieb wurde *Keolis Danmark A/S* beauftragt.

Das regionale Busunternehmen *Fynbus* bietet bislang nur in Ferienzeiten Tageskarten für Touristen und nur über deren App bzw. Webshop an, diese kosten jedoch nur 50 DKK (6,72 €, 2020) und sind auf der ganzen Insel Fünen gültig!

In Odense empfiehlt sich auch ein Besuch im Dänischen Eisenbahnmuseum direkt nördlich des Bahnhofs.

While the Letbane project for Aalborg in North Jutland, presented in the first edition of this atlas, was abandoned in 2015, planning in Odense on the island of Funen was progressing, and the first line should open at the end of 2021. It runs from west to east, past the train station and through the city centre before serving a business and retail area, the campus of the University of Southern Denmark, and the newly built University Hospital (OUH) in the southeast. The route eventually ends at the single-track Hjallese railway station, where interchange with regional trains to/from Ringe is provided on the same platform. The design standard of the Letbane corresponds to that of a modern tramway, with a dedicated right-of-way throughout and many sections featuring grass track. Two track triangles have already been installed for future extensions.

The Letbane will run every 7½ minutes during daytime hours and every 15 minutes in the early mornings and evenings. An operating contract was awarded to Keolis Danmark A/S.

The regional bus company 'Fynbus' currently only offers day tickets for tourists during holiday periods and only via their app or webshop, but they cost just 50 DKK (€6.72, 2020) and are valid on the entire island of Funen!

In Odense, a visit to the Danish Railway Museum just north of the railway station is certainly recommended.

Letbane > Fahrzeuge | *Rolling Stock* (750 V DC)						
Nummer *Number*	Anzahl *Quantity*	Hersteller *Manufacturer*	Typ *Class*	Länge *Length*	Breite *Width*	Ausgeliefert *Delivered*
01-16	16	Stadler	Variobahn <=>	29.2 m	2.65 m	2020-2021

ODENSE (Danmark | Dänemark | Denmark)

- 180 000 (79 km²)   ~ 205 000
- 2021
- 1435 mm
- 14.5 km
- 1
- Odense Letbane – *www.odenseletbane.dk*
- Fynbus – *www.fynbus.dk*

SDU (Syddansk Universitet)   (Aug. 2020)

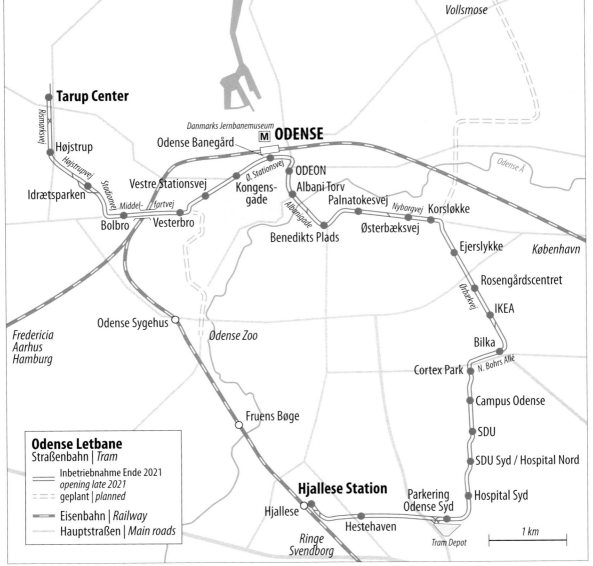

Odense Letbane
Straßenbahn | *Tram*

— Inbetriebnahme Ende 2021
  opening late 2021
--- geplant | *planned*

▬ Eisenbahn | *Railway*
— Hauptstraßen | *Main roads*

Metro (M3/M4) @ København H

KØBENHAVN

Die dänische Hauptstadt Kopenhagen liegt im äußersten Osten des Landes auf der Insel Seeland (Sjælland). Die Stadtgemeinde Kopenhagen umschließt die kleine selbstständige Gemeinde Frederiksberg, drumherum reihen sich zahlreiche kleinere Kommunen, die zusammen die Hauptstadtregion mit fast zwei Mio. Einwohnern bilden. Jenseits des Öresunds setzt sich die Metropolregion im südschwedischen Schonen (Skåne) rund um Malmö fort.

Im Großraum Kopenhagen übernimmt der S-tog nach dem Vorbild der Berliner S-Bahn einen wichtigen Teil des Nahverkehrs. Unterstützt wird er dabei seit 2002 von einer vollautomatischen, fahrerlosen Metro. Außerdem kommt den Regional- und Lokalbahnen im Großraum Kopenhagen/ Malmö (Öresundregion) eine bedeutende Rolle zu.

Von Hamburg aus fahren täglich drei Züge in 4 Stunden und 40 Minuten direkt nach Kopenhagen, seit Dezember 2019 stets über Fredericia und Odense und nicht mehr per Fähre über Puttgarden und Rødby. Erst mit Inbetriebnahme des Fehmarnbelt-Tunnels, dessen Bau derzeit beginnt, wird sich die Reisezeit ab Ende der 2020er Jahre erheblich verringern.

Seit 2015 gibt es nun auch in der dänischen Hauptstadtregion mit „DOT - Din Offentlige Transport" bis zu einem gewissen Grad ein einheitliches Erscheinungsbild des ÖPNV. Die Region ist in unzählige Tarifzonen eingeteilt, was aber für Besucher unerheblich ist, denn für diese empfiehlt sich ein City Pass, der für zwei Bereiche und fünf Zeitspannen angeboten wird: ein City Pass Small umfasst

The Danish capital Copenhagen is located in the extreme east of the country on the island of Zealand (Sjælland). The small independent municipality of Frederiksberg is an enclave surrounded by the city of Copenhagen, and around the two, a large number of other small municipalities are lined up, which together form the Capital Region with almost two million inhabitants. On the other side of the Øresund, the metropolitan region continues into Skåne, the southern Swedish region around Malmö.

In Greater Copenhagen, the S-tog, modelled after the Berlin S-Bahn, plays an important role in public transport. Since 2002, the urban rail network has been complemented by a fully automated driverless metro. In addition, the regional and local railways in the Copenhagen/Malmö area (Øresund Region) make up a significant part of the system, too.

Three trains run daily from Hamburg to Copenhagen, a journey taking 4 hours and 40 minutes. With the train ferry from Puttgarden to Rødby having ended service in December 2019, all trains now run via Fredericia and Odense. Travel times will only be significantly reduced in the late 2020s after the completion of the tunnel under the Fehmarn Belt, whose construction is just beginning.

In 2015, the 'DOT - Din Offentlige Transport' [Your public transport] brand was introduced, giving public transport in the Danish Capital Region a certain uniform identity. The region is divided into numerous fare zones, but this is rather irrelevant for the average visitor for

KØBENHAVN   (Danmark | Dänemark | Denmark)

 740 000 (83 km² – incl. Frederiksberg)

 ~ 2 100 000

 S-tog - 1934; Metro - 2002

 1435 mm

 S-tog ~ 170 km; Metro - 38 km

 S-tog - 6; Metro - 4

 S-tog - *www.dsb.dk/s-tog*
Metro - *www.m.dk*
    www.metroservice.dk

 DOT *(Din offentlige transport) - www.dinoffentligetransport.dk*
www.rejseplanen.dk

 Tram Museum
www.sporvejsmuseet.dk

City Pass (in DKK)	24 h	48 h	72 h	96 h	120 h
Small (Zone 1-4)	80	150	200	250	300
Large (Zone 1-99)	160	300	400	500	600

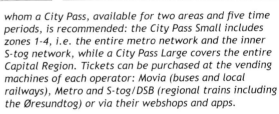
Metro (M3) @ Poul Henningsens Plads

die Zonen 1-4, d.h. das gesamte Metro-Netz und das innere S-tog-Netz, während ein *City Pass Large* die gesamte Hauptstadtregion abdeckt. Fahrkarten sind an Automaten der einzelnen Betreiber erhältlich: *Movia* (Busse und Lokalbahnen), *Metro* und *S-tog/DSB* (S-Bahn und Regionalzüge inkl. Øresundtog) bzw. online oder über diverse Apps.

[100 DKK = 13.44 €]

whom a City Pass, available for two areas and five time periods, is recommended: the City Pass Small includes zones 1-4, i.e. the entire metro network and the inner S-tog network, while a City Pass Large covers the entire Capital Region. Tickets can be purchased at the vending machines of each operator: Movia (buses and local railways), Metro and S-tog/DSB (regional trains including the Øresundtog) or via their webshops and apps.

Metro (M4) @ Nordhavn > Orientkaj

S-tog & (rechts | *right*) Øresundtag @ Østerport

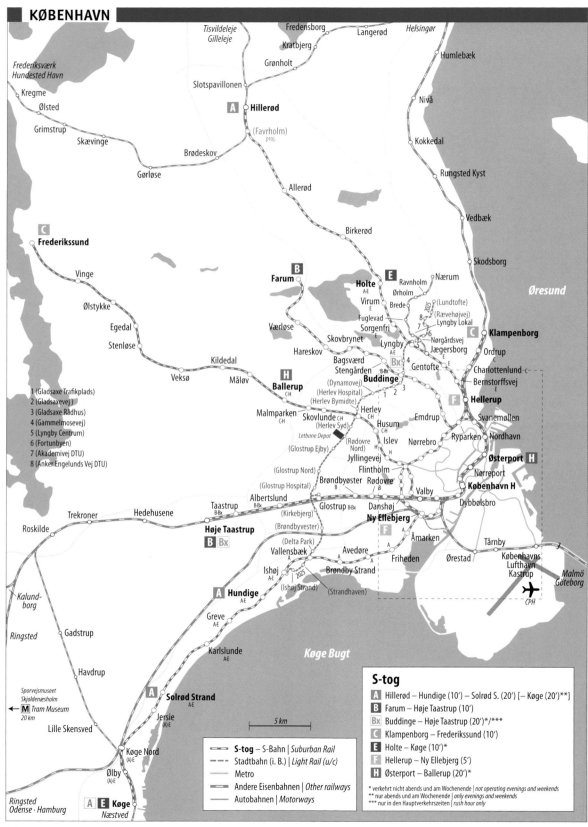

Øresund

Køge Bugt

1 (Gladsaxe Trafikplads)
2 (Gladsaxevej)
3 (Gladsaxe Rådhus)
4 (Gammelmosevej)
5 (Lyngby Centrum)
6 (Fortunbyen)
7 (Akademivej DTU)
8 (Anker Engelunds Vej DTU)

Sporvejsmuseet
Skjoldenæsholm
← M Tram Museum
20 km

5 km

S-tog

A	Hillerød – Hundige (10′) – Solrød S. (20′) [– Køge (20′)**]
B	Farum – Høje Taastrup (10′)
Bx	Buddinge – Høje Taastrup (20′)*/***
C	Klampenborg – Frederikssund (10′)
E	Holte – Køge (10′)*
F	Hellerup – Ny Ellebjerg (5′)
H	Østerport – Ballerup (20′)*

S-tog – S-Bahn | Suburban Rail
Stadtbahn (i. B.) | Light Rail (u/c)
Metro
Andere Eisenbahnen | Other railways
Autobahnen | Motorways

* verkehrt nicht abends und am Wochenende | not operating evenings and weekends
** nur abends und am Wochenende | only evenings and weekends
*** nur in den Hauptverkehrszeiten | rush hour only

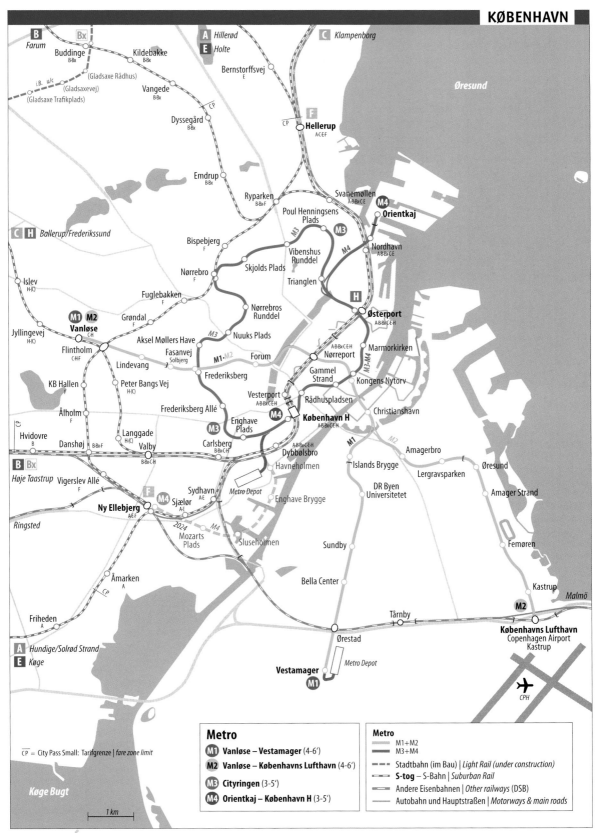

B Farum
Bx Buddinge B-Bx
Kildebakke B-Bx
A Hillerød
E Holte
C Klampenborg
Øresund

i.B. u/c (Gladsaxe Rådhus)
(Gladsaxevej)
(Gladsaxe Trafikplads)
Vangede B-Bx
Bernstorffsvej E

Dyssegård B-Bx
CP
CP Hellerup A-C-E-F
F

Emdrup B-Bx

Ryparken B-Bx-F
Svanemøllen A-B-Bx-C-E
M4 Orientkaj

Poul Henningsens Plads
M3
M3
Nordhavn A-B-Bx-C-E

C H Ballerup/Frederikssund
Bispebjerg F
Vibenshus Runddel
M4

Islev H-(C)
Nørrebro F
Skjolds Plads
Trianglen

Fuglebakken F
Nørrebros Runddel
H Østerport A-B-Bx-C-E-H

Jyllingevej H-(C)
M1 M2
Vanløse C-H
Grøndal F
Nuuks Plads
Marmorkirken

Flintholm C-H-F
Aksel Møllers Have
M3
A-B-C-E-H Nørreport
M3-M4

Lindevang
Fasanvej Solbjerg
M1·M2
Forum
Gammel Strand
Kongens Nytorv

KB Hallen F
Peter Bangs Vej H-(C)
Frederiksberg
Vesterport A-B-Bx-C-E-H
Rådhuspladsen

Ålholm F
Langgade H-(C)
Frederiksberg Allé
M4 København H A-B-Bx-C-E-H
Christianshavn

Hvidovre B
Danshøj B-Bx-F
Valby B-Bx-C-H
Carlsberg B-Bx-C-H
Enghave Plads
M3
A-B-Bx-C-E-H Dybbølsbro
M1
M2
Amagerbro

B Bx
Høje Taastrup
Vigerslev Allé
F Ny Ellebjerg A-E-F
Sydhavn A-E
M4 Sjælør A-E
Havneholmen
Islands Brygge
Lergravsparken
Øresund

Metro Depot
Enghave Brygge
DR Byen Universitetet
Amager Strand

Ringsted
2024 M4
Mozarts Plads
Sluseholmen
Sundby
Femøren

Åmarken A
CP
Bella Center
Kastrup

Friheden A
Ørestad
Tårnby
M2 Københavns Lufthavn
Copenhagen Airport Kastrup
Malmö

A Hundige/Solrød Strand
E Køge

Vestamager
M1
Metro Depot
✈ CPH

CP = City Pass Small: Tarifgrenze | fare zone limit

Metro

M1 **Vanløse – Vestamager** (4–6′)

M2 **Vanløse – Københavns Lufthavn** (4–6′)

M3 **Cityringen** (3–5′)

M4 **Orientkaj – København H** (3–5′)

Metro

M1+M2
M3+M4
--- Stadtbahn (im Bau) | Light Rail (under construction)
S-tog – S-Bahn | Suburban Rail
Andere Eisenbahnen | Other railways (DSB)
Autobahn und Hauptstraßen | Motorways & main roads

Køge Bugt
1 km

M1/M2 – Vanløse

Metro

Seit dem 19. Oktober 2002 verfügt auch die dänische Hauptstadt über eine U-Bahn und zwar in Form einer vollautomatischen, fahrerlosen Mini-Metro, die das Stadtzentrum in tief liegenden Röhrentunneln durchquert und auf Außenstrecken oberirdisch fährt. Während die unterirdischen Stationen der Linien M1 und M2, die alle nach einem einheitlichen Design gestaltet wurden, von Anfang an mit Bahnsteigtüren ausgestattet waren, wurde auf den oberirdischen anfangs ein Gleisüberwachungssystem ähnlich wie in Nürnberg installiert. Mittlerweile wurden diese Bahnhöfe allerdings mit halbhohen Bahnsteigtüren nachgerüstet.

Die Linien M1 und M2 fahren abwechselnd am westlichen Endpunkt Vanløse ab und verzweigen sich südöstlich des U-Bahnhofs Christianshavn in einen Ast nach Vestamager und einen zum Flughafen. Das ursprüngliche Netz von 20 km Länge (8,9 km unterirdisch) wurde etappenweise in Betrieb genommen, zuletzt der Abschnitt Lergravsparken – Lufthavnen am 28. September 2007. Der westliche Abschnitt zwischen Frederiksberg und Vanløse liegt auf einer Trasse, auf der früher der S-tog fuhr, der Flughafen-Ast hingegen nutzt eine alte Bahntrasse der Amagerbanen nach Kastrup und Dragør, auf der seit 1947 kein Personenverkehr mehr stattfand.

2009 begann der Ausbau des Netzes mit „Cityringen", einer 15,5 km langen, völlig unterirdisch verlaufenden Ringlinie (M3), die am 29. September 2019 in Betrieb ging. Später wurde das Projekt um einen 2,5 km langen Nordast von Østerport in das Nordhafengebiet erweitert, der seit dem 28. März 2020 von der Linie M4 bedient wird. Der vorläufige Endpunkt Orientkaj befindet sich in Hochlage. Mit der fortschreitenden städtebaulichen Entwicklung

Metro

Since 19 October 2002, the Danish capital has boasted a fully automated driverless mini-metro which runs through the city centre in deep tube tunnels, while the outer sections lie above ground. The M1 and M2 underground stations, which all have a standard design, were equipped with platform screen doors from the start, while the surface stations used to feature a track monitoring system similar to that in operation in Nuremberg. However, half-height platform screen doors have now been installed in all these stations.

Trains on the two lines M1 and M2 leave the western terminus Vanløse alternately before diverging just southeast of the metro station Christianshavn, with one branch going to Vestamager and the other to the airport. The original network, which has a total length of 20 km (8.9 km underground), was put into operation in stages, with the last section Lergravsparken – Lufthavnen having opened on 28 September 2007. The western section between Frederiksberg and Vanløse runs on an alignment previously used by the S-tog, while the leg to the airport uses an old railway line (Amagerbanen) to Dragør via Kastrup, which had not seen any passenger service since 1947.

In 2009, the expansion of the network was started with 'Cityringen', a 15.5 km completely underground circle line (M3) which opened on 29 September 2019. Later, the project was enhanced with a 2.5 km northern branch from Østerport to the Nordhavn [northern port] redevelopment area, which has been served by line M4 since 28 March 2020. The terminus at Orientkaj lies on a viaduct. As the redevelopment of the port area continues, the line may be extended with another 2-3

M4 – Orientkaj

des Hafengebiets könnte die Strecke mit 2 bis 3 weiteren Stationen verlängert werden. Südlich des Hauptbahnhofs wird die Ausfädelung zum neuen Betriebshof genutzt, um bis ca. 2024 einen zweiten Ast über das Südhafengelände zum Knoten Ny Ellebjerg anzuhängen. Daran könnte eine Verlängerung zum Krankenhaus in Hvidovre und/oder als Westtangente über Solbjerg und Nørrebro bis Emdrup anschließen.

Auch wenn die neuen Strecken der M3/M4 weitgehend nach denselben Parametern wie die M1/M2 errichtet wurden, gibt es keine Gleisverbindung zwischen den beiden Teilnetzen. Die Gestaltung der bis zu 35 m tiefen U-Bahnhöfe ist vor allem durch Verwendung von unterschiedlichen Farben und Materialien abwechslungsreicher als bei den Linien M1/M2.

Eigentümer der Metro ist *Metroselskabet*, an der der dänische Staat sowie die Städte Kopenhagen und

stations. To the south of the Central Railway Station, the junction built for the depot access tracks will also be used for a second branch, which by 2024 will run to the rail hub at Ny Ellebjerg via the southern port (Sydhavn) redevelopment area. From there, an extension could be built to Hvidovre Hospital and/or via Solbjerg and Nørrebro to Emdrup forming a kind of western tangential route.

The new M3/M4 routes were largely built to the same parameters as the older M1/M2, but there is no track connection between the two systems. The designs of the underground stations though, which lie up to 35 m deep, are more varied than the older ones, mainly through the use of different colours and materials.

The Metro is owned by 'Metroselskabet', a company in which the Danish state as well as the cities of Copenhagen and Frederiksberg are involved. The actual operation, at

M1/M2 – Kongens Nytorv

M2 – Øresund

M3/M4 – København H

Frederiksberg beteiligt sind. Der eigentliche Betrieb liegt bis mindestens 2027 in den Händen von *Metro Service A/S* – dahinter verbirgt sich ATM (Azienda Transporti Milanese) und Hitachi Rail STS (vormals Ansaldo STS).

Wie die durchgehend begehbaren 3-Wagen-Züge beider Generationen stammt das ursprüngliche Betriebssystem von der italienischen Firma Ansaldobreda (seit 2015 Hitachi Rail), welches 30 Züge pro Stunde und Richtung zulässt. Die neuen Strecken wurden hingegen mit CBTC (Computer-based train control) ausgerüstet, was bis zu 39 Züge pro Stunde und Richtung erlauben soll. Die Stromzufuhr mit 750 V Gleichstrom erfolgt über eine seitliche Stromschiene.

least until 2027, lies in the hands of 'Metro Service A/S', a joint venture between ATM (Azienda Trasporti Milanese) and Hitachi Rail STS (formerly Ansaldo STS).

Like the walk-through 3-car trains of both generations, the original operating system was delivered by the Italian company Ansaldobreda (since 2015 Hitachi Rail) and allows 30 trains per hour and direction. The new routes, however, were equipped with CBTC (computer-based train control), which increases the line capacity to 39 trains per hour and direction. 750 V dc power is supplied via a third rail.

M3/M4 – Kongens Nytorv

M3 – Aksel Møllers Have

M3 – Frederiksberg Allé

M3 – Trianglen

M3 – Enghave Plads

Metro > Fahrzeuge | _Rolling Stock_ (750 V DC)

Nummer _Number_	Anzahl _Quantity_	Hersteller _Manufacturer_	Typ _Class_	Länge _Length_	Breite _Width_	Ausgeliefert _Delivered_
M1/M2: 01-42	42	Ansaldo	Driverless	39.0 m	2.65 m	2001-2007, 2020
M3/M4: 01-39	39	Ansaldo	Driverless	39.0 m	2.65 m	2014-2018

Dybbølsbro (Fisketorvet) – Linje B ▶ Høje Taastrup

S-tog – S-Bahn

Der Kopenhagener S-tog [S-Zug] ähnelt in vielen Aspekten der Berliner und Hamburger S-Bahn. Er verkehrt durchweg auf eigenen Gleisen, oft parallel zu Fernbahnstrecken und erfüllt vorwiegend eine innerstädtische Verkehrsfunktion. Das Netz ist zwar anders als in Berlin und Hamburg mit Oberleitung elektrifiziert, jedoch ist die verwendete Spannung von 1500 V Gleichstrom nicht mit dem übrigen dänischen Bahnnetz (25 kV Wechselstrom) kompatibel. Die Gesamtnetzlänge beträgt 170 km mit 87 Stationen, wovon etwa 110 km (70 Stationen) im geschlossen bebauten Gebiet von Groß-Kopenhagen liegen, wo der durchschnittliche Stationsabstand etwa 1,6 km beträgt und die Züge mindestens alle 10 Minuten verkehren. Die Bahnsteige sind 160 m lang, auf der Ringbahn (Linie F) nur 90 m. Freitag- und Samstagnacht bzw. vor Feiertagen fährt der S-tog durchgehend im 30-Minuten-Takt.

Bis auf die eigentlich tangential verlaufende Ringbahn (Linie F) gehen alle Strecken radial vom Stadtzentrum aus. Sie sind durch die 1917-1921 eröffnete viergleisige Stammstrecke zwischen Østerport und Hovedbanegård (Hauptbahnhof) miteinander verbunden; diese ist auf 1,5 km (inkl. Bahnhof Nørreport) unterirdisch. Die beiden westlichen Gleise werden vom S-tog benutzt, die beiden östlichen von Regional- und Fernzügen. Der elektrische S-tog-Betrieb begann 1934 zwischen Hauptbahnhof und Klampenborg sowie zwischen Frederiksberg und Klampenborg. Nach und nach wurden andere Strecken auf S-Bahn-Standard gebracht, nur die Køge-Linie wurde zwischen 1972 und 1983 für den S-tog neu errichtet. 1989 erreichte der S-tog Frederikssund. Als Neubaustrecke auf der Trasse einer alten Güterbahn entstand im Zusammenhang mit dem Metro-Bau 2004-2006 der südliche Abschnitt

S-tog – Suburban Rail

The Copenhagen S-tog [S-train] is similar in many aspects to the Berlin and Hamburg S-Bahn systems. It runs entirely on its own tracks, often parallel to mainline routes, and its primary function lies in intra-city transport. Unlike in Berlin and Hamburg, however, the network is electrified with an overhead catenary, although the 1500 V dc voltage used is incompatible with the rest of the Danish electrified railway network, which uses 25 kV ac. The total network length is 170 km (with 87 stations), of which 110 km (70 stations) lies within the continuously built-up area of Greater Copenhagen, where the average station distance is about 1.6 km and trains run at least every 10 minutes. The platforms are 160 m long, except on the ring line (line F), where they are just 90 m. On Friday and Saturday nights as well as before holidays, the S-tog operates every 30 minutes all night.

Except for the ring line (line F), which is in fact a tangential line, the routes are all radial. They are connected via a four-track trunk route between Østerport and Hovedbanegård (Central Station), which opened between 1917 and 1921 and features a 1.5 km underground section (including Nørreport station); the two western tracks are used by the S-tog, and the two eastern ones by regional and long-distance trains. In 1934, electric S-tog operation began between the Central Station and Klampenborg, and between Frederiksberg and Klampenborg. Gradually, many other routes were upgraded to S-tog standard, too. The line to Køge, however, was purpose-built for the S-tog between 1972 and 1983. In 1989, the S-tog reached Frederikssund. In conjunction with the construction of the Metro system, and following an old freight railway, the ring line was extended from Flintholm to Ny Ellebjerg

København H – Linje H ▶ Østerport

der Ringbahn zwischen Flintholm und Ny Ellebjerg, womit das heutige Netz vollständig war. 2016 wurde die Station Carlsberg eröffnet, welche die nahe Station Enghave ersetzte, und zuletzt im Dezember 2020 die neue Station Vinge auf der Strecke nach Frederikssund. Während nach Inbetriebnahme der Fernbahn über Køge Nord eine Verlängerung des S-tog von Høje Taastrup nach Roskilde (11,5 km) wieder aktuell ist, wird auch die Möglichkeit einer Umrüstung auf fahrerlosen Betrieb untersucht.

Seit 2007 wird der S-Bahn-Betrieb ausschließlich mit Fahrzeugen der 4. Generation abgewickelt. Davon gibt es die kurze 4-Wagen-Version Litra SE (31 Einheiten), die u.a. auf der Ringbahn eingesetzt wird, und die lange 8-Wagen-Version Litra SA (104 Einheiten, 83,8 m), die meist als Doppeltraktionen verkehrt. Sie wurden gemeinsam von Alstom LHB und Siemens zwischen 1996 und 2006 in Deutschland hergestellt und zeichnen sich durch ihre ungewöhnliche Breite von 3,60 m aus, wodurch eine Querbestuhlung 3+3 möglich ist. Die Fußbodenhöhe liegt bei 1100 mm.

between 2004 and 2006, thus completing today's network. The most recent additions were Carlsberg station in 2016, which replaced the nearby Enghave station, and Vinge on the Frederikssund line in December 2020. After the completion of the new main line via Køge Nord, an extension of the S-tog system from Høje Taastrup to Roskilde (11.5 km) is again on the table; at the same time, the upgrading of the entire system to driverless operation is being examined.

Since 2007, the S-tog system has been operated exclusively with 4th generation trains. The fleet includes 31 units of the short 4-car LITRA SE — used for example on the ring line — as well as 104 units of the long 8-car LITRA SA (83.8 m), which operate mostly as double trainsets. The trains were jointly manufactured by Siemens and Alstom LHB in Germany between 1996 and 2006 and are remarkable for their extraordinary width of 3.60 m, resulting in a 3+3 transversal seating arrangement. The floor height is 1100 mm above the top of the rail.

Østerport

Carlsberg

Herlev Bymidte

Visualisierung © Hovedstadens Letbane/Gottlieb Paludan Architects

Hovedstadens Letbane – Stadtbahn

Nachdem das städtische Straßenbahnnetz im Jahr 1972 verschwunden war, wurde seit Anfang des Jahrtausends eine Stadtbahn als Tangentialverbindung durch die westlichen Vororte geplant. Die sog. *Letbane* [Leichtbahn von engl. *Light Rail*] wird auf einer 28 km langen Strecke (29 Stationen) entlang des Ring-3-Korridors (rund 9-12 km vom Kopenhagener Zentrum entfernt) acht Kommunen durchqueren: Lyngby-Taarbæk, Gladsaxe, Herlev, Rødovre, Glostrup, Brøndby, Vallensbæk und Ishøj. Am nördlichen Ende wird „Danmarks Tekniske Universitet" angeschlossen, auf dem mittleren Abschnitt liegen die Krankenhäuser Herlev und Glostrup direkt an der Strecke. An sechs Stationen wird es eine Umsteigemöglichkeit zu den radialen S-tog-Linien geben, wobei der Bahnhof Glostrup über eine Stichstrecke erreicht wird. Betriebshof und Leitstelle werden an der Grenze zwischen Glostrup und Herlev am Ballerup Boulevard errichtet.

Die Stadtbahn wird schlüsselfertig von einem Konsortium errichtet, an dem neben dem Generalunternehmer Per Aarsleff A/S auch Siemens beteiligt ist und u.a. die vierteiligen Fahrzeuge vom Typ Avenio liefert. Nachdem die Bauarbeiten schließlich 2018 begonnen haben, ist nach derzeitigem Stand eine Inbetriebnahme frühestens 2025 zu erwarten. Die Stadtbahn wird wie die Metro von *Metro Service A/S* betrieben werden. (Aktuelles unter www.dinletbane.dk)

Hovedstadens Letbane – Light Rail

With the urban tram system having been abandoned in 1972, from the start of the new millennium, a modern light rail line was planned as a tangential link through the western suburbs. On its 28 km route (29 stations) along the Ring 3 corridor (some 9-12 km from Copenhagen's city centre), the so-called 'Letbane' [light railway] will traverse eight municipalities: Lyngby-Taarbæk, Gladsaxe, Herlev, Rødovre, Glostrup, Brøndby, Vallensbæk and Ishøj. Along the northernmost stretch, it will serve 'Danmarks Tekniske Universitet', and along the middle stretch, there are two major hospitals at Herlev and Glostrup. At six stations, interchange with the radial S-tog lines will be provided; Glostrup station will be linked by a spur. The control centre and maintenance yard will be built on Ballerup Boulevard at the border between Glostrup and Herlev.

The light rail system is being implemented as a turnkey project by a consortium led by Per Aarsleff A/S, in which Siemens plays an important role, for example by delivering 4-section vehicles of their successful Avenio tram. With construction work having been launched in 2018, the Letbane may start running in 2025 at the earliest. Like the Metro, the Letbane will be operated by 'Metro Service A/S'.
(Follow the project at www.dinletbane.dk)

Letbane > Fahrzeuge | *Rolling Stock* (750 V DC)						
Nummer *Number*	Anzahl *Quantity*	Hersteller *Manufacturer*	Typ *Class*	Länge *Length*	Breite *Width*	Ausgeliefert *Delivered*
	29	Siemens	Avenio <=>	~37 m	2.65 m	*202x-*

Øresundståg @ Malmö Triangeln

Regional Railways

On weekdays, the Øresundstog (Öresundståg in Swedish) runs from Copenhagen (Østerport) to the airport every 10 minutes, with every other train continuing over the Öresund Bridge, opened in 2000, and the Malmö city tunnel, completed in 2010, to Malmö C. From there, at present, most trains operate through to various destinations in Sweden: via Landskrona and Helsingborg to Gothenburg; and via Hässleholm to Växjö and Kalmar as well as Karlskrona. On the Danish side, the trains provide an S-Bahn-style service north of Copenhagen on the Kystbane [Coast Line], going every 10 minutes to Nivå and every 20 minutes (express between Helle-rup and Kokkedal) to Helsingør (Elsinore). The service uses dual-system electric EMUs of class ET/X31K from Bombardier, which are equipped for both the Danish (25 kV 50 Hz ac) as well as the Swedish (15 kV 16 ⅔ Hz ac) overhead power supply system.

A dense regional and intercity rail service is also provided on the main route from Copenhagen to Roskilde and further west. With the new mainline route for long-distance trains in operation between Ny Ellebjerg and Ringsted via Køge Nord since mid-2019, more capacity for regional services is now available on the old route.

North of Copenhagen and on behalf of Movia, Lokaltog A/S operates four non-electrified local railways, three of which connect the S-tog terminus at Hillerød with some rather rural areas in Northern Zealand, while the fourth, **Nærumbanen**, starts at Jægersborg S-tog station and runs on a 7.8 km single-track line to Nærum; with a 20-minute headway (10 minutes during peak hours), it provides an S-tog-like service. This line uses RegioSprinter DMUs manufactured by Duewag (now Siemens). In the medium term, the Nærumbane may be integrated into the future Letbane network.

Regionalbahnen

Als **Øresundstog** (schwed. Öresundståg) fahren Züge von Kopenhagen (Østerport) wochentags tagsüber alle 10 Minuten bis zum Flughafen und alle 20 Minuten weiter über die im Jahr 2000 eröffnete Öresundbrücke und den 2010 vollendeten Citytunnel nach Malmö C, wo sie bislang noch über Landskrona und Helsingborg bis Göteborg oder über Hässleholm nach Växjö bzw. Kalmar sowie nach Karlskrona durchgebunden werden. Auf dänischer Seite übernehmen die Züge nördlich von Kopenhagen auf der Kystbane die Funktion einer S-Bahn, mit Zügen quasi alle 10 Minuten bis Nivå und alle 20 Minuten weiter bis Helsingør (Express Hellerup – Kokkedal). Zum Einsatz kommen hier 2-System-Elektrotriebwagen der Baureihe ET/X31K von Bombardier, die sowohl für das dänische (25 kV 50 Hz AC) als auch für das schwedische Bahnnetz (15 kV 16⅔ Hz AC) ausgerüstet sind.

Dichter Regional- und Intercity-Verkehr findet auch auf der Hauptstrecke Richtung Roskilde und in den Westen des Landes statt. Nach Inbetriebnahme der Neubaustrecke für den Fernverkehr zwischen Ny Ellebjerg über Køge Nord nach Ringsted Mitte 2019 steht dafür auf der alten Strecke mehr Kapazität zur Verfügung.

Nördlich von Kopenhagen betreibt Lokaltog A/S im Auftrag von Movia vier nicht elektrifizierte Lokalbahnstrecken, wovon drei in Hillerød an den S-tog anschließen und eher ländliche Gebiete im Norden Seelands erschließen, während die vierte, **Nærumbanen**, am S-Bahnhof Jægersborg beginnt und auf einer 7,8 km langen eingleisigen Strecke im 20-Minuten-Takt (10 Min. HVZ) durchaus eine S-Bahn-ähnliche Funktion wahrnimmt. Zum Einsatz kommen hier RegioSprinter von Duewag (heute Siemens). Die Nærumbane könnte mittelfristig in das zukünftige Letbane-Netz integriert werden.

Nærumbanen @ Nærum

#327 (KS - Københavns Sporveje) – Scandia, 1912 + Beiwagen | *trailer* #1321

Neben den Museen in Bergen, Trondheim, Oslo, Göteborg, Stockholm (derzeit geschlossen) und Helsinki findet man in Nordeuropa in einiger Entfernung zu den eigentlichen Straßenbahnen zwei sehenswerte Museen:
Im **Sporvejsmuseet** in **Skjoldenæsholm** sind viele Fahrzeuge der 1972 eingestellten Kopenhagener Straßenbahn zu sehen, die an Öffnungstagen auf einer rund 1,7 km langen Strecke verkehren. Neben Kopenhagener Wagen sind auch welche aus Odense und Aarhus sowie von ausländischen Betrieben (u.a. aus Hamburg) zu finden. Das Museum liegt etwa 50 km südwestlich der Hauptstadt und ist leider nicht mit öffentlichen Verkehrsmitteln erreichbar. Öffnungszeiten und Infos zum Busshuttle vom Bahnhof Borup gibt es unter

Besides the museums in Bergen, Trondheim, Oslo, Gothenburg, Stockholm (currently closed) and Helsinki, the Nordic countries also boast two fantastic museums located at some distance from the nearest tram city:
*At the **Sporvejsmuseet** in **Skjoldenæsholm**, numerous vehicles from Copenhagen's tram system, which was abandoned in 1972, have been preserved; many of them operate on a 1.7 km route on opening days. Besides Copenhagen cars, the museum's collection also includes trams from Odense and Aarhus as well as several foreign cities. The museum is located some 50 km southwest of the capital and is not accessible with public transport. Opening times and information about the shuttle bus from Borup train station are available at*

www.sporvejsmuseet.dk

#2412 (RBG - Rheinische Bahngesellschaft) – Düwag, 1957

PCC #3060 (HHA - Hamburger Hochbahn AG) – La Brugeoise et Nivelles, 1951

M20 #186 (GS - Göteborgs Spårvägar) – GS, 1930

Museispårvägen in **Malmköping**, 70 km nordöstlich von Norrköping und rund 80 km westlich von Stockholm gelegen (nicht mit der Bahn erreichbar), bietet eine große Auswahl historischer Straßenbahnfahrzeuge aller schwedischen Betriebe. Zur Blütezeit gab es in diesem Land neben den bestehenden immerhin noch weitere acht Städte mit einer elektrischen Straßenbahn: Gävle (1909-1956), Helsingborg (1903-1967), Jönköping (1907-1958), Karlskrona (1910-1949), Kiruna (1907-1958), Malmö (1906-1973), Sundsvall (1910-1952) und Uppsala (1906-1953).

An Öffnungstagen (Mai-August samstags, in den Sommerferien täglich) verkehrt die *Museispårväg* regelmäßig auf einer 2,6 km langen idyllischen Strecke nach Norden bis Hosjö. Mehr Infos unter

Museispårvägen in *Malmköping*, 70 km northeast of Norrköping and about 80 km west of Stockholm (not accessible by train), offers a large selection of historical tram vehicles from all the Swedish tramway companies. In its heyday, Sweden had eight other cities with an electric tramway: Gävle (1909-1956), Helsingborg (1903-1967), Jönköping (1907-1958), Karlskrona (1910-1949), Kiruna (1907-1958), Malmö (1906-1973), Sundsvall (1910-1952) and Uppsala (1906-1953).

On opening days (Saturdays May-August, daily during summer school holidays), the *Museispårväg* regularly runs on an idyllic 2.6 km route from the museum north to Hosjö. Further information at

www.sparvagssallskapet.se – www.muma.se

Das seit 2017 geschlossene **Stockholms Spårvägsmuseum** soll 2021 an einem neuen Standort im Osten der Stadt in einem ehemaligen Gaswerk neu eröffnet werden.

Stockholms Spårvägsmuseum, closed since 2017, may reopen in 2021 at a new location in the east of the city, on the terrains of a former gasworks.

F1 #43 (HSS - Helsingborgs Stads Sparvägar) – ASEA, 1948

A30 #302 (SL - Storstockholms Lokaltrafik) – Hammarby, 1983

Urbos #02 „Åsa-Hanna" @ Lund C > Universitetssjukhuset (Sept. 2020)

LUND

Die beschauliche Universitätsstadt Lund liegt nur 15 km nordöstlich von Malmö, der drittgrößten Stadt Schwedens, in der Region Skåne (dt. Schonen). Beide Städte sind rund sieben Mal pro Stunde per Bahn miteinander verbunden, darunter der über die Öresundbrücke nach Dänemark durchgebundene *Öresundståg* sowie der in der Region Skåne wie eine S-Bahn verkehrende *Pågatåg*.

Während sowohl in Helsingborg als auch in Malmö Projekte zur Wiedereinführung der Straßenbahn (in Helsingborg fuhren von 1903 bis 1967 und in Malmö von 1906 bis 1973 elektrische *spårvagnar*) wieder in der Schublade verschwunden sind, eröffnete Lund am 12. Dezember 2020 (corona-bedingt nur digital!) seine erste Straßenbahnstrecke und wurde somit zur aktuell vierten Tram-Stadt in Schweden. Der Bau der Strecke hatte im Februar 2017 begonnen. Lund hatte hingegen keine Straßenbahn der ersten Generation, auch wenn es um 1905 konkrete Initiativen diesbezüglich gab.

Als „LundaExpressen" verbindet die Linie 1 heute den Bahnhof mit Forschungseinrichtungen und Neubaugebieten im Nordosten der Stadt und hält an neun standardisierten Haltestellen mit meist 45 m langen Bahnsteigen. Für die Tram wurde eine Bustrasse (*Lundalänken*), die vom Universitätskrankenhaus bis Solbjer führte, umgebaut. Rund um die Haltestellen Solbjer und Brunnshögstorget waren bei Inbetriebnahme der Tram weitreichende städtebauliche Projekte im Gange, weiter nordöstlich fährt die Straßenbahn hingegen durch weitgehend unbebautes Gebiet. Der Betriebshof liegt rund 700 m hinter der Endstation ESS, was für „European Spallation Source" steht. Der Straßenbahn steht durchgehend ein eigener Gleiskörper zur Verfügung, meist als Rasengleis, nahe des

The tranquil university town of Lund lies in the Skåne region, only 15 km northeast of Malmö, Sweden's third largest city. Both cities are connected by train around seven times an hour, including the Öresundståg, which runs through to Denmark via the Öresund Bridge, and the Pågatåg, which runs like an S-Bahn in the Skåne region.

While recent projects to reintroduce trams to both Helsingborg and Malmö have been shelved (Helsingborg had electric 'spårvagnar' from 1903 to 1967 and Malmö from 1906 to 1973), Lund officially opened its first tram line on 12 December 2020 (due to Covid-19 with just a digital celebration!), becoming the fourth city in Sweden to currently boast a tram system. The construction of the line had begun in February 2017. Lund, however, never had a first-generation tramway, although there had been initiatives in this regard in around 1905.

Labelled 'LundaExpressen', line 1 now runs from the train station to the research institutes and new housing developments in the northeast of the city serving nine standardised stops with mostly 45 m platforms. A former busway (Lundalänken) leading from the university hospital to Solbjer was rebuilt to accommodate the new tram tracks. Extensive urban development projects were going on around the Solbjer and Brunnshögstorget stops when the tram was inaugurated, but further northeast the trams run through largely undeveloped areas. The depot is located some 700 m beyond the terminus ESS, which stands for 'European Spallation Source'. The tram has its own right-of-way throughout, mostly as a grass track, though paved on its approach to the train station, where emergency vehicles may use the tram lanes. A wide cycle path was laid out along the entire route, which

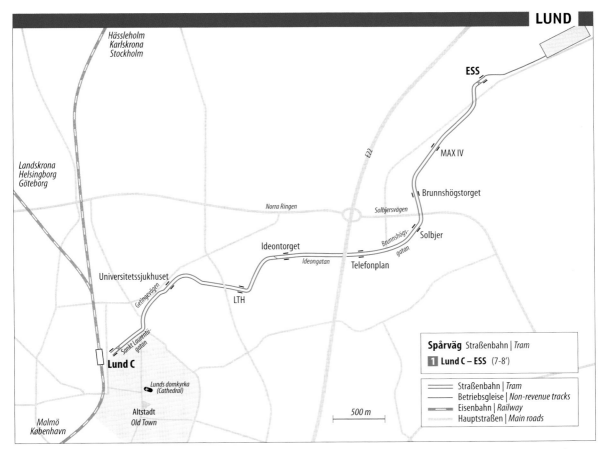

Hässleholm
Karlskrona
Stockholm

ESS

Landskrona
Helsingborg
Göteborg

MAX IV

Brunnshögstorget

Norra Ringen

Solbjersvägen

Brunnshögs-gatan

Solbjer

Ideontorget

Ideongatan

Telefonplan

Universitetssjukhuset

Getingevägen

LTH

Sankt Laurenti-gatan

Lund C

Lunds domkyrka
(Cathedral)

Altstadt
Old Town

Malmö
København

500 m

Spårväg Straßenbahn | *Tram*

1 **Lund C – ESS** (7-8′)

Straßenbahn | *Tram*
Betriebsgleise | *Non-revenue tracks*
Eisenbahn | *Railway*
Hauptstraßen | *Main roads*

Bahnhofs gepflastert und im Notfall befahrbar. Entlang der gesamten Strecke wurde ein breiter Radweg angelegt, der bei Notfällen auch von Einsatzfahrzeugen genutzt werden kann. Anfangs angedachte Erweiterungen von Solbjer Richtung Osten nach Dalby sowie über das Stadtzentrum nach Süden bis Staffanstorp wurden vorerst zurückgestellt.

Die neue Straßenbahn gehört zum städtischen ÖPNV-Netz von Lund und ist somit in das regionale Tarifsystem von Skånetrafiken integriert. Eine 24-Stunden-Karte (*24-timmarsbiljett*) für Lund kostet lediglich 54 SEK (5,30 €), dazu kommen allerdings einmalig 30 SEK für die im Kundencenter oder in Kiosken erhältliche aufladbare *reskort*. Den Betrieb der neuen Straßenbahn übernahm *Vy Buss* (vormals *Nettbuss*) im Auftrag von Skånetrafiken.

can also be used by emergency vehicles. Two extensions initially planned from Solbjer east to Dalby and via the city centre south to Staffanstorp have been postponed for the time being.

The new tram line is part of Lund's urban public transport network and is therefore integrated into Skånetrafiken's regional fare system. A 24-hour ticket (24-timmarsbiljett) for Lund only costs 54 SEK (€5.30), but there is a one-time fee of 30 SEK for the rechargeable reskort, which is available in the customer centre and in kiosks. An operating contract for the new tram line was signed between Skånetrafiken and Vy Buss (formerly Nettbuss).

LUND (Sverige | Schweden | Sweden)

95 000 (26.5 km²)   125 000

el.   2020   1435 mm

km   5.2 km   1

Spårväg Lund
www.sparvaglund.se

Skånetrafiken
www.skanetrafiken.se

Lund C – Öresundtåg & Pågatåg

Urbos #02 „Åsa-Hanna" @ Lund C (Clemenstorget, Sept. 2020)

Nachdem das erste Fahrzeug („Åsa-Hanna") erst Ende Juli 2020 vom spanischen Hersteller CAF angeliefert worden war, standen zur Eröffnung lediglich vier Fahrzeuge zur Verfügung, so dass anfangs nur alle 20 Minuten gefahren werden konnte. Mit Auslieferung der restlichen Wagen wird das Angebot auf einen 7½-Minuten-Takt verdichtet.

With the first vehicle ('Åsa-Hanna') having only been delivered by the Spanish manufacturer CAF in late July 2020, just four vehicles were available for the opening, so initially a timetable with a tram only every 20 minutes was possible. With the ongoing delivery of the remaining cars, headways will be reduced to 7½ minutes.

Urbos #02 „Åsa-Hanna" @ ESS (Sept. 2020)   (Foto: Per Gunnar Andersson)

Urbos #02 „Åsa-Hanna" @ Universitetssjukhuset (Sept. 2020)

LTH (Foto PG Andersson)

LTH > Universitetssjukhuset (Foto PG Andersson)

Brunnshögstorget (Sept. 2020)

ESS (Sept. 2020)

Spårväg > Fahrzeuge | Rolling Stock (750 V DC)

Nummer Number	Anzahl Quantity	Hersteller Manufacturer	Typ Class	Länge Length	Breite Width	Ausgeliefert Delivered
01-07	7	CAF	Urbos 100 <=>	33.0 m	2.65 m	2020-2021

Brunnshögstorget (Okt. 2020) *(Foto Per Gunnar Andersson)*

Tram Depot (Okt. 2020) *(Foto PG Andersson)*

Urbos #03 „Blåtand" (Okt. 2020) *(Foto PG Andersson)*

In Malmö verkehrt seit 1987 in den Sommermonaten samstags und sonntags im Kungsparken westlich der Innenstadt eine Museums-straßenbahn vom Technischen Museum zur Stadtbibliothek.

On Saturdays and Sundays during the summer months, a heritage tramway has been operated since 1987, running in Malmö's Kungsparken to the west of the city centre on a route between the Technical Museum and the City Library.

[www.mss.se]

Trolleybus #6993 „Ellen" @ Landskrona Stationen
(Foto Per Gunnar Andersson)

LANDSKRONA

In Skåne liegt rund 30 km nordwestlich von Lund auch die kleine Stadt Landskrona (30.000 Einw.), wo seit dem 27. September 2003 ein Obus (schwed. *Trådbuss* – „Drahtbus") fährt, und zwar vom Stadtzentrum zum neuen Bahnhof am östlichen Rand der Stadt, der den alten zentrumsnahen Kopfbahnhof am Fährhafen ersetzte. Die einzige Linie, die Linie 3 im Stadtbusnetz, ist knapp 3 km lang und wurde anfangs mit drei Obussen des Typs Trollino 12 (Nr. 6991-6993) von Solaris/Ganz betrieben. 2010 kam ein vierter (Nr. 6990) hinzu und 2013 ergänzte ein fünfter (Nr. 6994) die Flotte (beide von Solaris/Škoda). Letzterer ist mit einer speziellen Batterie ausgestattet, die den Betrieb auf bis zu 20 km langen, nicht elektrifizierten Strecken ermöglicht. Die Strecke zum Depot muss von vier Bussen im Batteriebetrieb, von Bus Nr. 6990 mit Dieselhilfsmotor zurückgelegt werden. Die Busse sind Eigentum von *Skånetrafiken*.

Der Stadtbusverkehr in Landskrona wird derzeit von *Nobina AB* betrieben, tariflich gehört die Stadt zum Verkehrsverbund *Skånetrafiken* (www.skanetrafiken.se). Der Obus verkehrt tagsüber alle 12 Minuten, in der Hauptverkehrszeit alle 6 Minuten.

Obusse gab es in Schweden früher nur in Göteborg (1940-1964) und Stockholm (1941-1964).

With a population of just 30,000, Landskrona also lies in Skåne, some 30 km northwest of Lund. On 27 September 2003, a trolleybus line (in Swedish 'Trådbuss' – 'wire bus') came into service between the city centre and the new railway station, which is situated on the eastern outskirts of the town. This replaced the old terminal station at the ferry port, which lies close to the city centre. This single line, line 3 in the urban bus network, is about 3 km long and was initially operated with three 'Trollino 12' trolleybuses (nos. 6991-6993) from Solaris/Ganz. A fourth bus (no. 6990) was added to the fleet in 2010, and a fifth (no. 6994) in 2013 (both from Solaris/Škoda). The latter is equipped with a special battery which allows operation on non-electrified lines up to a distance of 20 km. Four buses have to switch to battery mode to go to the depot, while no. 6990 is equipped with a diesel auxiliary motor. The vehicles are owned by 'Skånetrafiken'.

Urban bus transport in Landskrona is currently operated by 'Nobina AB', and the town is part of the 'Skånetrafiken' fare system (www.skanetrafiken.se). The trolleybuses run every 12 minutes (every 6 minutes during rush hour).

Trolleybuses had previously only existed in Sweden in Gothenburg (1940-1964) and Stockholm (1941-1964).

Map:
Göteborg
Lasarettet Norra — LANDSKRONA ③
Vilan — Repslagarg. — Kolonigatan — **Stationen**
Säbygatan
Malmö
Rådhustorget
Sofia Albertina
Centrum ● ③
Skeppsbron ◇ Bus Depot

Trådbuss – Obus | Trolleybus	
Eisenbahn | Railway	
Güterbahn | Freight railway	
Straßen | Roads	

500 m

M32 Sirio #465 @ Valand

GÖTEBORG

Schwedens zweitgrößte Stadt liegt im Westen des Landes in der Region Västra Götaland beiderseits des Göta älv. Das relativ große Stadtgebiet umfasst beinahe den gesamten durchgehend bebauten Raum, im Osten schließt die Gemeinde Partille und im Süden Mölndal an; in letzterer liegen auch fünf Haltestellen der Straßenbahn.

Göteborg erreicht man von Hamburg aus mit der Bahn mit einmaligem Umsteigen in Kopenhagen, allerdings dauert die Fahrt rund neun Stunden.

Für den Nahverkehr in Västra Götaland ist Västtrafik verantwortlich, dessen Tarifangebot alle verfügbaren Verkehrsmittel (auch Fähren und Regionalbahnen) umfasst. Ein „Zon A dygnsbiljett" (24- bzw. 72-Stunden-Ticket für Göteborg, Partille, Mölndal und Öckerö) kostet 110 bzw. 220 SEK (10,90/21,80 €). Die gesamte Region (Zon ABC) kann man für 330 bzw. 660 SEK erkunden. Fahrscheine gibt es in Kiosken oder in Västtrafik-Kundenbüros, manche auch an Automaten im Fahrzeug (nur bargeldlos!).

Spårvagn – Straßenbahn

Göteborg hat das größte Straßenbahnnetz in Nordeuropa, das sich außerdem durch einen sehr hohen Anteil an Eigentrassen auszeichnet. Nur im Innenstadtbereich liegen die Gleise im Straßenraum, meist auch hier abmarkiert, während auf den Außenstrecken lange kreuzungsfreie Abschnitte zur Verfügung stehen, so dass man durchaus auch von einer Stadtbahn sprechen kann. An fast allen Haltestellen überqueren jedoch die Fahrgäste die Gleise.

Sweden's second largest city, Gothenburg, located in the west of the country in the Västra Götaland Region, lies on either side of Göta älv. The relatively large municipal territory covers almost the entire continuously built-up area, with only Partille in the east and Mölndal (with five tram stops) in the south lying directly adjacent to it.

From Central Europe, Gothenburg can be reached by train via Copenhagen, but a journey from Hamburg takes around nine hours.

Public transport in Västra Götaland is organised by 'Västtrafik', whose fare system includes every available means of transport (including ferries and local trains). A 'zon A dygnsbiljett' (24- or 72-hour ticket for Gothenburg, Partille, Mölndal and Öckerö) costs 110 and 220 SEK (€10.90/21.80), respectively. The entire region (Zon ABC) can be explored for 330/660 SEK. Tickets can be bought at kiosks and Västtrafik customer offices, and some tickets also from vending machines in the trams (cashless only!).

Spårvagn – Tram

Gothenburg has the largest tram network in Northern Europe. It is characterised by a large proportion of dedicated rights-of-way, and only in the city centre are the tracks embedded in the roadway, although mostly on marked-off lanes. As there are some rather long grade-separated segments on the outer sections, the system may be classified as 'light rail'. At almost every stop, however, passengers have to cross the tracks.

M31 #314 @ Östra Sjukhuset

1879 nahm die englische Firma *Gothenburg Tramway Ltd.* die erste Pferdestraßenbahn Göteborgs in Betrieb. Das ursprünglich meterspurige Netz wurde 1900 von der Stadt übernommen und ab 1902 umgespurt und elektrifiziert. Bereits 1907 wurden die ersten Strecken über die damaligen Stadtgrenzen hinweg eröffnet, nämlich nach Långedrag im Südwesten (heute Teil von Göteborg) und Mölndal. Von 1940 bis 1964 fuhren in Göteborg auch Obusse.

In den 1960er Jahren entstand ähnlich wie in deutschen Städten vergleichbarer Größe die Idee, aus dem vorhandenen Straßenbahnnetz eine Stadtbahn zu machen, d.h. die Innenstadtstrecken in Tunnel zu verlegen und die

In 1879, the English company 'Gothenburg Tramway Ltd.' opened the first horse tramway in the Swedish city. The network, initially metre-gauge, was taken over by the city in 1900, and regauging and electrification started in 1902. In as early as 1907, the first lines were built beyond the city boundaries, namely to Långedrag in the southwest (now part of Gothenburg) as well as to Mölndal. From 1940 to 1964, Gothenburg also had trolleybuses.

In the 1960s, like in many German cities of a comparable size, the idea came up to develop the existing tram network into a light rail system by putting the city centre routes underground, and building outer sections

GÖTEBORG (Sverige | Schweden | Sweden)

 580 000 (448 km²)   ~ 800 000

 1902

 1435 mm

 79 km   12

 Göteborgs Spårvägar AB
www.goteborgssparvagar.se

 Västtrafik
www.vasttrafik.se

 Göteborgs spårvägsmuseum
www.ringlinien.org

M5 #92 (ASEA, 1917) @ Kungsportsplatsen > Valand

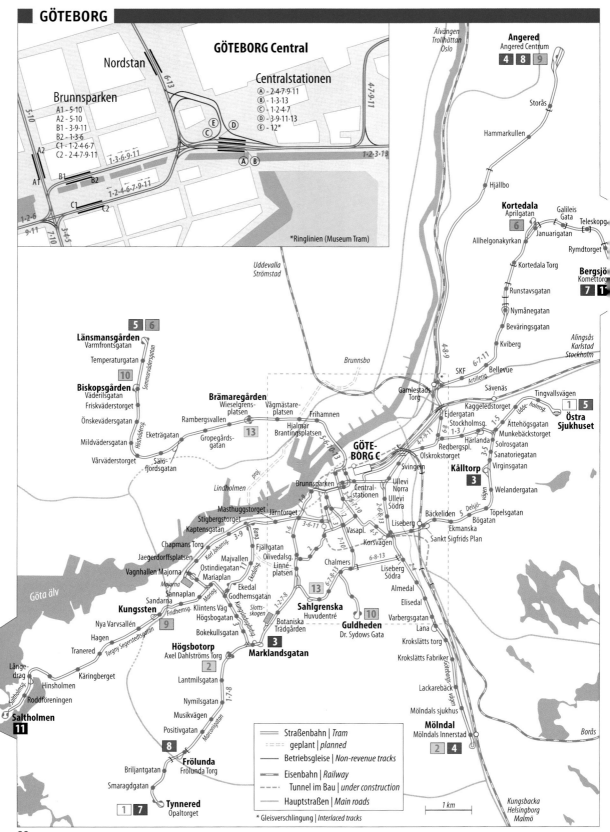

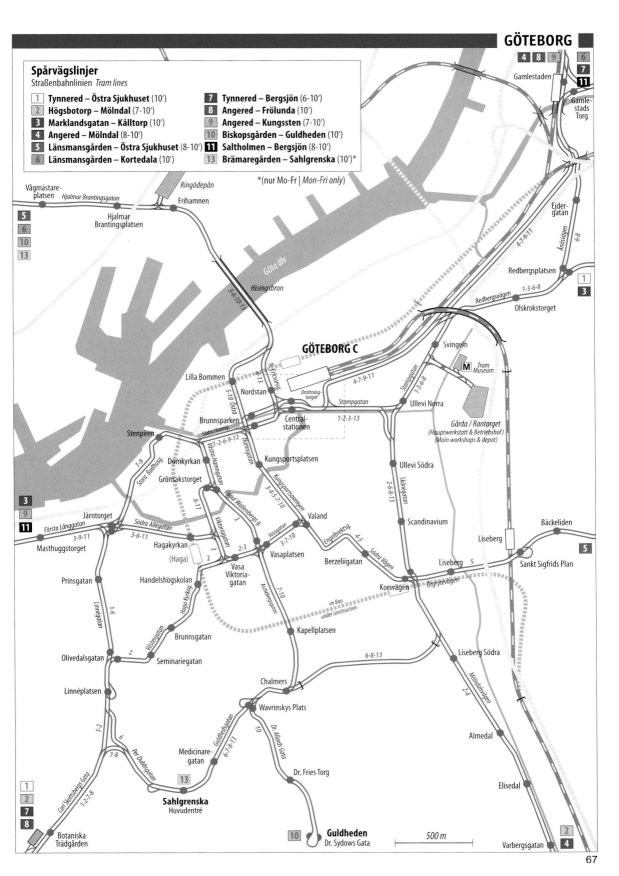

M29 #815 + M28 #701 @ Lilla Bommen (> Frihamnen, 2013)

Außenstrecken weitgehend kreuzungsfrei zu trassieren. Langfristig sollte daraus eine U-Bahn werden. So entstanden etappenweise Neubaustrecken nach Länsmansgården (bis 1964), nach Angered teils entlang einer ehemaligen Schmalspurbahn (1969-1978; ab Hjällbo im Linksverkehr wegen des Mittelbahnsteigs im einzigen unterirdischen Bahnhof Hammarkullen, analog zu Zürich!), nach Bergsjön mit mehreren Tunneln (1957-1970) sowie im Süden nach Tynnered (1962-1966).

In den 1970er Jahren wurde jedoch klar, dass der Bau der geplanten Innenstadttunnel technisch schwierig und nicht finanzierbar war, so dass man stattdessen eine Schnellstraßenbahn (Snabbspårväg) anstrebte. Das Netz wurde seither nur geringfügig vergrößert: 1982 vom Kaggeledstorget zum Östra Sjukhuset [Ostkrankenhaus], 2002 die Tunnelverbindung Chalmers – Korsvägen und 2003 oberirdisch weiter bis Ullevi als Teil einer angedachten

mostly without any level crossings. In the long term, this should have created a proper metro/tunnelbana system. Following this plan, several new sections were built: to Länsmansgården (by 1964); to Angered (1969-1978), partly along an old narrow-gauge railway (beyond Hjällbo in left-hand operation as an island platform had already been built in the only underground station, Hammarkullen); to Bergsjön with several tunnels (1957-1970); and to Tynnered in the south (1962-1966).

By the 1970s, it had become clear that the construction of the planned city centre tunnels was technically and financially too difficult, so a 'rapid tram' (Snabbspårväg) system became the new goal instead. The network has since only been expanded with short sections: in 1982, from Kaggeledstorget to Östra Sjukhuset (Eastern Hospital); in 2002, the tunnel connection between Chalmers and Korsvägen; and in 2003, an aboveground con-

M28 #766+723 @ Kålltorp (2013)

Flexity M33B #491 @ Centralstationen   *(Foto Rikard Ågren)*

Flexity M33B #491 @ Kungsladugårdsgatan (Klintens väg > Godhemsgatan) (Foto Rikard Agren)

Ringlinie („Kringen"-Projekt). Zuletzt wurde am 16. August 2015 die Verbindung Järntorget – Brunnsparken über Stenpiren (1.1 km) eröffnet. Mittelfristig ist eine Neubaustrecke am Nordufer des Göta älv geplant, von Brunnsbo über Hjalmar Brantingsplatsen/Frihamnen nach Lindholmen und dann entweder im Tunnel oder auf einer neuen Brücke über den Fluss zum Stigbergstorget und gegebenenfalls weiter bis Linnéplatsen. In der Innenstadt soll ein kurze Spange entlang der Engelbrektsgatan und eine längere entlang der Nya alléen entstehen. Erwähnenswert ist auch die Verlegung der Tramtrasse Mitte 2021 von der Götaälv-Brücke auf die neue Hisingsbron.

Samstags (im Sommer täglich) verkehren historische Straßenbahnen als Linie 12 zwischen Centralstationen und dem Vergnügungspark in Liseberg. Der Verein Ringlinien betreibt auch ein kleines Museum neben dem Straßenbahn-Betriebshof in Gårda.

Göteborgs Spårvägar besitzt einen Wagenpark mit etwa 260 Fahrzeugen (alle 2,65 m breit und bis 2020 Einrichtungswagen), wobei die ältesten mittlerweile über 50 Jahre alt sind und in den kommenden Jahren durch die neuen Flexity-Straßenbahnen von Bombardier ersetzt werden:

tinuation of the same route to Ullevi, conceived as part of a future ring line ('Kringen' project). More recently, the 1.1 km link between Järntorget and Brunnsparken via Stenpiren was opened on 16 August 2015. In the medium term, a new route may be built along the north bank of the Göta älv, namely from Brunnsbo via Hjalmar Brantingsplatsen/Frihamnen to Lindholmen, and then either in a tunnel or on a new bridge across the river to Stigbergstorget and possibly on to Linnéplatsen. In the city centre, a short link will be built along Engelbrektsgatan and a longer link along Nya alléen. The relocation of tram tracks from the old Götaälv Bridge to the new Hisingsbron in mid-2021 is also worth mentioning.

On Saturdays (every day in summer) historical trams labelled 'line 12' run between the Central Station and the amusement park at Liseberg. The 'Ringlinien' association also maintains a small museum next to the tram depot in Gårda.

'Göteborgs Spårvägar' has a fleet of about 260 vehicles (all 2.65 m wide and until 2020 all single-ended). The oldest ones, now over 50 years old, will be replaced by new Flexity trams from Bombardier in the near future:

Tram > Fahrzeuge | Rolling Stock (750 V DC)						
Nummer Number	Anzahl Quantity	Hersteller Manufacturer	Typ Class	Länge Length	Breite Width	Ausgeliefert Delivered
701...770	55	ASJL/Asea	M28 =>	14.2 m	2.65 m	1965-1967
801...860	56	Hägglund	M29 =>	14.2 m	2.65 m	1969-1972
300-305, 307-380	80	Asea/ABB	M31* =>	30.6 m	2.65 m	1984-1992
401-435, 437-465	64	Ansaldobreda	M32 (Sirio) =>	29.5 m	2.65 m	2005-2013
490-499	3 / 10	Bombardier/Kiepe	M33B (Flexity) <=>	33.0 m	2.65 m	2020-
501-530	30	Bombardier/Kiepe	M33 (Flexity) =>	33.0 m	2.65 m	2021-

* mit 1998-2002 in M21-Wagen eingebautem Niederflurmittelteil | with low-floor section added to M21 stock in 1998-2002

M31 #366 @ Valand

M29 #804 + M28 #711 @ Mölndal

MB01 #208 (ASEA, 1928) @ Centralstationen (2007)

M32 #414 @ Valand > Kungsportsplatsen (2007)

M29 #831 @ Valand > Kungsportsplatsen

X61 Coradia Nordic #61401 @ Göteborg C

Pendeltåg – S-Bahn

Nach dem Vorbild von Stockholm wird auch in Göteborg vom Hauptbahnhof ausgehend auf drei Strecken ein Pendeltåg-Verkehr angeboten:

Alingsåspendeln: Göteborg C – Alingsås (45 km; 30')
Kungsbackapendeln: Göteborg C – Kungsbacka (28 km; 15-30')
Alependeln: Göteborg C – Älvängen (31 km; 15-30')

Den S-Bahn-Linien sind keine Liniennummern zugeordnet. Sie sind Teil des westschwedischen Regionalbahnnetzes (Västtågen) und es stehen keine eigenen S-Bahn-Gleise zur Verfügung. Dazu kommen auf den meisten Strecken Regionalbahnen im Stundentakt. Im Västra Götaland (sowie nach Kungsbacka) gelten die Tarife von *Västtrafik*.

Der Betrieb wird bis mindestens 2024 von *SJ Götalandståg* durchgeführt. Als Pendeltåg verkehren heute vorwiegend Fahrzeuge der Baureihe X61 (Coradia Nordic, 74,3 m lang), aber auch Triebwagen der Baureihe X11 aus den 1990er Jahren sind noch im Einsatz.

Derzeit ist mit dem Projektnamen „Västlänken" eine 8 km lange Tunnelstrecke unter dem Zentrum von Göteborg im Bau. Frühestens ab 2026 werden ähnlich wie in Malmö Vorort- und Regionalzüge durch die Stadt fahren und dabei an drei unterirdischen Stationen halten.

Pendeltåg – *Suburban Rail*

Like Stockholm, Gothenburg also has a Pendeltåg network, with three lines running from the Central Station into the surrounding region:

The different Pendeltåg lines have no line numbers. They are part of the West Swedish regional rail network (Västtågen), and there are no separate tracks for the Pendeltåg either. On most routes, this service is complemented with hourly regional trains. In Västra Götaland (plus Kungsbacka), Västtrafik fares apply.

Until at least 2024, trains will be operated by SJ Götalandståg primarily using EMUs of class X61 (Coradia Nordic, 74.3 m long), while some class X11 trains from the 1990s are also still in service.

Currently, 'Västlänken', an 8 km rail tunnel below central Gothenburg is under construction. Rather like the city tunnel in Malmö, the three centrally located underground stations will be served by suburban and regional trains, but not before 2026.

X11 #3140 @ Mölndal

M06 #40 @ Atriumhusen

NORRKÖPING

Die kleine Stadt Norrköping liegt knapp 160 km südwestlich von Stockholm im Östergötlands län, beide Städte sind häufig sowohl mit Fernzügen auf der Hauptstrecke Richtung Malmö (1h 15') als auch durch Regionalzüge (1h 50') miteinander verbunden. Als *Östgötapendeln* fährt 2-3 Mal stündlich eine Regionalbahn Richtung Linköping und darüber hinaus. Diese ist wie die Straßenbahn von Norrköping in den Tarifverbund der *Östgöta Trafiken* integriert. Eine 24-Stunden-Karte (*24-timmarsbiljett*) für Norrköping (*stadszon*) kostet gerade mal 52 SEK (5,10 €), dazu kommen allerdings einmalig 30 SEK für die im Kundencenter oder in Kiosken erhältliche aufladbare *reskort*.

Mit unter 100.000 Einwohnern gehört Norrköping zu den kleineren Städten weltweit mit einem Tram-Netz. Dieses wurde von der AEG gebaut und 1904 in Betrieb genommen. Bis in die 1950er Jahre entstand so ein Netz mit vier Linien, darunter die ehemalige Ringlinie 1. 1967 überlebte die Straßenbahn die Umstellung auf Rechtsverkehr.

1975 bzw. 1980 wurde in zwei Etappen eine 1,5 km lange Neubaustrecke auf Eigentrasse vom Folkets Park bis Klockaretorpet eröffnet. Einen wesentlichen Zuwachs bekam das Netz schließlich mit der Verlängerung von Ljura bis Trumpetaregatan (2,2 km) am 21. Oktober 2010 und weiter bis Kvarnberget (1,5 km) genau ein Jahr später, nachdem die ehemalige Schleife Ljura erst 2006 angelegt worden war.

Trotz des privaten Betriebs durch *Transdev Sverige AB* sind die Infrastruktur und die Fahrzeuge Eigentum der

The small city of Norrköping is located in Östergötland County, some 160 km southwest of Stockholm. The two cities are frequently linked by both long-distance trains on the main line towards Malmö (1h 15') as well as by regional trains (1h 50'). Labelled 'Östgötapendeln', a regional train runs 2-3 times an hour to Linköping and beyond. Like the Norrköping tram, this service is integrated into the 'ÖstgötaTrafiken' fare system. A 24-hour ticket (24-timmarsbiljett) for Norrköping (stadszon) costs a mere 52 SEK (€5.10), but you need to add an initial 30 SEK for a 'reskort' (reloadable travelcard), which is available at the customer centre and in kiosks.

With less than 100,000 inhabitants, Norrköping is one of the smaller cities in the world with a tram network. Built by AEG and opened in 1904, by the 1950s it had evolved into a network of four lines, including the former ring line, no. 1. In 1967, the Norrköping tramway survived the Swedish change to right-hand traffic.

In 1975 and 1980, a 1.5 km extension on a dedicated right-of-way from Folkets Park to Klockaretorpet was brought into service in two stages. A more substantial increase in the overall network length came with the extension from Ljura to Trumpetaregatan (2.2 km) on 21 October 2010, and further south to Kvarnberget (1.5 km) exactly a year later, the former loop at Ljura having only been built in 2006.

Although privately operated by 'Transdev Sverige AB', the infrastructure and vehicles are owned by the city.

NORRKÖPING (Sverige | Schweden | Sweden)

97 000 (37 km²)   145 000

⟨el.⟩ 1904   1435 mm

km̲ 18.5 km   2

🏢 Transdev Sverige AB
www.transdev.se

📑€ ÖstgötaTrafiken
www.ostgotatrafiken.se

Östgötapendeln: Coradia Nordic @ Norrköping

Stockholm
Nyköping

2 Fridvalla

Vidablick **3**

Heleneborgsgatan
De Geersgatan
Finspängsvägen
Slåttergatan
Rågången
Rågången
Sandbyhov
Breda vägen
Eneby centrum
Slåtterg.
Tabergsbergsv.
Högvg.
Cedersborgsvägen
Hagaskolan
Marielund
Värmlandsg.
Norra Promenaden

NORRKÖPING

Resecentrum
Styrmansgatan
Norr Tull
Rådhuset
Trädgårdsg.
Matteusskolan
Nya torget
Djäkneparksskolan
Drottningg.
Östra Promenaden
Hörsalsparken
Väster Tull
Stortorget
Vägträffen
Linköpingsvägen
Nygatan
Strömbacken
Söder Tull
Central-badet
Nygatan
Broocmansplan
Ljura Centrum
Albrektsvägen
Ljura spårvägsbro
Linköping
Malmö
Trozelligatan
Ljuragatan
SMHI
H. Brantings g.
Lokegatan
Hageby vårdcentral
Torsten
Fogelqvists gata
Bastuban
Skarphagsgatan
Odenzg.
Hageby centrum
Folkets Park
Hagebygatan
Hyvlaregatan

3 Klockaretorpet

Trumpetaregatan
Navestadsgatan
Atriumhusen
Ringdansens centrum

2 Kvarnberget

Spårvägslinjer
Straßenbahnlinien *Tram lines*

2 **Fridvalla – Kvarnberget** (10′)

3 **Vidablick – Klockaretorpet** (10′)

═══ Straßenbahn | *Tram*
─── Betriebsgleise | *Tracks not used in regular passenger service*
▦▦▦ Eisenbahnstrecken | *Railway routes*
─── Hauptstraßen | *Main roads*

1 km

* Gleisverschlingung | *Interlaced tracks*   × außer Betrieb | *out of service*

M97 #66 @ Saltängsbron (Rådhuset)

Stadt. Der Fahrzeugpark besteht heute aus älteren Due-wag-Wagen (ex Duisburg bzw. Dessau) mit eingefügtem Niederflurmittelteil sowie Wagen vom Typ Flexity Classic, wie man sie auch aus Frankfurt am Main (S-Wagen) kennt. Die sechs baugleichen Stockholmer Wagen wurden Ende 2020 von Norrköping übernommen.

Kurzzeitig kamen in Norrköping 2011 aushilfsweise Tatra-T6A2-Wagen aus Berlin zum Einsatz, nachdem drei M06-Wagen (Nr. 33-35) nach Stockholm ausgeliehen waren, um bei der neuen Spårväg City auszuhelfen. Die drei ursprünglich als Prototypen (R1.1) für München gebauten M98-Wagen von Adtranz (Nr. 22-24) sind seit 2015 außer Dienst; der 1998 nach Norrköping verkaufte Prototyp GT6N war bereits im Jahr 2011 nach Bremen zurückgekehrt.

Today's fleet consists of older Duewag cars taken over from Duisburg and Dessau in 1997 and extended with a centre low-floor section, and modern Flexity Classic trams, which are almost identical to the S-cars in Frankfurt am Main. In addition, the six identical Stockholm cars were transferred to Norrköping in late 2020.

For a short period in 2011, Tatra T6A2 cars from Berlin were in service in Norrköping to tackle a vehicle shortage that had arisen after three M06 cars (nos. 33-35) had been lent to Stockholm to operate on the newly-opened Spårväg City. The three M98 cars (nos. 22-24), i.e. the R1.1 prototypes built for Munich, were withdrawn from service in 2015; the GT6N prototype, purchased in 1998, had already returned to Bremen in 2011.

M97 #65 @ Hageby vårdcentral

M06 #36 @ Resecentrum (Bahnhof | *Railway Station*)

M06 #39 @ Nya Torget

Tram > Fahrzeuge | *Rolling Stock* (750 V DC)

Nummer *Number*	Anzahl *Quantity*	Hersteller *Manufacturer*	Typ *Class*	Länge *Length*	Breite *Width*	Ausgeliefert *Delivered*
61-70	10	Duewag	M97 => ex Duisburg/Dessau	25.6 m	2.40 m	(1966) 1997
31-46	16	Bombardier	M06 (Flexity Classic) <=>	30.0 m	2.40 m	2007-2012
47-52	6	Bombardier	M06 (Flexity Classic) <=> ex Stockholm	30.0 m	2.40 m	(2011-2012) 2020

M06 #44 @ Skarphagsgatan > Folkets Park

Spårväg City: A35 #466 @ Djurgårdsbron

STOCKHOLM

Die schwedische Hauptstadt, im Osten des Landes gelegen, wartet mit einem vorbildlichen öffentlichen Nahverkehr auf und bietet eine Vielfalt an Schienenverkehrsmitteln wie kaum eine andere Stadt in Europa. Wer aus Deutschland mit der Bahn anreisen möchte, ist von Hamburg aus mit Umsteigen in Kopenhagen über 10 Stunden unterwegs.

Während in der eigentlichen Stadt Stockholm fast eine Million Menschen leben, schließen sich an allen Seiten direkt mehrere Städte wie Solna, Sundbyberg, Huddinge, Botkyrka, Danderyd oder Nacka an, was die Einwohnerzahl auf etwa 1,5 Mio. ansteigen lässt. Der Verwaltungsbezirk Stockholms län, der sich von Södertälje im Süden bis nördlich des Flughafens Arlanda und weit nach Nordosten hinter Norrtälje erstreckt, zählt rund 2,4 Mio. Einwohner.

Die Organisation des Nahverkehrs im Stockholms län obliegt *AB Storstockholms Lokaltrafik* (SL), dem einzigen Ansprechpartner für die Fahrgäste, auch wenn der eigentliche Betrieb der einzelnen Verkehrsmittel in privaten Händen ist. SL ist Eigentümer sämtlicher Fahrzeuge und des Großteils der Infrastruktur.

Im SL-Gebiet gilt ein Einheitstarif für das ganze *län*: für eine 24-Stunden-Karte (160 SEK) oder eine 72-Stunden-Karte (315 SEK) braucht man nicht unbedingt eine elektronische *SL Access-kort* für 20 SEK, nur für eine 7-Tage-Karte (415 SEK). Für den Pendeltåg zum Flughafen Arlanda ist ein Zuschlag von 120 SEK fällig (der private, direkte *Arlanda Express* kostet 299 SEK!).

The Swedish capital, situated in the east of the country, boasts an excellent public transport system, and for urban rail enthusiasts it offers a variety of railway modes hard to find anywhere else in Europe. A train journey from Hamburg to Stockholm takes more than 10 hours, with a change of trains in Copenhagen.

The city of Stockholm proper has about a million inhabitants, but it is surrounded on every side by several independent cities such as Solna, Sundbyberg, Huddinge, Botkyrka, Danderyd and Nacka, which bring the overall population up to about 1.5 million. Stockholms län (Stockholm County), which extends from Södertälje in the south to areas north of the airport Arlanda and far northeast beyond Norrtälje, is home to more than 2.4 million people.

Local transport in Stockholm County is organised by 'AB Storstockholms Lokaltrafik' (SL), which from the passengers' point of view is the sole transport agent. However, the actual operation of the different transport modes has been transferred to various private companies. SL is the owner of all the vehicles, though, and of the majority of the infrastructure.

In the SL region, a flat fare applies for the entire 'län': for 24-hour (160 SEK) and 72-hour tickets (315 SEK) the electronic 'SL Access kort' (20 SEK) is not necessary, but it is for a 72-hour pass (415 SEK). For the Pendeltåg to Arlanda Airport a supplement of 120 SEK is payable (the privately operated, direct Arlanda Express costs 299 SEK!).

[100 SEK ≈ € 9.77]

Spårväg City: A34 #2 @ **Styrmansgatan** (Sept. 2020)

STOCKHOLM
(Sverige | Schweden | Sweden)

 980 000 (187 km²)

 ~ 1 500 000

 Tram - 1901; Tunnelbana - 1950

 1435 mm

 Tram ~ 38.8 km;
Tunnelbana - 105.7 km

 Tram - 5; Tunnelbana - 7

 AB Stockholms Spårvägar
- *www.ss.se*
Arriva Sverige AB
- *www.arriva.se*
MTR Nordic AB
- *www.mtrnordic.se*

 AB Storstockholms Lokaltrafik (SL)
www.sl.se

Transport Projects
www.sll.se/framtid

 Tram Museum
sparvagsmuseet.sl.se

Tunnelbana (Gröna linjen): C20 @ Sockenplan

Lidingöbanan: A36 #554 @ Torsvik

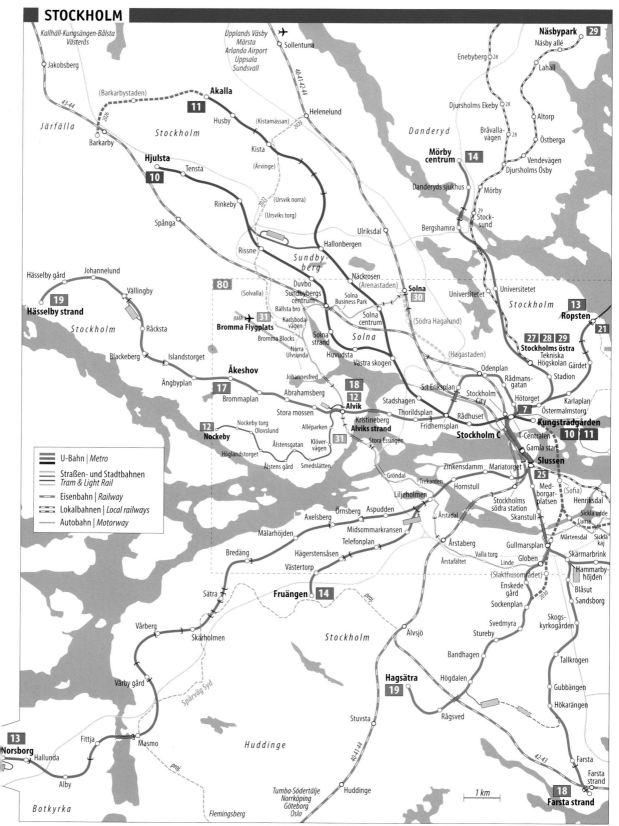

STOCKHOLM

Kallhäll·Kungsängen·Bålsta
Västerås

Jakobsberg

(Barkarbystaden)

43-44

Järfälla

Barkarby

Hjulsta
10
Tensta

Spånga

Upplands Väsby
Märsta
Arlanda Airport
Uppsala
Sundsvall

Sollentuna

Akalla
11
Husby   (Kistamässan)
Kista

Helenelund

40-41-42-44

Stockholm

(Ärvinge)

Rinkeby   (Ursvik norra)

(Ursviks torg)

Rissne

Sundby-
berg

Näckrosen
Ulriksdal   (Arenastaden)
Hallonbergen

Duvbo
Sundbybergs
centrum   Solna Business Park

Solna
30

Näsbypark 29
Näsby allé

Eneberget 28
Lahäll

Djursholms Ekeby 28   Altorp
Danderyd   Brävalla-   Östberga
vägen
Mörby   Vendevägen
centrum 14   Djursholms Ösby
Danderyds sjukhus   Mörby

Bergshamra   29 Stock-
sund

Universitetet   Universitetet

Stockholm 13
Ropsten

21

Hässelby gård   Johannelund

19   Vällingby
Hässelby strand
Stockholm   Råcksta

Blackeberg   Islandstorget

Ängbyplan

17
Brommaplan

80

(Solvalla)

BMA ✈
Bromma Flygplats 31
Bromma Blocks

Johannesfred
Åkeshov
Abrahamsberg   18
12
Alvik

Solna   Solna centrum
strand
(Södra Hagalund)

Solna

Huvudsta
Västra skogen

(Hagastaden)

Odenplan

Rådmans-
gatan

27 28 29
Stockholms östra
Tekniska
Högskolan
Gärdet

Stadion

Karlaplan

Stadshagen   S:t Eriksplan
Thorildsplan   Stockholm
City

12   Nockeby torg
Nockeby   Olovslund
Alléparken
Kristineberg
Alviks strand
Stora Essingen   Klöver-   31
vägen
Ålstensgatan
Höglandstorget
Ålstens gård   Smedslätten

Rådhuset   Hötorget   Östermalmstorg
7
Fridhemsplan   Stockholm C   Kungsträdgården
T-Centralen   10 11
Gamla stan

Slussen
25

Gröndal   Zinkensdamm   Mariatorget   Med-
Trekanten   borgar-   (Sofia)
Liljeholmen   platsen   Henriksdal
Hornstull   Sickla udde
Stockholms   Luma
södra station
Örnsberg   Aspudden   Skanstull   Sickla
Axelsberg   Årstadal   kaj
Årstaberg   Märtensdal
Mälarhöjden   Midsommarkransen   Gullmarsplan   Skärmarbrink
Telefonplan   Valla torg   Linde   Globen   Hammarby-
Bredäng   Hägerstensåsen   Årstafältet   (Slakthusområdet)   höjden
Västertorp   Enskede   Blåsut
gård   Sandsborg
Sätra   Sockenplan   Skogs-
Fruängen 14   Svedmyra   kyrkogården
Älvsjö   Sureby   Tallkrogen
Vårberg   Bandhagen   Gubbängen
Skärholmen   Stockholm
Hökarängen
Vårby gård   Hagsätra   Högdalen
19
Spårväg Syd   Stuvsta   Rågsved

13
Norsborg   Fittja   Masmo   42-43   Farsta
Hallunda
Huddinge   Farsta
Alby   strand
18
Botkyrka   Tumba·Södertälje   Farsta strand
Norrköping   1 km
Flemingsberg   Göteborg
Oslo   Huddinge

U-Bahn | Metro
Straßen- und Stadtbahnen
Tram & Light Rail
Eisenbahn | Railway
Lokalbahnen | Local railways
Autobahn | Motorway

78

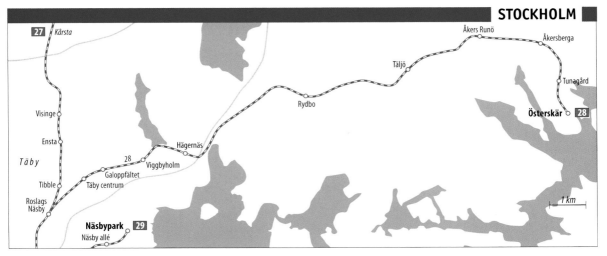

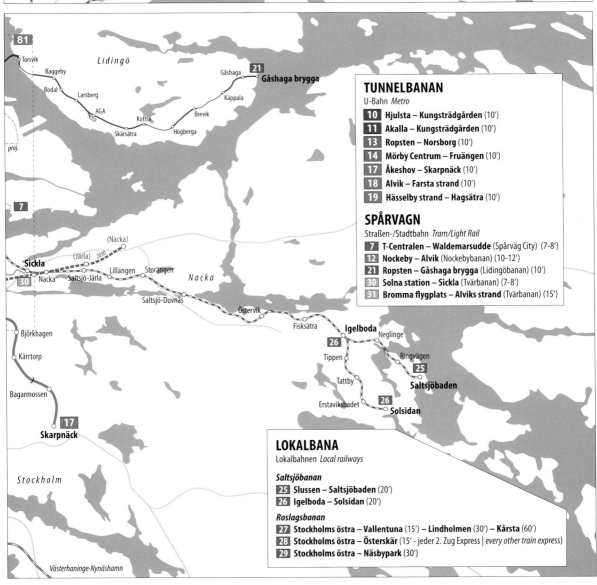

TUNNELBANAN
U-Bahn *Metro*

10 Hjulsta – Kungsträdgården (10′)
11 Akalla – Kungsträdgården (10′)
13 Ropsten – Norsborg (10′)
14 Mörby Centrum – Fruängen (10′)
17 Åkeshov – Skarpnäck (10′)
18 Alvik – Farsta strand (10′)
19 Hässelby strand – Hagsätra (10′)

SPÅRVAGN
Straßen-/Stadtbahn *Tram/Light Rail*

7 T-Centralen – Waldemarsudde (Spårväg City) (7-8′)
12 Nockeby – Alvik (Nockebybanan) (10-12′)
21 Ropsten – Gåshaga brygga (Lidingöbanan) (10′)
30 Solna station – Sickla (Tvärbanan) (7-8′)
31 Bromma flygplats – Alviks strand (Tvärbanan) (15′)

LOKALBANA
Lokalbahnen *Local railways*

Saltsjöbanan
25 Slussen – Saltsjöbaden (20′)
26 Igelboda – Solsidan (20′)

Roslagsbanan
27 Stockholms östra – Vallentuna (15′) – Lindholmen (30′) – Kårsta (60′)
28 Stockholms östra – Österskär (15′ - jeder 2. Zug Express | *every other train express*)
29 Stockholms östra – Näsbypark (30′)

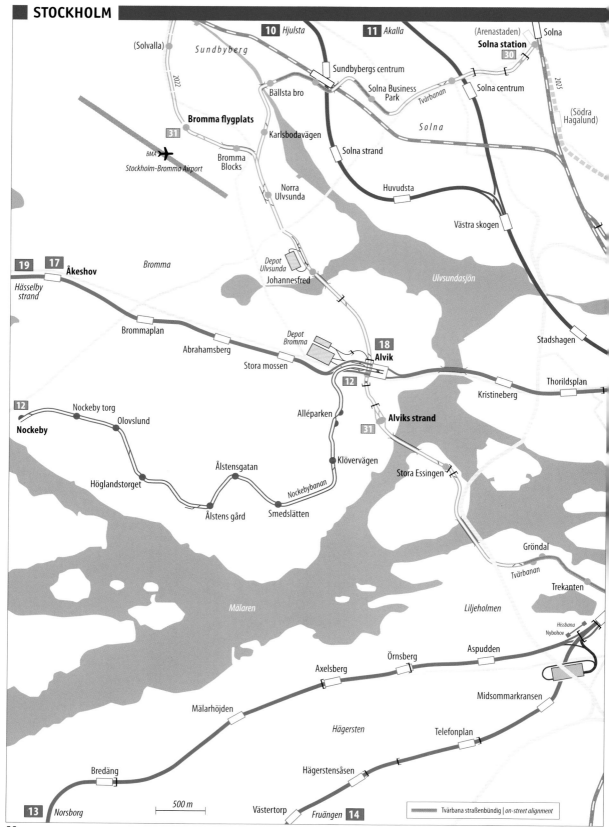

10 Hjulsta

11 Akalla

(Arenastaden) · Solna

Solna station

30

(Solvalla)

Sundbyberg

Sundbybergs centrum

Solna Business Park

Tvärbanan

Solna centrum

Bällsta bro

Bromma flygplats

31

Karlsbodavägen

Solna

(Södra Hagalund)

Solna strand

2025

BMA ✈
Stockholm-Bromma Airport

Bromma Blocks

Huvudsta

Norra Ulvsunda

Västra skogen

Ulvsundasjön

2022

19 **17** **Åkeshov**

Bromma

Depot Ulvsunda

Johannesfred

Stadshagen

Hässelby strand

Brommaplan

Abrahamsberg

Depot Bromma

18
Alvik

Thorildsplan

Stora mossen

12

Kristineberg

12

Nockeby torg

Olovslund

Alléparken

Alviks strand

12
Nockeby

Ålstensgatan

31

Höglandstorget

Klövervägen

Stora Essingen

Nockebybanan

Ålstens gård

Smedslätten

Gröndal

Tvärbanan

Trekanten

Mälaren

Liljeholmen

Hissbana
Nybohov

Aspudden

Örnsberg

Axelsberg

Midsommarkransen

Mälarhöjden

Hägersten

Telefonplan

Bredäng

Hägerstensåsen

13 Norsborg

500 m

Västertorp

Fruängen **14**

▬▬▬ Tvärbana straßenbündig | on-street alignment

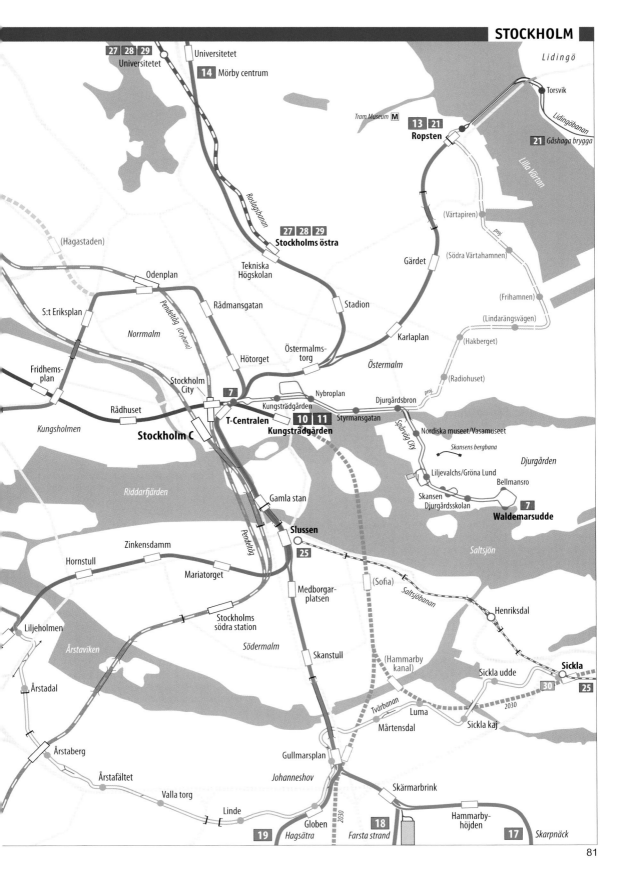

27 **28** **29** Universitetet
Universitetet

14 Mörby centrum

Lidingö

Tram Museum **M**

13 **21**
Ropsten

Torsvik

Lidingöbanan

21 *Gåshaga brygga*

Lilla Värtan

Roslagsbanan

(Hagastaden)

27 **28** **29**
Stockholms östra

(Värtapiren)

proj.

Gärdet

(Södra Värtahamnen)

Tekniska
Högskolan

Odenplan

(Frihamnen)

Rådmansgatan

Stadion

(Lindarängsvägen)

S:t Eriksplan

(Hakberget)

Norrmalm

Pendeltåg (Citybanan)

Hötorget

Östermalms-
torg

Östermalm

Karlaplan

(Radiohuset)

Fridhems-
plan

Stockholm
City

7

Nybroplan

proj.

Djurgårdsbron

Rådhuset

Kungsträdgården

Styrmansgatan

Spårväg City

Nordiska museet/Vasamuseet

Kungsholmen

T-Centralen

10 **11**

Kungsträdgården

Stockholm C

Skansens bergbana

Djurgården

Liljevalchs/Gröna Lund

Bellmansro

Riddarfjärden

Gamla stan

Skansen
Djurgårdsskolan

7

Waldemarsudde

Zinkensdamm

Slussen

25

Saltsjön

Hornstull

Mariatorget

(Sofia)

Saltsjöbanan

Henriksdal

Medborgar-
platsen

Pendeltåg

Stockholms
södra station

Södermalm

Skanstull

(Hammarby
kanal)

Liljeholmen

Sickla udde

Sickla

Årstaviken

30

25

Årstadal

Tvärbanan

Luma

2030

Sickla kaj

Mårtensdal

Årstaberg

Gullmarsplan

Årstafältet

Johanneshov

Skärmarbrink

Valla torg

Hammarby-
höjden

17

Skarpnäck

Linde

2030

Globen

19 *Hagsätra*

18 *Farsta strand*

Spårväg City: A35 #466 @ T-Centralen

Straßen- und Stadtbahnen

Auch wenn moderne Straßenbahnen erst seit dem 21. August 2010 in der Stockholmer Innenstadt zu sehen sind, geht die Geschichte dieses Verkehrsmittels auf das Jahr 1877 zurück, als die erste Pferdebahn in Betrieb ging. Ab 1901 erschienen die ersten elektrischen Wagen und in den folgenden Jahrzehnten wurde das innerstädtische Netz durch zahlreiche Vorortlinien ergänzt. 1933 wurde sogar ein Tram-Tunnel unter Södermalm zwischen Slussen und Skanstull in Betrieb genommen. Wie in vielen anderen Städten begann der Niedergang Mitte der 1950er Jahre, als auch der Bau einer U-Bahn in die Wege geleitet wurde. Das endgültige Aus für die Stockholmer Straßenbahn kam im September 1967, als Schweden von Links- auf Rechtsverkehr umstellte. Einzig die auf eigener Trasse verkehrenden Vorortbahnen, nämlich die Nockeby- und die Lidingöbana, konnten sich vor einer Stilllegung retten.

● **Spårväg City** (Linie 7) - 3,8 km
In der Innenstadt konnte man schließlich ab 1991 wieder Straßenbahnen sehen, als die **Djurgårdslinje** zwischen Norrmalmstorg und Waldemarsudde den Betrieb mit historischen Fahrzeugen aufnahm. Als Linie 7 (heute 7N) verband sie das Stadtzentrum mit dem Freilichtmuseum Skansen, dem Vergnügungspark Gröna Lund und anderen Museen. Daraus entstand schließlich eine reguläre Linie mit modernen Fahrzeugen, die **Spårväg City**. Die zuvor knapp 3 km lange Strecke wurde 2010 im Stadtzentrum um 400 m entlang der Hamngatan zu einer provisorischen Endstelle an der Ostseite des Sergels torg verlängert, bevor sie am 3. September 2018 ihre heutige Endstelle über dem U-Bahnhof T-Centralen erreichte (300 m). Die Spårväg City wurde anfangs mit sechs aus Norrköping und Frankfurt am Main geliehenen Fahrzeugen des Typs Flexity Classic

Tram & Light Rail

Although modern trams only started running through Stockholm's city centre on 21 August 2010, the history of this means of transport dates back to 1877, when the first horse-drawn tramway was put into operation. The first electric cars appeared in 1901, and in the following decades, the urban network was complemented by numerous suburban tram lines. In 1933, a tram tunnel was even opened in Södermalm, running between Slussen and Skanstull. Like in many other cities, the decline of the tram system began in the mid-1950s, coinciding with the construction of the first Tunnelbana line. The definitive end for Stockholm's trams came in September 1967, when Sweden switched from left- to right-hand traffic. The only lines which survived were the two suburban lines which ran on dedicated rights-of-way, namely the Nockebybana and the Lidingöbana.

● **Spårväg City** (Line 7) - 3.8 km
Trams finally returned to the city centre in 1991, when the **Djurgårdslinje** began operations between Norrmalmstorg and Waldemarsudde using old vehicles. Line 7 (now 7N) provided a link between the city centre and the open air museum Skansen, the amusement park Gröna Lund and other museums in that area. Eventually, this became a regular line with modern vehicles, the **Spårväg City**. In 2010, the 3 km long line was extended in the city centre by 400 m along Hamngatan to a temporary terminus on the eastern side of Sergels torg, before reaching its current terminus above the metro station T-Centralen on 3 Sept 2018 (300 m). Initially, Spårväg City was launched with six Bombardier Flexity Classic vehicles (type A34) borrowed from Norrköping and Frankfurt. They were replaced with six identical cars in 2011/12 and from

Lidingöbanan: A36 #553 @ Skärsätra

(Typ A34) von Bombardier eröffnet. Diese wurden 2011/12 durch sechs baugleiche Neuwagen ersetzt. Ab 2013 wurde der Fahrzeugpark durch A35-Wagen von CAF ergänzt. Die sechs A34-Wagen wurden schließlich Ende 2020 nach Norrköping abgegeben. Die Linie 7 wird gemeinsam mit den historischen Straßenbahnen von *AB Stockholms Spårvägar* betrieben und ist komplett straßenbündig, jedoch teilweise abmarkiert.

Im Osten war eine 4,3 km lange Neubaustrecke über den neuen Stadtteil Norra Djurgårdsstaden im ehemaligen Hafengebiet geplant, die in Ropsten direkt an die Lidingö- bana angeschlossen werden sollte, doch das Projekt liegt derzeit auf Eis.

● **Lidingöbanan** (Linie 21) - 9,2 km
Die Lidingöbana gehört zu den ältesten Bahnstrecken im Großraum Stockholm. Ein 1971 geschlossener Nordast nach Kyrkviken entstand sogar schon 1907, der aktuelle südliche Ast nach Gåshaga kam zwischen 1914 und 1916 hinzu. Die Brücke über den Lilla Värtan nach Ropsten wurde 1925 in Betrieb genommen, die Bahnen fuhren bis zur Schließung des städtischen Netzes 1967 ins Stadtzentrum durch. Seither muss man in Ropsten auf die U-Bahn umsteigen. Im Juni 2013 ging die Lidingöbana außer Betrieb, um modernisiert und teils zweigleisig ausgebaut zu werden. Sie wurde am 24. Oktober 2015 mit den neuen vierteiligen A36-Fahrzeugen wieder in Betrieb genommen.

2013, the tram fleet was expanded with A35 vehicles from CAF. The six A34 vehicles, however, were eventually transferred to Norrköping in late 2020. Like the historical trams, line 7 is operated by 'AB Stockholms Spårvägar'. Its route is completely embedded in the roadway, although parts of it run on dedicated lanes.

On the eastern side, a 4.3 km new line was planned to serve the new district of Norra Djurgårdsstaden in the former port area; at Ropsten, the tram might be directly connected to the Lidingöbana, but the project is currently on hold.

● *Lidingöbanan (Line 21) - 9.2 km*
The Lidingöbana, now a tram line, was one of the oldest railway lines in the Stockholm area. The northern branch to Kyrkviken, closed in 1971, was opened in as early as 1907, while the existing southern branch to Gåshaga was added between 1914 and 1916. The bridge over the Lilla Värtan to Ropsten was taken into operation in 1925, and until the closure of the urban tram network in 1967, Lidingö cars used to run through into the city centre. Since then, a transfer to the Tunnelbana has been required at Ropsten. In June 2013, the Lidingöbana was taken out of service to be modernised, and for some sections to be double-tracked. It reopened on 24 October 2015 with new four-section A36 vehicles.

Spårväg > Fahrzeuge | *Rolling Stock* (750 V DC)						
Nummer *Number*	Anzahl *Quantity*	Hersteller *Manufacturer*	Typ *Class*	Länge *Length*	Breite *Width*	Ausgeliefert *Delivered*
401-437	37	Bombardier	A32 (Flexity Swift) <=>	29.7 m	2.65 m	1999-2010
451-493	15 / 43*	CAF	A35 (Urbos AXL) <=>	31.2 m	2.65 m	2013-
551-559	7 / 9*	CAF	A36 (Urbos AXL) <=>	39.5 m	2.65 m	2015-

* Juni 2020: A35/A36-Bestellung ergänzt; Option auf insg. 136 Wagen | *June 2020: A35/A36 order increased; option for a total of 136 cars*

Tvärbanan: A35 #482 & A32 #402 @ Globen

● **Tvärbanan** (Linien 30 & 31) - 20,1 km

Die am 8. Januar 2000 zwischen Gullmarsplan und Lilje-holmen eröffnete „Querbahn" stellt eine tangentiale Verbin-dung zwischen verschiedenen Ästen der radial aus dem Stadtzentrum in die Vororte führenden Tunnelbana dar. Sie wurde sechs Monate später bis Alvik verlängert und zwei Jahre danach bis Sickla udde und erreichte somit eine Länge von 11,6 km. Der ursprüngliche Abschnitt verläuft größtenteils auf eigenem Gleiskörper, nur zwischen Lilje-holmen und Gröndal ist ein kurzer Abschnitt straßenbündig mit gemischtem Verkehr. Zwei Brücken stellen im Westen eine Verbindung der beiden Ufer des Mälarsees über die Insel Stora Essingen her.

Die tangentiale Strecke wurde 2013 von Alvik bis Solna centrum erweitert, die Endstelle am S-Bahnhof Solna wurde 2014 erreicht. Auf der 6,6 km langen Verlängerung findet man zwei Tunnel und im Bereich des S-Bahnhofs Sundbyberg sowie im Solna Business Park straßenbündige Abschnitte. Am südlichen Ende wurde die Tvärbana am 2. Oktober 2017 zwar um 800 m zur Station Sickla verlängert, eine einst angedachte betriebliche Verknüpfung mit der Saltsjöbana wurde jedoch letztendlich nicht umgesetzt.

Im Norden ist derzeit ein Ast (Kistagrenen) über Rissne und Kista zur Pendeltåg-Station Helenelund vorgesehen. Der erste 1,1 km lange und teils aufgeständerte Abschnitt bis zum Flughafen Bromma wurde zwar am 13. Dezember 2020 offiziell eröffnet, der Fahrgastbetrieb konnte jedoch aufgrund fehlender Genehmigungen der Flughafenbehör-de bislang nicht aufgenommen werden. Dieser Ast wird anfangs von der Linie 31 befahren; dazu wurde 2017 die Haltestelle Alviks strand dreigleisig ausgebaut, um die Züge dort enden zu lassen. Aus der ursprünglichen Linie 22 wurde nun die Linie 30.

● **Nockebybanan** (Linie 12) - 5,7 km

Die Linie 12 („Tolvan") war neben der Lidingöbana die einzige Strecke, die nach dem Jahr 1967 überlebt hat.

● *Tvärbanan* (Lines 30 & 31) - 20.1 km

The 'diagonal line' opened between Gullmarsplan and Liljeholmen on 8 January 2000 as a tangential connection between different branches of the radial Tunnelbana system. Six months later, it reached Alvik, and two years later, Sickla udde, thereby attaining a total length of 11.6 km. The initial section runs mostly on a dedicated right-of-way, with just a short section between Liljeholmen and Gröndal embedded in the roadway and sharing lanes with road traffic. In the west, two bridges connect the two shores of Lake Mälaren via the island of Stora Essingen.

The tangential route was extended from Alvik to Solna centrum in 2013, and to the current terminus at Solna Pendeltåg station in 2014. On the 6.6 km extension there are two tunnels, and in the area of the Sundby-berg railway station and in the Solna Business Park, sections with on-street running. At the southern end, the Tvärbana was extended by 800 m to the Sickla station on 2 October 2017, but a once-planned joint operation with the Saltsjöbana was not implemented in the end.

In the north, a branch ('Kistagrenen') via Rissne and Kista to the Pendeltåg station Helenelund is currently being built. The first 1.1 km partly elevated section to Bromma Airport was officially opened on 13 December 2020, but pending permits from the airport authorities have indefinitely delayed the start of passenger service. The branch is initially served by line 31, which has its southern terminus at Alviks strand, a stop expanded to three tracks in 2017. The original line 22 has now become line 30.

● *Nockebybanan* (Line 12) - 5.7 km

Besides the Lidingöbana, line 12 (popularly known as 'Tolvan') was the only line to survive the 1967 general tramway closure. Although it runs entirely on its own right-of-way, for safety reasons, operation was then switched from left- to right-hand traffic. However, the trams switch

Nockebybanan: A32 #432 @ Alléparken

Sie fährt zwar stets auf eigenem Gleiskörper, wurde aber damals dennoch aus Sicherheitsgründen auf Rechtsverkehr umgestellt. Allerdings wechselt sie an der Haltestelle Alléparken auf Linksverkehr, um im Bahnhof Alvik bahnsteiggleiches Umsteigen zur weiterhin links fahrenden Tunnelbana zu ermöglichen.

Die Nockebybana wurde in mehreren Stufen zwischen 1914 und 1929 eröffnet. Ursprünglich fuhr sie wie das Bahnen aus Ängby und Ulvsunda als Vorortbahn ins Stadtzentrum, doch nachdem der westliche Ast nach Ängby bereits 1952 Teil der ersten Tunnelbana-Strecke geworden war, blieb die Nockebybana vom übrigen Straßenbahnnetz abgeschnitten.

Wie auf der Tvärbana (dort auch als Doppeltraktionen) verkehren auf der Nockebybana Stadtbahnwagen sowohl vom Typ A32 als auch A35. Sechs A32-Wagen (432-437) waren einige Jahre bei der RijnGouweLijn im niederländischen Gouda im Einsatz. Beide Strecken sind nördlich der Haltestelle Alvik durch einen Tunnel miteinander verbunden, so erreichen die Fahrzeuge der Nockebybana über den Betriebshof Bromma auch den neuen Betriebshof in Ulvsunda. Seit 2012 werden die Tvärbana und die Nockebybana von *Arriva Sverige AB*, einer Tochtergesellschaft der Deutschen Bahn, betrieben.

● Als **Spårväg syd** [Tram Süd] ist mittelfristig eine Stadtbahn zwischen den S-Bahn-Stationen Flemingsberg und Älvsjö geplant, die u.a. Masmo, Kungens kurva, Skärholmen und Fruängen erschließen soll. Die Streckenführung steht seit Ende 2020 weitgehend fest. Der Bau soll jedoch frühestens Mitte der 2020er Jahre beginnen.

sides at Alléparken, so that at Alvik cross-platform interchange can be provided between the Nockebybana and the Tunnelbana, the latter still operating on the left.

The Nockebybana was opened in stages between 1914 and 1929. Initially, like the suburban trams from Ängby and Ulvsunda, it operated through into the city centre, but it was isolated from the remaining tram network in 1952 when the western branch to Ängby became part of the first Tunnelbana line.

The Tvärbana and the Nockebybana are both operated with light rail vehicles of type A32 and A35, but on the Tvärbana they also run as double units. Six of the A32 units (432-437) were in service for some years on the RijnGouweLijn in the Dutch city of Gouda. The two routes are connected via a tunnel just north of Alvik station, allowing trains from the Nockebybana to reach the new depot at Ulvsunda via the Bromma depot. Since 2012, the Tvärbana and the Nockebybana have been operated by 'Arriva Sverige AB', a subsidiary of the German DB.

● Promoted as **Spårväg syd** [southern tram], a light rail line is planned in the medium term to provide a link between the Pendeltåg stations Flemingsberg and Älvsjö, serving areas like Masmo, Kungens kurva, Skärholmen and Fruängen. The route has largerly been determined in late 2020, but construction might only start in the mid-2020s.

Tvärbanan: A35 #474 @ Arstaberg

Saltsjöbanan & Tvärbanan @ Sickla

Lokalbahnen

● **Saltsjöbanan** (Linien 25 & 26) - 18,4 km
Die Vororte östlich von Stockholm in der Nachbargemeinde
Nacka werden von der normalspurigen Saltsjöbana bedient.
Die Züge fahren ab Slussen im 20-Minuten-Takt nach
Saltsjöbaden (15,6 km), während der Ast von Igelboda nach
Solsidan (2,8 km) als Shuttle betrieben wird.

Die Strecke nach Saltsjöbaden entstand bereits 1893 als
Dampfeisenbahn, der Ast nach Solsidan kam 1913 hinzu,
als die gesamte Strecke elektrifiziert wurde. Die Strecke ist
bis heute größtenteils eingleisig mit mehreren Ausweichen.
Seit 2012 ist *Arriva Sverige AB* auch Betreiber dieser Bahn.

Seit 1976 werden Wagen vom Typ C10/C11, davon
einige von der Tunnelbana übernommene, eingesetzt. Da
diese nur 2,80 m breit sind, haben sie seitliche „Blumen-
bretter".

In der Vergangenheit gab es immer wieder Vorschläge,
die Strecke auf Stadtbahnbetrieb umzustellen und mit der
Tvärbana zu verbinden, immerhin wurde die neue Endstelle
der Tvärbana in Sickla direkt neben dem Bahnsteig der
Saltsjöbana angelegt. Gleich daneben entsteht nun ein tief
liegender U-Bahnhof für die blaue Tunnelbana-Linie.

● **Roslagsbanan** (Linien 27-29) - 65,3 km
Das Lokalbahnnetz im Nordosten des *Stockholms län* hat
eine Spurweite von nur 891 mm. Tagsüber fahren vom
Bahnhof Stockholms östra [Ostbahnhof] zehn Züge pro
Stunde ab und bedienen drei Äste: zwei Züge Richtung
Näsbypark (L29) mit Halt an allen Stationen; vier Richtung
Österskär (L28), wobei jeder zweite Zug als Express fährt;
vier Richtung Kårsta (L27), wobei bis Roslags Näsby nicht
überall gehalten und nur stündlich bis Kårsta durchgefahren
wird (sonst bis Vallentuna bzw. Ormsta oder Lindholmen).

Local Railways

● *Saltsjöbanan (Lines 25 & 26) - 18.4 km*
*The suburbs east of Stockholm in the neighbouring
municipality of Nacka are served by the standard-gauge
Saltsjöbana. Trains run every 20 minutes from Slussen to
Saltsjöbaden (15.6 km), while the branch from Igelboda
to Solsidan (2.8 km) is operated as a shuttle.*

*The route to Saltsjöbaden dates back to 1893, when it
opened as a steam railway, while the branch to Solsidan
was added in 1913, when the entire route was electrified.
The route is still mostly single-track with several passing
loops. Since 2012, 'Arriva Sverige AB' has also been the
operator of this railway line.*

*Since 1976, cars of type C10/C11 have been used,
some of which were transferred from the Tunnelbana to
the Saltsjöbana. As the cars are only 2.80 m wide, they
were extended on the sides with 'flower boards'.*

*In the past, there have been proposals to convert the
Saltsjöbana to light rail operation and connect it to the
Tvärbana; in the end, this idea was shelved, but when
the Tvärbana was extended to Sickla, its terminus was
placed right next to the Saltsjöbana platform to provide
convenient interchange. Adjacent to it, a deep-level
underground station is currently under construction for
the eastern extension of the blue Tunnelbana line.*

● *Roslagsbanan (Lines 27-29) - 65.3 km*
*This local railway network in the northeastern parts of
Stockholm County has a track gauge of just 891 mm.
During daytime service, ten trains an hour depart
from Stockholms östra [Eastern Station] to serve three
branches: two trains go to Näsbypark (L29), stopping at
all stations; four to Österskär (L28), with every other*

28	Österskär	4 min		27	Täby kyrkby
28S	Österskär	22 min		27	Täby kyrkby
28	Österskär	15:05		27	Täby kyrkby
27	Täby kyrkby	15:30		27	Täby kyrkby

selecta

Roslagsbanan: X10p #141 & 136 @ Stockholms östra

Der längste Ast, der nach Kårsta, ist 41,7 km lang, eine kurze Strecke im Vergleich zum einst 327 km langen Gesamtnetz. Die heutigen Strecken der Roslagsbana entstanden zwischen 1888 und 1906 und wurden ab 1895 mit 1500 V Gleichstrom elektrifiziert. Bis 1960 fuhr die Roslagsbana als Straßenbahn direkt ins Stadtzentrum. In den 1970er Jahren sollte das Netz zugunsten einer Verlängerung der roten Tunnelbana-Linie geschlossen werden, überlebte aber und wurde in den letzten Jahren modernisiert. Die Roslagsbana ist heute bis Viggbyholm durchgehend zweigleisig, der Rest nach Österskär sowie die beiden anderen Äste sind vorwiegend eingleisig. Die Roslagsbana wird seit 2013 auch von *Arriva Sverige AB* betrieben.

Es kommen 2,60 m breite und knapp 60 m lange 3-Wagen-Triebzüge der Baureihe X10p zum Einsatz (in der Hauptverkehrszeit auch Doppeltraktionen). Sie wurden 1988-1995 von ABB (heute Bombardier) hergestellt und später teilweise im mittleren Bereich des mittleren Wagens abgesenkt, um stufenloses Einsteigen zu ermöglichen. Die Wagen werden mittelfristig durch neue X15p-Triebzügen von Stadler Rail ersetzt. Sie haben ähnliche Abmessungen, sind mit 2,75 m jedoch etwas breiter.

train running express; and four trains run on the branch to Kårsta (L27), skipping some stops up to Roslags Näsby, and with only one train an hour going all the way to Kårsta (otherwise they terminate at Vallentuna, Ormsta or Lindholmen).

The longest route, that to Kårsta, is 41.7 km, just a short stretch compared to the total route length of 327 km which the entire network once had. The routes of the Roslagsbana which still exist were built between 1888 and 1906, and electrified from 1895 with 1500 V dc. Before 1960, the Roslagsbana used to continue into the city centre like a tramway. In the 1970s, the entire system was supposed to have been closed down in favour of an extension to the red Tunnelbana line, but in the end it survived, and in recent years it has been modernised. The Roslagsbana is now double-track all the way to Viggbyholm, while the rest of the Österskär branch, as well as the other two branches, remain mostly single-track. Since 2013, the Roslagsbana has also been operated by 'Arriva Sverige AB'.

The service is provided with 2.60 m wide and 60 m long 3-car trainsets of class X10p (also operating as 6-car trains during peak hours). They were manufactured by ABB (now Bombardier) between 1988 and 1995, and numerous units were later rebuilt with a partially low-floor section in the middle carriage to allow step-free boarding. In the medium term, they will be replaced by new X15p EMUs from Stadler Rail with similar dimensions, but at 2.75 m they are slightly wider.

Roslagsbanan: X15p (Abb. © Stadler Rail)

Blå linjen: C14 @ Solna strand (ex Vreten)

Tunnelbanan – U-Bahn

Das Stockholmer U-Bahn-Netz ist verglichen zur Einwohnerzahl des Großraums eines der größten Europas. Es hat eine Gesamtlänge von 105,7 km mit 100 Stationen, von denen viele, vor allem die unterirdischen, künstlerisch gestaltet wurden. Nach 25 Jahren Pause hat nun ein ehrgeiziger Ausbau des Netzes begonnen – bis 2030 sollen insgesamt fast 20 km neuer Strecken entstehen. Das Netz besteht aus drei Liniengruppen, die nach ihren Kennfarben bezeichnet werden und jeweils mehrere Äste aufweisen. Zu jeder Gruppe gehören 2-3 Linien, die in Fahrplänen mit Nummern bezeichnet werden. Jede dieser sieben Linien verkehrt tagsüber alle 10 Minuten, mit zusätzlichen Zügen während der Hauptverkehrszeiten. Die Tunnelbana wird seit 2009 von *MTR Nordic AB* betrieben.

Die Bahnsteige sind mit 145 m Länge im Vergleich zu westeuropäischen Metros sehr lang und bieten Platz für 8- bzw. 9-Wagen-Züge. Die Stromzufuhr erfolgt über eine abgedeckte, von oben bestrichene Stromschiene. Wie bei den schwedischen Eisenbahnen herrscht auch auf dem Tunnelbana-Netz Linksverkehr. Auf allen Strecken können dieselben Züge eingesetzt werden:

Tunnelbanan – Metro

In relation to the population of the metropolitan area, the Stockholm Tunnelbana system is one of the largest in Europe. With a total length of 105.7 km, it has 100 stations, many of which, especially the underground ones, are decorated with artwork. After a break of 25 years, an ambitious expansion programme has just started – by 2030, a total of almost 20 km of new routes is to be built. The network consists of three groups of lines, each of which is named after its respective colour and has several branches. In each group, there are 2-3 'lines', which are referred to in timetables by numbers. During daytime hours, each of the seven lines runs every 10 minutes, with additional trains during peak hours. Since 2009 the Tunnelbana has been operated by 'MTR Nordic AB'.

At 145 m, the platforms are rather long compared to Western European metros, and they can accommodate 8- or 9-car trains. Power is supplied via a covered third rail, with collection from the top side. Operation is on the left hand side just like on the Swedish railway network. The same rolling stock can be used on every line:

Nummer *Number*	Anzahl *Quantity*	Hersteller *Manufacturer*	Typ *Class*	Länge *Length*	Breite *Width*	Ausgeliefert *Delivered*
2651...2818	~	ASEA/Hägglund	C6	17.6 m	2.80 m	1970-1974
1260...1399	~	ASEA/Hägglund	C14-C15	17.6 m	2.80 m	1985-1989
2001-2270	270 (x3)*	Adtranz (Bombardier)	C20	46.4 m	2.90 m	1998-2004
2301-2396	96 (x4)**	Bombardier	C30 (Movia)	70.0 m	2.90 m	2018-2024

Tunnelbanan > Fahrzeuge | Rolling Stock (750 V DC)

* 3-Wagen-Einheit; Langzug aus 9 Wagen | *3-car unit; full-length train made up of 9 cars*
** 4-Wagen-Einheit; Langzug aus 8 Wagen | *4-car unit; full-length train made up of 8 cars*

1) Ältere Wagen vom Typ C6 sowie C14-C15, in der Regel als 8-Wagen-Züge. Die C6-Wagen wurden in den 1990ern modernisiert. Bei den C14-Wagen wurden Teile älterer Fahrzeuge wiederverwendet.
2) Das Bild der Tunnelbana prägt seit der Jahrtausend-wende der Typ C20 (Vagn 2000), der aus durchgängig begehbaren 3-Wagen-Einheiten besteht, die in der Regel als 9-Wagen-Züge die gesamte Bahnsteiglänge ausfüllen.
3) Im Mai 2013 bestellte SL bei Bombardier vierteilige Einheiten des Typs MOVIA (C30), die in Doppeltraktion seit 2020 auf der roten Linie eingesetzt werden; diese sollte für den fahrerlosen Betrieb mit CBTC ausgerüstet werden, was aber vorerst aufgeschoben wurde.

● **Gröna linjen** (Linien 17-19) - 41,5 km
Die grüne Linie ist die älteste des Tunnelbana-Netzes. Sie entstand zwischen 1950 und 1960 durch Ausbau mehrerer Vorortstraßenbahnstrecken (daher stammen die heutigen Liniennummern) auf Metro-Standard und einer unterirdischen Verbindung durch das Stadtzentrum. Ähnlich wie die Osloer T-bane vermittelt sie deshalb auf den Außenstrecken durch einfach gestaltete oberirdische Haltestellen und enge Kurvenradien oft den Eindruck einer Hochflur-Stadtbahn. Der Tunnel unter der Insel Södermalm zwischen Slussen und Skanstull war bereits 1933 für die Straßenbahn errichtet worden. Nach 1960 wurde die grüne Linie nur geringfügig erweitert: 1971 von Farsta nach Farsta strand und 1994, als bislang letzte Erweiterung des Tunnelbana-Netzes überhaupt, unterirdisch von Bagarmossen bis Skarpnäck. Mittelfristig wird die grüne Linie den Ast nach Hagsätra an die blaue Linie abgeben, dafür aber einen Nordast, der als gelbe Linie (4,1 km) beworben wird und u.a. das Karolinska Universitetssjukhuset (Uni-Klinikum) erschließt, dazugewinnen.

● **Röda linjen** (Linien 13 & 14) - 39,7 km
Zwischen 1964 und 1978 wurde die rote Linie errichtet. Bis auf den Ast nach Fruängen, der auch aus einer Vorortstra-ßenbahn hervorging, zeichnet sich diese Strecke durch große Radien und eine weitgehend unterirdische Trassie-rung auch in den Außenbereichen aus. Zwischen T-Cen-tralen und Slussen verkehren die grüne und die rote Linie parallel, aber stets auf eigenen Gleisen. Während man in Gamla stan [Altstadt] und Slussen am selben Bahnsteig im

1) Older cars of class C6 and C14-C15, which usually form 8-car trains. The C6 cars were modernised in the 1990s. The C14s were manufactured reusing parts of older cars.
2) The trains of class C20 (Vagn 2000) have shaped the image of the Tunnelbana since the turn of the millen-nium. The walk-through 3-car sets generally form 9-car trains, which take up the entire length of the platform.
3) In May 2013, SL ordered four-section MOVIA trains (class C30) from Bombardier, which started running in regular service on the Red Line in double formation in 2020. The Red Line was planned to be equipped with the new CBTC system to allow driverless operation, but this project has been postponed.

● *Gröna linjen* (Lines 17-19) - 41.5 km
The Green Line is the oldest Tunnelbana route. It was created between 1950 and 1960 by upgrading several suburban tram lines to metro standard (hence today's line numbers) and building an underground connection through the city centre. Like the Oslo T-bane, it therefore gives the impression of a high-floor light rail system, especially on the outer sections, where simple surface stations and rather tight curves can be found. The tunnel under the island Södermalm between Slussen and Skanstull had already been built in 1933 for the old tram system. After 1960, the Green Line was only slightly expanded: in 1971, from Farsta to Farsta strand, and in 1994, on an under-ground route from Bagarmossen to Skarpnäck; at present, this remains the last extension to the entire Tunnelbana network. In the medium term, the Green Line will hand its Hagsätra branch over to the Blue Line, while a 4.1 km northern branch will be added. Currently promoted as the Yellow Line, it will serve, among other places, the Karolinska Universitetssjukhuset [University hospital].

● *Röda linjen* (Lines 13 & 14) - 39.7 km
The Red Line was built between 1964 and 1978. Except for the Fruängen branch, which was also developed from a former suburban tram line, this route is characterised by large curve radii and a mostly underground alignment, on the outer sections too. Between T-Centralen and Slussen, the Green and Red Lines operate in parallel but on their own tracks. While at Gamla stan [Old Town] and Slussen, cross-platform interchange is available in

Gröna linjen: C20 @ Globen

Röda linjen: C30 @ Liljeholmen   (Foto Thomas Johansson)

Richtungsverkehr umsteigen kann, bietet der U-Bahnhof T-Centralen, wo zwei Mittelbahnsteige übereinander liegen, eine bequeme Umsteigemöglichkeit in entgegengesetzter Richtung. Zur Entlastung des Betriebshofs Nyboda bei Liljeholmen wurde 2016 ein zweiter Betriebshof in Norsborg eröffnet, der größtenteils unterirdisch in einem Felstunnel liegt. Als Teil des Tunnelbana-Netzes führt von der Station Liljeholmen die sog. **Hissbana** [Liftbahn], eine unterirdische Schrägkabelbahn, hinauf zum Wohngebiet Nybohov.

● **Blå linjen** (Linien 10 & 11) - 24,5 km
Die blaue Linie ergänzte das Tunnelbana-Netz zwischen 1975 und 1985, wobei die ursprüngliche Linie von T-Centralen über Hallonbergen nach Hjulsta führte. Erst zehn Jahre später entstand der Abschnitt durch Sundbyberg zwischen Västra skogen und Rinkeby. Die blaue Linie verläuft bis auf zwei Abschnitte im Bereich Kista unterirdisch, wobei tief liegende, künstlerisch ausgestaltete Felsgewölbestationen wie schon teilweise bei der roten Linie vorherrschen. Die Bahnsteige sind auf dieser Linie sogar 180 m lang.

Vom stadtseitigen Endpunkt Kungsträdgården war bereits von Anfang an eine Verlängerung Richtung Osten über Skeppsholmen und/oder Slussen Richtung Nacka geplant, eine Erweiterung, deren Bau nun im Jahr 2020 begonnen hat. Dabei wird Skeppsholmen allerdings keinen U-Bahnhof bekommen. Nach der rund 100 m tief liegenden Station Sofia auf Södermalm wird sich die Strecke verzweigen, ein Ast führt wie geplant über Sickla nach Nacka (8 km), der andere zum Gullmarsplan, wo die blaue Linie 70 m unterhalb der bestehenden oberirdischen Station halten wird; der nördliche Ausgang bringt die Fahrgäste direkt nach Mårtensdal. Die Neubaustrecke (3 km) endet kurz vor der Station Sockenplan, ab wo sie die bestehende oberirdische Strecke der grünen Linie nach Hagsätra übernimmt. Die Altstrecke mit den aus der Zeit der Vorortstraßenbahn stammenden Haltestellen Enskede gård und Globen wird stillgelegt. Beide Äste sollen 2030 in Betrieb gehen.

Am anderen Ende der blauen Linie soll eine 4 km lange unterirdische Verlängerung zum S-Bahnhof Barkarby bereits 2026 fertig werden. Diese erschließt das Neubaugebiet Barkarbystaden in der Kommune Järfälla und schafft eine bessere Verbindung aus der Region westlich von Stockholm zu den Arbeitsplätzen in Kista und Solna.

the same direction, at T-Centralen, where two island platforms lie on top of the other, the two lines stop next to each other in the opposite direction. To relieve the Nyboda depot near Liljeholmen, a second depot was opened in 2016 in Norsborg, located underground inside a rock tunnel. Another part of the Tunnelbana network is the so-called 'Hissbana' [lift railway], an underground cable-hauled cabin that shuttles between Liljeholmen station and the neighbourhood of Nybohov, which is located on a hill.

● *Blå linjen (Lines 10 & 11) - 24.5 km*
Built between 1975 and 1985, the Blue Line completed today's Tunnelbana network. The original line went from T-Centralen to Hjulsta via Hallonbergen. The section through Sundbyberg from Västra skogen to Rinkeby was only opened ten years later. Except for two sections in the Kista area, the Blue Line runs completely underground and features many rather deep and artistically enhanced rock cavern stations, a type of station also found on some sections of the Red Line. At 180 m, the platforms on the Blue Line are even longer than those on the other two routes.

An eastern extension from the city centre terminus Kungsträdgården via Skeppsholmen and/or Slussen to Nacka had been planned from the beginning, but its construction was only launched in 2020. Skeppsholmen, however, will be passed without a station. After the 100 m deep Sofia station on Södermalm, the line will split into two branches: one branch will run via Sickla to Nacka (8 km) as originally planned, while the other will go to Gullmarsplan, where the Blue Line will stop 70 m below the existing above-ground station; the northern exit will lead directly to Mårtensdal. The new route (3 km) ends shortly before Sockenplan station, from where it takes over the existing surface segment of the Green Line to Hagsätra. The old route with Enskede gård and Globen stations, which date back to the suburban tramway era, will be abandoned. Both branches are scheduled to go into operation in 2030.

At the other end of the Blue Line, a 4 km underground extension to Barkarby Pendeltåg station should be ready in 2026. It will serve the new district of Barkarbystaden in the municipality of Järfälla and provide a better connection for commuters from the region west of Stockholm to their workplaces in Kista and Solna.

Blå linjen: C20 @ Rinkeby

Gröna linjen: C20 @ Enskede gård

Röda linjen: C20 @ Alby

Röda linjen: C20 @ Mörby centrum

Röda linjen: Stadion

Röda linjen: C20 @ Mälarhöjden

Blå linjen: Kista

X60 @ Stockholms södra

Pendeltåg – S-Bahn

Ein durchgehender S-Bahn-Verkehr begann in Stockholm im Jahr 1968. Es entwickelten sich im Laufe der Jahre zwei Hauptlinien, die zwischen Karlberg und Älvsjö gemeinsam verkehrten, nämlich J35 Bålsta – Nynäshamn und J36 Märsta – Södertälje centrum; beide fuhren auf dem zentralen Abschnitt werktags alle 15 Minuten, weiter außerhalb alle 30 Minuten. Dazu kam im Süden die teils nur stündlich bediente Anschlusslinie J37 Södertälje centrum – Gnesta. Im Dezember 2012 wurde gemeinsam mit dem benachbarten Uppsala län eine direkte halbstündliche Verbindung von Älvsjö nach Uppsala über den Flughafen Arlanda eingeführt (Linie J38), womit man günstiger als mit dem *Arlanda Express* zum Flughafen kommt, auch wenn dafür ein Zuschlag fällig ist. An diesen Linien änderte sich auch nichts, als am 10. Juli 2017 die sog. **Citybana**, eine 6 km lange, zweigleisige Tunnelverbindung zwischen Stockholms södra und der Verzweigung Tomteboda im Norden in Betrieb ging, womit der Engpass südlich des Hauptbahnhofs Stockholm C, wo nur zwei Gleise für Fern- und Nahverkehr zur Verfügung standen, entschärft werden konnte. Östlich des Hauptbahnhofs entstand unter dem U-Bahnhof T-Centralen in 40 m Tiefe der viergleisige S-Bahnhof Stockholm City, ein zweigleisiger wurde schräg unterhalb des U-Bahnhofs Odenplan errichtet. Bereits 2005 war eine zweite Eisenbahnbrücke in Årsta eröffnet worden, um die Kapazität der sonst viergleisigen Hauptstrecke aus dem Süden bzw. Westen (Västra stambanan) zu erhöhen. Die Nordstrecke (Ost-kustbanan) ist ebenfalls viergleisig bis Upplands Väsby, wo seit 1999 die Strecke zum Flughafen abzweigt. Der viergleisige Ausbau des Bålsta-Astes (Mälarbanan) soll 2028 abgeschlossen sein.

Pendeltåg – Suburban Rail

*A suburban rail service with cross-city lines was launched in Stockholm in 1968. Over the years, two main lines that shared the section between Karlberg and Älvsjö had evolved, namely J35 Bålsta – Nynäshamn and J36 Märsta – Södertälje centrum. On weekdays, these lines used to run every 15 minutes on their central portions, and every 30 minutes on their outer sections. In addition, line J37 provided a shuttle service between Södertälje centrum and Gnesta in the south of the region, but usually with a train just once an hour. In December 2012, together with the neighbouring Uppsala County, SL introduced a direct service from Älvsjö to Uppsala via Arlanda Airport (line J38, every 30 minutes), which is a cheaper way to get to the airport than the Arlanda Express, even including the supplementary fare which is payable. The same lines continued to operate when the so-called **Citybana** opened on 10 July 2017 – a 6 km, double-track tunnel connection between Stockholms södra and the junction at Tomteboda in the north. This eliminated the bottleneck to the south of Stockholm's Central Station, where there were just two tracks for both long-distance and local trains. On the eastern side of the Central Station and below the Tunnel-bana T-Centralen station, a 4-track suburban station called Stockholm City was built at a depth of 40 m, while a 2-track underground station was placed diagonally below Odenplan metro station. Already in 2005, a second railway bridge had been opened in Årsta to increase the capacity of the mainline route from the south and west of Sweden (Västra stambanan), the rest of which had been widened to four tracks on its approach to Stockholm in previous years. The northern route (Ostkustbanan) also has four tracks to Upplands Väsby, from where the airport*

Stockholm Odenplan

Das Liniennetz wurde im Dezember 2017 reformiert und ist dadurch leider etwas unübersichtlich geworden, zumal neben den teils nur zeitweise verkehrenden Linien 40-44 und 48 noch Expressfahrten wie 42X und 43X hinzukommen. Nach Upplands Väsby im Norden kommt man 8x/h, nach Tumba im Südwesten sogar 10x/h, nach Nynäshamn oder Bålsta hingegen meist nur halbstündlich. Lediglich die Pendeltåg-Stationen Knivsta und Uppsala liegen außerhalb des SL-Tarifgebiets, während für Arlanda C (Flughafen) ein Zuschlag fällig ist. Andere Regionalbahnen sind nicht im SL-Verbundtarif integriert.

Der Pendeltåg-Betrieb wird ausschließlich mit X60-Triebwagen vom Typ Coradia Nordic von Alstom abgewickelt. Die 6-teiligen, durchgehend begehbaren Fahrzeuge sind 106,5 m lang, 3,26 m breit und verkehren auch in Doppeltraktionen. Der Einstieg ist an allen Türen stufenlos. Die S-Bahn-Fahrzeuge sind Eigentum von SL, mit dem Betrieb wurde 2016 die Firma *MTR Nordic AB* beauftragt.

line has diverged since 1999. The quadrupling of the Bålsta branch (Mälarbanan) may be completed in 2028.

The Pendeltåg network was restructured in December 2017 and is now unfortunately a bit difficult to grasp, with lines 40-44 and 48, some of which only run at certain times, being mixed with some express journeys labelled 42X and 43X, for example. From the city centre, 8 trains per hour go to Upplands Väsby in the north, and to Tumba in the southwest even 10tph, while Nynäshamn and Bålsta can only be reached twice an hour. Only the Pendeltåg stations Knivsta and Uppsala lie outside the SL fare area, while for Arlanda C (airport) a supplement is payable. Other regional trains, however, are not integrated into the SL fare system.

The Pendeltåg is now operated exclusively with X60 'Coradia Nordic' EMUs from Alstom. The 6-car, walk-through trainsets are 106.5 m long, 3.26 m wide and can run as double units. Access into the train is step-free at all the doors. The trains are owned by SL, while operation was transferred to 'MTR Nordic AB' in 2016.

Stockholm Odenplan

X60 @ Helenelund

Stockholm City

Stockholm City

Stockholm City

Arlanda Central

X60 @ Arstaberg

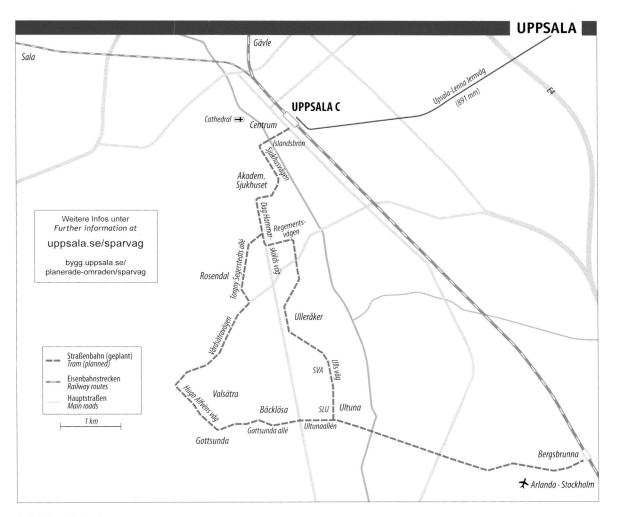

UPPSALA

In der rund 70 km nördlich von Stockholm gelegenen Universitätsstadt Uppsala (175.000 Einw.) ist der Bau einer Straßenbahn geplant. Die beiden Städte sind mehrmals stündlich über den Flughafen Arlanda durch Regionalzüge von SJ, aber auch durch den Pendeltåg von SL miteinander verbunden.

Das Netz der neuen Straßenbahn soll den Hauptbahnhof mit den südlichen Stadtteilen verbinden und gleichzeitig mehrere Forschungseinrichtungen anschließen, darunter das Uppsala Universitätskrankenhaus, die SLU (Schwedische Landwirtschaftshochschule), den Uppsala Science Park und das Uppsala Biomedical Centre. Durch bislang teils unbebautes Gebiet soll die Tram schließlich den Bahnhof Bergsbrunna (Uppsala Södra) erreichen, der auf der viergleisig auszubauenden Strecke nach Stockholm geplant ist.

Sollten noch im Jahr 2021 die entsprechenden Beschlüsse gefasst und die Finanzierung sichergestellt werden, könnte 2022 mit der Detailplanung begonnen werden, so dass der eigentliche Bau 2024-2028 erfolgen und schließlich mit einer Inbetriebnahme im Jahr 2029 gerechnet werden könnte. Gleichzeitig sollen auch der neue Bahnhof Bergsbrunna sowie die zusätzlichen Gleise zwischen Uppsala und Bergsbrunna fertig sein.

The construction of a tram system is planned in the university town of Uppsala (175,000 inhabitants), some 70 km north of Stockholm. The two cities are connected several times an hour by SJ regional trains running via Arlanda Airport, but also by the SL Pendeltåg.

The new tramway is intended to link the city's railway station to the southern suburbs while also serving several academic institutions, such as the Uppsala University Hospital, the Swedish University of Agricultural Sciences (SLU), the Uppsala Science Park and the Uppsala Biomedical Centre. Through as yet undeveloped areas, the tram will reach Bergsbrunna (Uppsala Södra) station, which is to be added along the main line to Stockholm, which is planned to be quadrupled.

If the respective decisions are taken and financing is secured in 2021, detailed planning could start in 2022, and the actual construction of the route could take place from 2024 to 2028 for a possible opening in 2029. By that time, the new train station Bergsbrunna should also have been completed, as well as additional tracks between Uppsala and Bergsbrunna.

Erste vollständig ausgerüstete Straßenbahn | *first fully equipped tram car* (Sept 2020) (Foto Pasi Tiitola / Tampere Tramway Ltd)

TAMPERE

Tampere (schwedisch Tammerfors) ist Finnlands größte Stadt außerhalb des Großraums Helsinki. Helsinki und Tampere sind per Bahn mindestens stündlich miteinander verbunden, eine Fahrt (ca. 180 km) dauert je nach Zuggattung 90-120 Minuten.

Anders als in Turku gab es in Tampere in früheren Zeiten keine elektrische Straßenbahn, allerdings fuhren in dieser Stadt von 1948 bis 1976 Obusse. Neben Turku und Helsinki war Viipuri (Vyborg) von 1912 bis 1957 die dritte finnische Straßenbahnstadt, allerdings fiel diese Stadt im 2. Weltkrieg an die Sowjetunion und gehört auch heute zu Russland.

Nachdem Anfang des neuen Jahrtausends eine Regionalstadtbahn (Tram-Train) mit einem Tunnel durch das Stadtzentrum untersucht worden war, beschloss der Stadtrat am 7. November 2016 schließlich den Bau einer modernen Straßenbahn, die in einer ersten Phase vom Pyynikintori in der westlichen Innenstadt über den Bahnhof nach Hervanta im Süden, wo sich ein Universitätscampus befindet, verlaufen sollte. Dazu kam ein östlicher Ast zur

Tampere (Tammerfors in Swedish) is the largest city in Finland outside the Helsinki metropolitan area. Helsinki and Tampere (approximately 180 km) are linked by train at least every hour, with a journey taking 90-120 minutes, depending on the type of train chosen.

Unlike Turku, Tampere did not have a first-generation electric tramway, but instead operated trolleybuses from 1948 to 1976. Besides Turku and Helsinki, Viipuri (Vyborg) was yet another Finnish city with a tramway, which existed from 1912 to 1957, but it was ceded to the Soviet Union in World War II and is today a part of Russia.

After a regional tram-train system with a tunnel through the city centre had been examined at the beginning of the new millennium, the city council eventually decided on 7 November 2016 to build a modern tramway that, in the initial stage, would run from Pyynikintori in the western part of the city centre via the railway station to Hervanta in the south, where a large university campus is located. This main route was

(Foto Samu Rytkönen / Tampere Tramway Ltd)

Hiedanranta > Santalahti
neuer Damm | *new embankment*
(Abb. raitiotieallianssi.fi)

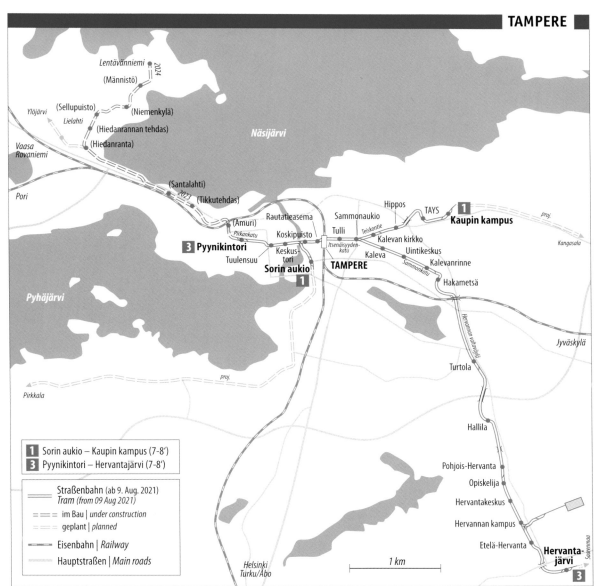

1 Sorin aukio – Kaupin kampus (7-8′)
3 Pyynikintori – Hervantajärvi (7-8′)

———	Straßenbahn (ab 9. Aug. 2021) *Tram (from 09 Aug 2021)*
= = =	im Bau | *under construction*
= = =	geplant | *planned*
—•—	Eisenbahn | *Railway*
	Hauptstraßen | *Main roads*

Erschließung des Uni-Klinikums (TAYS). Am 25. November 2019 fiel die Entscheidung, auch einen kurzen Ast im Zentrum zum Sorin aukio in die erste Ausbauphase aufzunehmen. 2017 war der Auftrag zum Bau der Fahrzeuge an Škoda Transtech vergeben worden, diese werden in Otanmäki, rund 450 km nördlich von Tampere, gefertigt. Die 37 m langen dreiteiligen Zweirichtungsfahrzeuge verfügen über eine Klimaanlage und sind bei Bedarf durch ein weiteres Mittelteil auf 47 m verlängerbar. Ähnliche Wagen verkehren bereits in Helsinki und bei der Schöneicher-Rüdersdorfer

TAMPERE (Suomi | Finnland | Finland)

🥾	240 000	🥾	~ 350 000
⟨el.⟩	2021		
⎮⊢	1435 mm		
km	14.2 km		
⋈	2		

Tampereen Ratikka
- www.tampereenratikka.fi
- www.raitiotieallianssi.fi

Nysse – www.nysse.fi

complemented with an eastern branch to the university hospital (TAYS). On 25 November 2019, the decision was taken to add to the first phase yet another short branch in the city centre to Sorin aukio. In 2017, the contract to supply the vehicles had been awarded to Škoda Transtech, which is manufacturing the trams in Otanmäki, some 450 km north of Tampere. The 37 m bidirectional three-section vehicles feature air-conditioning and can be extended to 47 m by adding another middle section if necessary. Similar cars are already running in Helsinki and on the Schöneicher-Rüdersdorfer

Testfahrt am 21. Okt. 2020 | *test ride on 21 Oct 2020*
(LAJINSA ENSIMMÄINEN = Der erste seiner Art | *The first of its kind*)   (Foto Aarne Alameri)

Straßenbahn östlich von Berlin. Das von der Bevölkerung in einem Voting gewählte ziegelrote Design spielt auf die industrielle Tradition und die damit verbundenen typischen Backsteinbauten in Tampere an.

Im April 2019 bekam die *VR Group*, hinter der sich die finnische Staatsbahn verbirgt, den Zuschlag, die Straßenbahn 10 Jahre lang zu betreiben. Die Eröffnung der Linien 1 (4 km) und 3 (11,3 km) soll am 9. August 2021 stattfinden. Erste Tests auf der vollendeten Strecke durch Hervanta, wo auch der Betriebshof angesiedelt ist, fanden im Frühjahr 2020 mit einem aus Hannover ausgeliehenen TW 6000 statt, bevor im Mai 2020 die erste Artic-Tram angeliefert wurde, mit der im Laufe des Jahres zahlreiche Testfahrten absolviert wurden.

Am 19. Oktober 2020 beschloss der Stadtrat den Weiterbau Richtung Westen. Bis 2023 soll die Tram Santalahti erreichen und ein Jahr später die Endstation in Lentävänniemi. Für die letzte Phase wird zwischen Santalahti und Hiedanranta/Lielahti ein Damm im See Näsijärvi aufgeschüttet.

Längerfristig könnte der Ast zum Sorin aukio über Härmälä Richtung Pirkkala und zum Flughafen verlängert werden. Außerdem werden Erweiterungen Richtung Ylöjärvi, Kangasala und Saarenmaa untersucht.

Die neue Straßenbahn ist in das Tarifsystem der Region Tampere *Nysse* integriert, doch ganz im Trend der nordischen Länder gibt es wohl 24-Stunden-Tickets ab 2021 nur noch über die „Nysse Mobile" App (Zonen AB - 7 €).

tram system east of Berlin. The brick-red design chosen by the local population was inspired by Tampere's industrial tradition and the red-brick buildings associated with it.

In April 2019, the VR Group (a holding which includes the Finnish State Railway) was awarded a contract to operate the tram for 10 years. Lines 1 (4 km) and 3 (11.3 km) are scheduled to open on 9 August 2021. The first tests on the completed route through Hervanta, where the depot is located, took place in spring 2020 with a class TW 6000 tram borrowed from Hanover. The first Artic tram was delivered in May 2020, allowing numerous test runs to be carried out for the rest of the year.

On 19 October 2020, the city council decided to move forward with the western extension. The tram should reach Santalahti by 2023, and a year later, the terminus at Lentävänniemi. For the latter section, an embankment will be erected on the lakeshore of Näsijärvi between Santalahti and Hiedanranta/Lielahti.

In the longer term, the branch to Sorin aukio could be extended via Härmälä to Pirkkala and the airport. Extensions towards Ylöjärvi, Kangasala and Saarenmaa are also being examined.

The new tram is integrated into the 'Nysse' fare system of the Tampere Region, but keeping in line with the Nordic trend, from 2021, 24-hour tickets may only be available via the 'Nysse Mobile' app (zones AB - €7).

Ratikka > Fahrzeuge | *Rolling Stock* (750 V DC)						
Nummer *Number*	Anzahl *Quantity*	Hersteller *Manufacturer*	Typ *Class*	Länge *Length*	Breite *Width*	Ausgeliefert *Delivered*
01-19	19	Škoda Transtech	ForCity Smart Artic X34 <=>	37.3 m	2.65 m	2020-2021

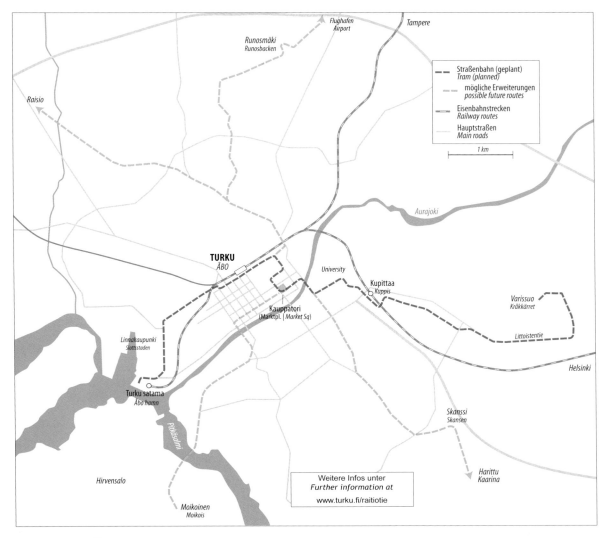

TURKU ÅBO

In der offiziell zweisprachigen Hafenstadt Turku (schwedisch Åbo) im Westen Finnlands leben etwa 195.000 Menschen. Die ca. 160 km Entfernung zwischen Turku und der Hauptstadt Helsinki legen die häufig verkehrenden Züge der VR in etwa zwei Stunden zurück.

Während eine moderne Straßenbahn im etwas größeren Tampere kurz vor der Inbetriebnahme steht, gehen die Planungen in Turku nur langsam voran. Anders als in Tampere gab es hier allerdings bereits von 1908 bis 1972 eine elektrische Straßenbahn. Das Netz war meterspurig und bestand aus zwei Ost-West-Linien und einer Ringlinie.

Nach Untersuchung verschiedener Korridore entschied die Stadt im April 2020, die Strecke nach Westen zum Hafen mit dem Entwicklungsgebiet Linnakaupunki sowie die Strecke nach Osten über die Universität nach Varissuo als erste in Angriff zu nehmen. Ein endgültiger Beschluss soll aber erst 2024 gefasst werden, so dass die Inbetriebnahme wohl frühestens 2029 erfolgen könnte.

The port city of Turku (Åbo in Swedish) in western Finland is officially bilingual and has a population of approximately 195,000. The 160 km route between Turku and the capital Helsinki is frequently served by VR trains, a journey which takes about two hours.

While a new tram system is about to open in slightly larger Tampere, planning in Turku is advancing at a slow pace. Unlike Tampere, however, Turku once had an electric tramway, which operated from 1908 to 1972. The network used metre gauge and consisted of two east-west lines and a circular one.

After examining various possible routes, the city council decided in April 2020 to move forward with a western line to the port, serving the redevelopment area known as Linnakaupunki, as well as an eastern line via the university area to Varissuo. The final decision will only be taken in 2024 for a possible opening in 2029.

Tram: Artic #424 @ Lasipalatsi Glaspalatset

HELSINKI HELSINGFORS

Das Zentrum der finnischen Hauptstadt liegt auf einer Halbinsel am Finnischen Meerbusen, dem östlichen Teil der Ostsee, der die Stadt vom nur 82 km entfernten Tallinn trennt. Das Stadtgebiet erstreckt sich vor allem Richtung Norden und über mehrere Inseln auch nach Osten. Im Westen schließt die weitläufige Stadt Espoo, im Norden rund um den Flughafen die Stadt Vantaa an. Zusammen ergeben die drei Städte mit der kleinen, von Espoo umschlossenen Gemeinde Kauniainen den Großraum „Hauptstadtregion Helsinki" mit ca. 1,1 Mio. Einwohnern. Auch wenn der Anteil der schwedischsprachigen Bevölkerung in Helsinki nur 6 % ausmacht, ist die gesamte Hauptstadtregion offiziell zweisprachig, was sich auch im Bereich des Nahverkehrs bemerkbar macht, z.B. Hakaniemi (finnisch, immer an erster Stelle und meist in Fettdruck) bzw. Hagnäs (schwedisch).

Über die Hauptstadtregion hinaus erstreckt sich der Verkehrsverbund HSL (Helsingin seudun liikenne), der sich in vier Ringzonen (A-D) gliedert, wobei Zone A fast den gesamten Bereich des aktuellen Straßenbahnnetzes umfasst, Zone B das gesamte Metro-Netz und Zone C den Flughafen sowie die bevorstehende Verlängerung der Metro nach Kivenlahti. Für Besucher bieten sich Tageskarten entweder für die Zonen AB (von 1 Tag/8 € bis 7 Tage/32 €) oder ABC (von 1 Tag/11 € bis 7 Tage/44 €) an. Diese sind auch weiterhin als konventionelle Tickets an Fahrscheinautomaten und in Kiosken erhältlich.

The centre of the Finnish capital lies on a peninsula in the Gulf of Finland, the eastern part of the Baltic Sea, which separates the city from Tallinn, only 82 km away. The municipal area extends mainly to the north of the city centre, and over several islands to the east. In the west, the urban area continues directly into the sprawling city of Espoo, and further north around the airport, into the city of Vantaa. Together, the three cities plus the small Kauniainen, an enclave within Espoo, form the metropolitan area known as the 'Helsinki Capital Region', which has some 1.1 million inhabitants. Although Swedish speakers account for only 6 % of Helsinki's population, the entire capital region is officially bilingual, which is also reflected in the field of transport, e.g. Hakaniemi (Finnish, always first and mostly in bold type) vs. Hagnäs (Swedish).

The fare system administered by the regional transport authority HSL (Helsingin seudun liikenne) extends beyond the actual Capital Region. The area is divided into four zones, A-D, with zone A roughly corresponding to the area served by the current tram system, while zone B includes the entire Metro network, and zone C the airport and the future Metro extension to Kivenlahti. For urban rail enthusiasts, a day ticket for zones AB (from 1 day/€8 to 7 days/€32) or for zones ABC (from 1 day/€11 to 7 days/€44) is therefore recommended. They are still available as conventional one-use tickets from vending machines and in kiosks.

Metro: **Matinkylä** Mattby

Während die Straßenbahn nur den Innenstadtbereich sowie die inneren Vororte nördlich davon abdeckt, stellt die Metro eine schnelle Verbindung in die östlichen Vororte und in die westliche Nachbarstadt Espoo her. Die S-Bahn hat innerhalb Helsinkis 15 Bahnhöfe und erschließt sonst vor allem Espoo und Vantaa sowie die umliegende Region. Neben dem Inlandsfernverkehr (mindestens stündlich nach Turku und Tampere) ist Helsinki auch mehrmals täglich mit dem modernen Schnellzug *Allegro* mit St. Petersburg verbunden.

While the tramway only covers the city centre and the inner suburbs north of it, the Metro provides a rapid link between the city centre and the eastern suburbs as well as Espoo, the neighbouring city to the west. Suburban trains stop at 15 stations in Helsinki, but otherwise mainly serve Espoo, Vantaa and the surrounding region. In addition to the domestic long-distance train service (at least every hour to Turku and Tampere), Helsinki is also connected to St. Petersburg several times a day by the Allegro, a modern express train.

HELSINKI HELSINGFORS
(Suomi | Finnland | Finland)

  660 000 (213 km²)

  ~ 1 100 000 (770 km² incl. Vantaa, Espoo)

  Tram – 1900; Metro – 1982

  Tram – 1000 mm; Metro – 1522 mm

  Tram ~ 46 km; Metro – 35 km

  Tram – 9 (+1); Metro – 2

  HKL (Helsingin kaupungin liikennelaitos) – *www.hkl.fi*

  HSL (Helsingin seudun liikenne) – *www.hsl.fi*

S-Bahn: **FLIRT @ Leinelä** Lejle

Raide-Jokeri: Artic XL
(© Škoda Transtech/HSL | *raidejokeri.info*)

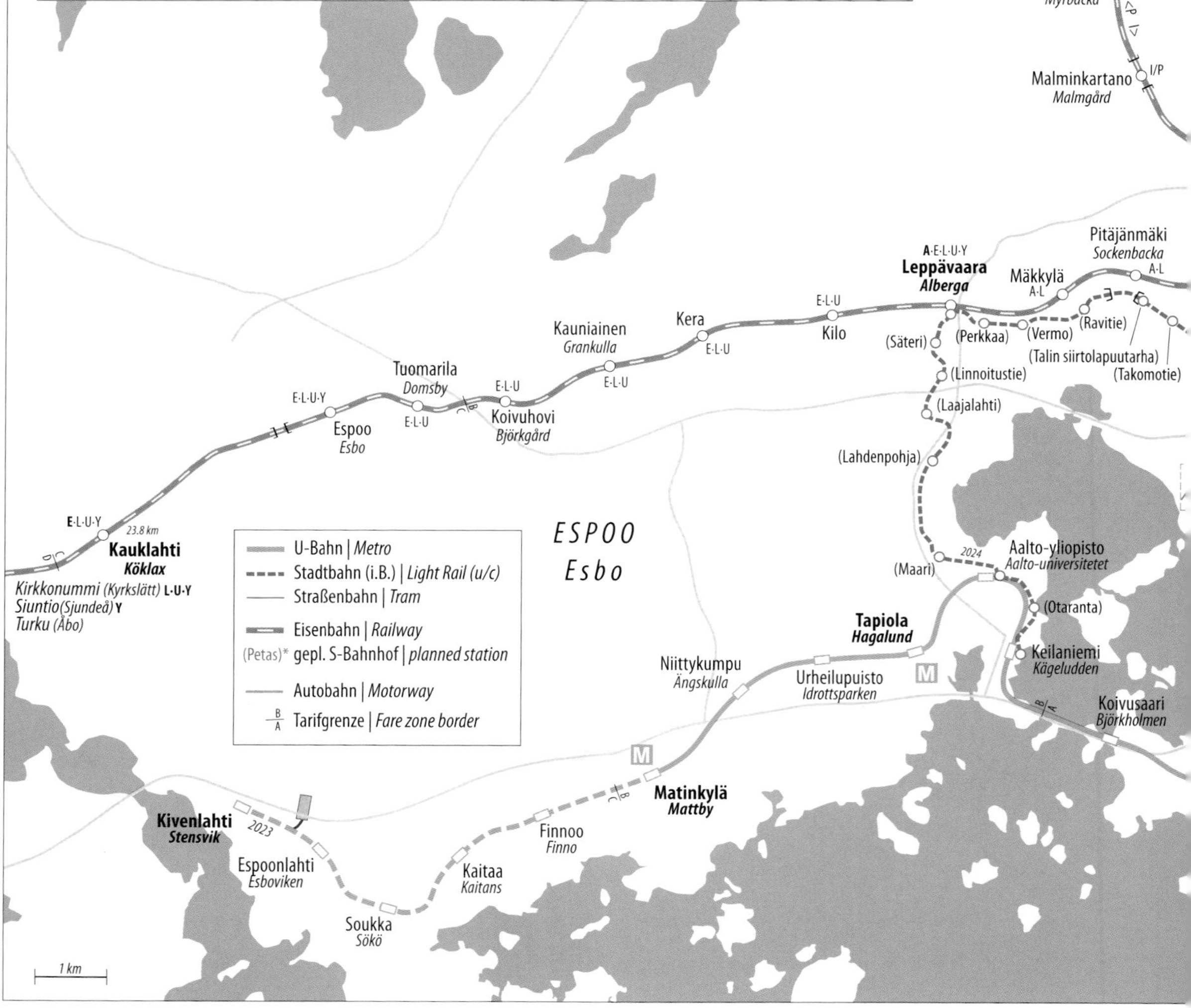

Kivistö I/P

(Petas)*

Vehkala I/P
Veckal

14.9 km
Vantaankoski I/P
Vandaforsen

Martinlaakso I/P
Mårtensdal

Louhela I/P
Klippsta

Myyrmäki I/P
Myrbacka

Malminkartano I/P
Malmgård

Pitäjänmäki
Sockenbacka A·L

A·E·L·U·Y
Leppävaara Mäkkylä
Alberga A·L

(Ravitie)

(Säteri) (Perkkaa) (Vermo)
(Talin siirtolapuutarha)
(Takomotie)

Kauniainen Kera E·L·U
Grankulla Kilo

E·L·U (Linnoitustie)

Tuomarila E·L·U (Laajalahti)
Domsby E·L·U

Koivuhovi (Lahdenpohja)
Björkgård

E·L·U·Y Espoo
Esbo

Aalto-yliopisto
Aalto-universitetet
2024

(Maari) (Otaranta)

E·L·U·Y *23.8 km*
Kauklahti
Köklax

Keilaniemi
Kägeludden

Kirkkonummi (Kyrkslätt) L·U·Y
Siuntio(Sjundeå) Y
Turku (Åbo)

ESPOO
Esbo

Tapiola
Hagalund

Koivusaari
Björkholmen

Niittykumpu
Ängskulla

Urheilupuisto
Idrottsparken

Matinkylä
Mattby

Finnoo
Finno

Kivenlahti
Stensvik 2023

Espoonlahti
Esboviken

Kaitaa
Kaitans

Soukka
Sökö

	U-Bahn	Metro
▬▬	Stadtbahn (i.B.)	*Light Rail (u/c)*
—	Straßenbahn	*Tram*
▭▬	Eisenbahn	*Railway*
(Petas)*	gepl. S-Bahnhof	*planned station*
—	Autobahn	*Motorway*
ᴮ⁄ᴀ	Tarifgrenze	*Fare zone border*

1 km

20.3 km Rekola *Räckhals* K·T

Kerava (Kervo) **K**
Riihimäki **D·T**
Lahti (Lahtis) **Z**
Tampere (Tammerfors) **R**
St. Petersburg

(Ruskeasanta)*
(Rödsand)

↑ **M** Finnisches Eisenbahnmuseum
Finnish Railway Museum
in Hyvinkää (D·R·T)

Koivukylä
Björkby K·T

<I P>

(Lapinkylä)*
(Lappböle)

I/P

HEL ✈

Helsinki-Vantaan lentoasema
Helsingfors-Vanda flygplats

Lentoasema
Flygplatsen
Airport

Leinelä
Lejle

I/P

<I P>

I/P·K·T Hiekkaharju
Sandkulla

(Viinikkala)*
(Vinikby)

I/P

Aviapolis

D·I/P·K·R·T·Z **Tikkurila**
Dickursby

VANTAA
Vanda

C
8

M	**M1**	**Matinkylä – Vuosaari** (5-8′)
		Mattby – Nordsjö
M	**M2**	**Tapiola – Mellunmäki** (5-8′)
		Hagalund – Mellungsbacka

Liniennummern kaum genutzt
Line numbers barely used

I/P·K·T Puistola
Parkstad

proj.

Majvik

I/P·K·T Tapanila
Mosabacka

Malmi
Malm
I/P·K·T

Mellunmäki
Mellungsbacka
M

Pukinmäki
Bocksbacka
I/P·K·T

Kontula
Gårdsbacka

Kannelmäki
Gamlas
I/P

(Kustaan-
kartano)

HELSINKI
Helsingfors

(Pirjontie)

(Maunula)

(Teininpuisto)

(Viikinmäki)

Pohjois-Haaga
Norra Haga
I/P

(Pirkkola)

(Mäkitorpantie)

(Veräjämäki)

(Viikin tiedepuisto)

Myllypuro
Kvarnbäcken

(Ilkantie)

(Hämeenlinnanväylä)

Oulunkylä
Åggelby
I/P·K·T

Puotila
Botby gård

A·L

Valimo
Gjuteriet

A·E·I/P·L·U·Y

Huopalahti
Hoplax

(Latokartano)

2024

Käpylä
Kottby
I/P·K·T

(Karhunkaataja)

Tram
Depot

Vuosaari
Nordsjö
M

(Vihdintie)
(Kutomotie)

104

(Kauppamyllyntie)

Metro
Depot

Itäkeskus
Östra centrum

Ilmala

A·I/P·L

(Roihupelto)

Rastila
Rastböle

Siilitie
Igelkottsvägen

Pasila
Böle

Herttoniemi
Hertonäs

Kalasatama
Fiskehamnen

Sörnäinen
Sörnäs

Kulosaari
Brändö

(Yliskylä)
(Uppby)

Hakaniemi
Hagnäs

Kruunuvuoren-
silta

Laajasalo
Degerö

HELSINKI
Helsingfors

Helsingin yliopisto
Helsingfors universitet

proj.

Kamppi
Kampen

Rautatientori
Järnvägstorget

(Haakoninlahti)
(Håkansviken)

Ruoholahti
Gräsviken

Lauttasaari
Drumsö

Anm.: Auf allen unseren Helsinki-Plänen stehen schwedische Haltestellennamen zwecks besserer Lesbarkeit *kursiv*!
Note: On all our Helsinki maps, Swedish station names are shown in italics for better legibility!

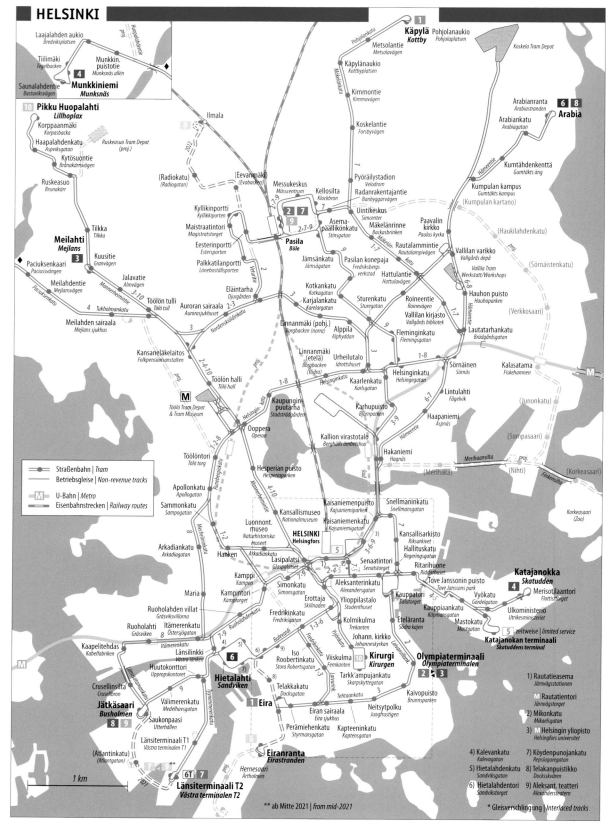

HELSINKI

Käpylä *Kottby* — Pohjolanaukio *Pohjolaplatsen*

Koskela Tram Depot

Pohjolankatu
Metsolantie *Metsolavägen*
Käpylänaukio *Kottbyplatsen*
Kimmontie *Kimmovägen*
Koskelantie *Forsbyvägen*

Arabianranta *Arabiastranden* — **Arabia**
Arabiankatu *Arabiagatan*
Kumtähdenkenttä *Gumtäkts äng*
Kumpulan kampus *Gumtäkts kampus*
(Kumpulan kartano)

Laajalahden aukio *Bredviksplatsen*
Tiilimäki *Tegelbacken*
Munkkin. puistotie *Munksnäs allén*
Munkkiniemi *Munksnäs*
Saunalahdentie *Bastuviksvägen*

Pikku Huopalahti *Lillhoplax*
Korppaanmäki *Korpasbacka*
Haapalahdenkatu *Äspviksgatan*
Kytösuontie *Brånakärrsvägen*
Ruskeasuo *Brunakärr*

Ruskeasuo Tram Depot (proj.)
Ilmala

Pyöräilystadion *Velodrom*
Radanrakentajantie *Banbyggarvägen*
Uintikeskus *Simcenter*
Asema-päällikönkatu *Stinsgatan*
Mäkelänrinne *Backasbrinken*
Paavalin kirkko *Paulus kyrka*
(Haukilahdenkatu)

(Radiokatu) *(Radiogatan)*
(Eevanmäki) *(Evabacken)*
Messukeskus *Mässcentrum*
Kellosilta *Klockbron*

Kyllikinportti *Kyllikkiporten*
Maistraatintori *Magistratstorget*
Eesterinportti *Estersporten*
Palkkatilanportti *Lönebostälsporten*
Eläintarha *Djurgården*

Pasila *Böle*
Pasilan konepaja *Fredriksbergs verkstad*
Hattulantie *Hattulavägen*
Rautalammintie *Rautalampivägen*
(Sörnäistenkatu)
Vallilan varikko *Vallgårds depå*
Vallila Tram Werkstatt/Workshops

Meilahti *Mejlans*
Tilkka
Kuusitie *Granvägen*
Jalavatie *Almvägen*
Meilahdentie *Mejlansvägen*
Paciuksenkatu
Meilahden sairaala *Mejlans sjukhus*
Paciuksenkaari *Paciussvängen*

Jämsänkatu *Jämsägatan*
Kotkankatu *Kotkagatan*
Karjalankatu *Karelargatan*
Sturenkatu *Sturegatan*
Roineentie *Roinevägen*
Vallilan kirjasto *Vallgårds bibliotek*
Hauhon puisto *Hauhoparken*
(Verkkosaari)
Lautatarhankatu *Brädgårdsgatan*

Töölön tulli *Tölö tull*
Auroran sairaala *Aurorasjukhuset*
Tukholmankatu
Meilahden sairaala *Mejlans sjukhus*

Linnanmäki (pohj.) *Borgbacken (norra)*
Alppila *Alphyddan*
Fleminginkatu *Flemingsgatan*

Kansaneläkelaitos *Folkpensionsanstalten*

Linnanmäki (etelä) *Borgbacken (södra)*
Urheilutalo *Idrottshuset*
Sörnäinen *Sörnäs*
Kalasatama *Fiskehamnen*

Töölön halli *Tölö hall*
Kaarlenkatu *Karlsgatan*
Helsinginkatu *Helsingegatan*
Lintulahti *Fågelvik*
(Junonkatu)

HELSINKI *Helsingfors*

Kaupungin-puutarha *Stadsträdgården*
Karhupuisto *Björnparken*
Haapaniemi *Aspnäs*
(Sompasaari)

Töölö Tram Depot & Tram Museum
Ooppera *Operan*
Kallion virastotalo *Berghälls ämbetshus*
Hakaniemi *Hagnäs*
Merihaansilta
(Merihaka)
(Nihti)
(Korkeasaari)
Finlandsbro

Töölöntori *Tölö torg*
Hesperian puisto *Hesperiaparken*

Korkeasaari (Zoo)

Apollonkatu *Apollogatan*
Sammonkatu *Sampogatan*
Kaisaniemenpuisto *Kajsaniemiparken*
Kaisaniemenkatu *Kajsaniemigatan*
Snellmaninkatu *Snellmansgatan*

Kansallismuseo *Nationalmuseet*
Luonnont. museo *Naturhistoriska museet*

Kansallisarkisto *Riksarkivet*
Hallituskatu *Regeringsgatan*

Arkadiankatu *Arkadiagatan*
Hanken
Arkadiankatu
Lasipalatsi *Glaspalatset*
Senaatintori *Senatstorget*
Ritarihuone *Riddarhuset*
Tove Janssonin puisto *Tove Janssons park*

Katajanokka *Skatudden*
Merisotilaantori *Flottisttorget*
Vyökatu *Gördelgatan*
Ulkoministeriö *Utrikesministeriet*
Mastokatu *Mastgatan*
Katajanokan terminaali *Skatuddens terminal*
zeitweise | limited service

Kamppi *Kampen*
Kampintori *Kamptorget*
Maria
Ruoholahden villat *Gräsviksvillorna*
Ruoholahti *Gräsviken*
Itämerenkatu *Östersjögatan*

Simonkatu *Simonsgatan*
Erottaja *Skillnaden*
Fredrikinkatu *Fredriksgatan*
Kolmikulma *Trekanten*
Johann. kirkko *Johanneskyrkan*

Aleksanterinkatu *Alexandersgatan*
Ylioppilastalo *Studenthuset*
Kauppatori *Salutorget*
Kauppiaankatu *Köpmansgatan*
Eteläranta *Södra kajen*

Olympiaterminaali *Olympiaterminalen*

Kaapelitehdas *Kabelfabriken*
Huutokonttori *Uppropskontoret*
Länsilinkki *Västra länken*
Iso Roobertinkatu *Stora Robertsgatan*
Viiskulma *Femkanten*
Tarkk'ampujankatu *Skarpskyttegatan*
Kaivopuisto *Brunnsparken*

Kirurgi *Kirurgen*

Hietalahti *Sandviken*
Telakkakatu *Dockskären*
Eiran sairaala *Eira sjukhus*
Neitsytpolku *Jungfrustigen*

Cruselinsiltä *Crusellbron*
Välimerenkatu *Medelhavsgatan*
Saukonpaasi *Utterhällan*

Jätkäsaari *Busholmen*

Eira
Eiran katu
Perämiehenkatu *Styrmansgatan*
Kapteeninkatu *Kaptensgatan*
Tehtaankatu

Länsiterminaali T1 *Västra terminalen T1*
(Atlantinkatu) *(Atlantgatan)*

Eiranranta *Eirastranden*
Hernesaari *Ärtholmen*

Länsiterminaali T2 *Västra terminalen T2*

1 km

** ab Mitte 2021 | from mid-2021

Legend:
- Straßenbahn | Tram
- Betriebsgleise | Non-revenue tracks
- M U-Bahn | Metro
- Eisenbahnstrecken | Railway routes

1) Rautatieasema *Järnvägsstationen*
M Rautatientori *Järnvägstorget*
2) Mikonkatu *Mikaelsgatan*
3) M Helsingin yliopisto *Helsingfors universitet*
4) Kalevankatu *Kalevagatan*
5) Hietalahdenkatu *Sandviksgatan*
6) Hietalahdentori *Sandvikstorget*
7) Köydenpunojankatu *Repslagaregatan*
8) Telakanpuistikko *Docksvären*
9) Aleksant. teatteri *Alexandersteatern*

* Gleisverschlingung | Interlaced tracks

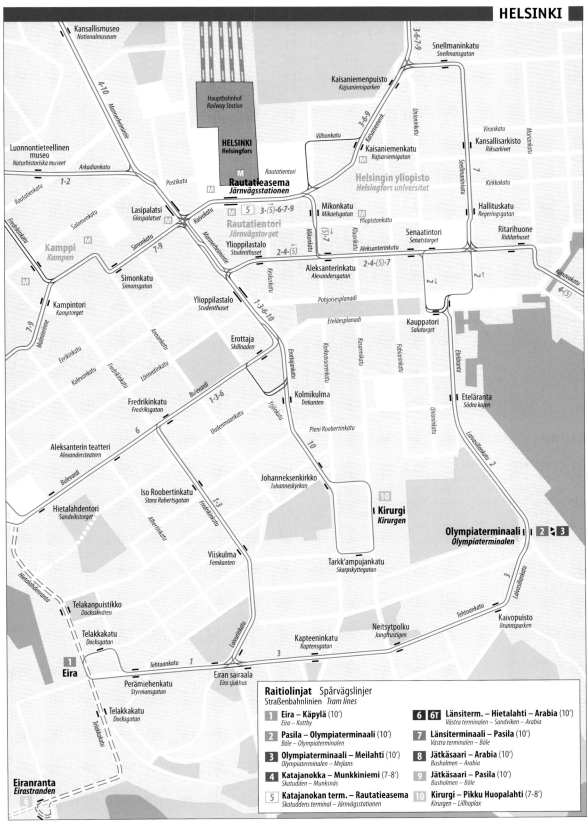

Kansallismuseo
Nationalmuseum

Snellmaninkatu
Snellmansgatan

3·6·7·9

4·10

Kaisaniemenpuisto
Kajsaniemiparken

Mannerheimintie

3·6·9

Kaisaniemenk.

Unioninkatu

Vironkatu

Mar..katu

Luonnontieteellinen museo
Naturhistoriska museet

Arkadiankatu

Hauptbahnhof
Railway Station

Vilhonkatu

Kaisaniemenkatu
Kajsaniemigatan

Kansallisarkisto
Riksarkivet

HELSINKI
Helsingfors

1·2

Rautatienkatu

Postikatu

Rautatientori

Snellmaninkatu

7

Kirkkokatu

M Rautatieasema
Järnvägsstationen

Helsingin yliopisto
Helsingfors universitet

Lasipalatsi
Glaspalatset

Kaivokatu

M 5 3·(5)·6·7·9

Mikonkatu
Mikaelsgatan

Yliopistonkatu

Hallituskatu
Regeringsgatan

Fredrikinkatu

Salomonkatu

Kamppi
Kampen

Rautatientori
Järnvägstorget

7·9

Simonkatu

Mannerheimintie

Ylioppilastalo
Studenthuset

2·4·(5)

Mikonkatu

(5)·7

Kluuvikatu

Aleksanterinkatu

Senaatintori
Senatstorget

Ritarihuone
Riddarhuset

Kanavakatu

2↓

2↑

4·(5)

Simonkatu
Simonsgatan

Aleksanterinkatu
Alexandersgatan

2·4·(5)·7

Kampintori
Kamptorget

7·9

Malminrinne

Ylioppilastalo
Studenthuset

1·3·6·10

Keskuskatu

Pohjoisesplanadi

Erottajankatu

Eerikinkatu

Annankatu

Erottaja
Skillnaden

Eteläesplanadi

Korkeavuorenkatu

Kasarmikatu

Fabianinkatu

Kauppatori
Salutorget

Kalevankatu

Fredrikinkatu

Lönnrotinkatu

Bulevardi

1·3·6

Kolmikulma
Trekanten

Yrjönkatu

Eteläranta
Södra kajen

Fredrikinkatu

Fredrikinkatu
Fredriksgatan

6

Uudenmaankatu

Pieni Roobertinkatu

10

Unioninkatu

Aleksanterin teatteri
Alexandersteatern

Bulevardi

Johanneksenkirkko
Johanneskyrkan

Laivasillankatu

2

Hietalahdenranta

Iso Roobertinkatu
Stora Robertsgatan

Albertinkatu

Hietalahdentori
Sandvikstorget

1·3

10

Kirurgi
Kirurgen

Olympiaterminaali
Olympiaterminalen

2 ◄ 3

Viiskulma
Femkanten

Tarkk'ampujankatu
Skarpskyttegatan

3

Laivasillankatu

Telakanpuistikko
Docksskvären

Neitsytpolku
Jungfrustigen

Tehtaankatu

Kaivopuisto
Brunnsparken

Telakkakatu
Docksgatan

Laivurinkatu

Kapteeninkatu
Kaptensgatan

3

1

1

Tehtaankatu

Hietalahdenranta

1

Eira

Peramiehenkatu
Styrmansgatan

Eiran sairaala
Eira sjukhus

Telakkakatu
Docksgatan

Telakkakatu

Raitiolinjat Spårvägslinjer
Straßenbahnlinien *Tram lines*

1 **Eira – Käpylä** (10') *Eira – Kottby*	**6** **6T** **Länsiterm. – Hietalahti – Arabia** (10') *Västra terminalen – Sandviken – Arabia*
2 **Pasila – Olympiaterminaali** (10') *Böle – Olympiaterminalen*	**7** **Länsiterminaali – Pasila** (10') *Västra terminalen – Böle*
3 **Olympiaterminaali – Meilahti** (10') *Olympiaterminalen – Mejlans*	**8** **Jätkäsaari – Arabia** (10') *Busholmen – Arabia*
4 **Katajanokka – Munkkiniemi** (7-8') *Skatudden – Munksnäs*	**9** **Jätkäsaari – Pasila** (10') *Busholmen – Böle*
5 **Katajanokan term. – Rautatieasema** *Skatuddens terminal – Järnvägsstationen*	**10** **Kirurgi – Pikku Huopalahti** (7-8') *Kirurgen – Lillhoplax*

Valmet #96 @ **Rautatieasema** Järnvägsstationen (Hauptbahnhof) *Central Station*

Raitiotie – Straßenbahn

Der Innenstadtbereich von Helsinki wird größtenteils von der Straßenbahn erschlossen. Das etwa 46 km lange Netz wird derzeit von neun Linien befahren, wobei die Linien 2 und 3 am Olympiaterminaali betrieblich miteinander verknüpft sind. Dazu kommt die nur zeitweise verkehrende Linie 5. Die Straßenbahn verkehrt von etwa 6 Uhr morgens bis Mitternacht. Insgesamt handelt es sich um einen klassischen Straßenbahnbetrieb mit eigenem Gleiskörper nur auf einigen Außenstrecken; auf einigen Hauptstrecken sind die Gleise allerdings vom übrigen Verkehr durch Bodenmarkierungen getrennt. An allen Haltestellen stehen jedoch Bahnsteige zur Verfügung, die ein stufenloses Einsteigen in die Niederflurwagen ermöglichen.

Die ersten Pferdestraßenbahnen fuhren in Helsinki 1891, ab 1900 wurde das meterspurige Netz elektrisch betrieben. In den folgenden Jahren wurden einige Strecken zweigleisig ausgebaut und neue kamen hinzu, bis 1930 die größte Ausdehnung erreicht war. 1945 wurde die zuvor privat betriebene Straßenbahn in den neu gegründeten städtischen Verkehrsbetrieb HKL (*Helsingin kaupungin liikennelaitos*) eingegliedert.

In den letzten Jahrzehnten kamen mehrere kleinere Netzergänzungen hinzu: 1976 nach Pasila/Ostseite (1 km; SL 7), 1980 nördlicher Ast in Katajanokka (700 m; SL 4), 1985 Pasila/Westseite (1,9 km; SL 2/7), 1991 von Ruskeasuo bis Pikku Huopalahti (800 m; SL 10), 1992 zum Fährterminal Katajanokka (400 m; SL 5); 2004 von Arabiankatu bis Arabianranta (500 m; SL 6 & 8). Die wichtigste Neubaustrecke war 2008 der 2,1 km lange Nordabschnitt

Raitiotie – Tram

The inner city of Helsinki is to a large extent covered by the tramway. The approximately 46 km network is currently served by nine lines, with lines 2 and 3 operationally linked at Olympiaterminaali; plus line 5, which only operates sporadically. The trams run from about 06:00 in the morning until midnight. Overall, the Helsinki tram is a classic system with separate rights-of-way only on some outer sections, although on some trunk routes, the track lanes are separated from other traffic by road markings. However, proper platforms are available at all the stops, so level boarding is possible with low-floor vehicles.

The first horse-drawn trams in Helsinki appeared in 1891, and the metre-gauge network was electrified from 1900. In the following years, some routes were doubled and new ones were added, until in 1930, the network reached its maximum expansion. In 1945, the tramway, up to then privately operated, was incorporated into the newly established municipal transport company HKL (Helsingin kaupungin liikennelaitos).

Several smaller sections have been added to the network in recent decades: in 1976, to Pasila/east side (1 km, line 7); in 1980, the northern branch in Katajanokka (700 m; line 4); in 1985, to Pasila/west side (1.9 km; line 2/7); in 1991, from Ruskeasuo to Pikku Huopalahti (800 m; line 10); in 1992, to the ferry terminal at Katajanokka (400 m; line 5), and in 2004, from Arabiankatu to Arabianranta (500 m, lines 6 & 8). The most important new route, however, was the 2.1 km northern

Valmet #83 @ Lasipalatsi Glaspalatset

Artic #437 @ Jätkäsaari/Saukonpaasi Busholmen/Utterhällen

der neuen Linie 9 von der Helsinginkatu bis Pasila. 2012 begann die Erschließung des ehemaligen Hafengebiets auf der Insel Jätkäsaari, einerseits von Ruoholahti bis zur aktuellen Schleife Saukonpaasi (750 m), andererseits von Kamppi zum Länsiterminaali T1 [Westhafen] (1,9 km); letztere Strecke wurde 2017 um 500 m zum Länsiterminaali T2 verlängert, gleichzeitig wurde die Verbindung Huutokonttori – Schleife Saukonpaasi (630 m) in Betrieb genommen. Derzeit ist noch ein Lückenschluss zwischen den beiden Endstellen im Bau (2021). Ebenfalls im Bau befindet sich der erste Abschnitt zur Erschließung des Entwicklungsgebiets Munkkisaari bis Eiranranta (2021). Bis 2022 soll auch eine knapp 1,2 km lange Strecke von Pasila bis Ilmala für die Linie 9 vollendet werden; mittelfristig wird für diese Linie östlich von Pasila in der Asemapäällikönkatu ein zweites Gleis verlegt, damit sie nicht mehr den Umweg über Messukeskus [Messezentrum] nehmen muss. Im Zeitraum 2021-2024 soll außerdem eine rund 4 km lange Neubaustrecke zur Erschließung der ehemaligen Hafengebiete am nordöstlichen Rand der inneren Stadt von Sompasaari über Kalasatama bis Pasila umgesetzt werden.

Am südlichen Ende schließt die Kalasatama-Tram an ein ambitioniertes Stadtbahnprojekt an: Über mehrere Brücken (**Crown Bridges**), darunter die 1200 m lange Kruunuvuorensilta, und die Insel Korkeasaari, auf der sich der Zoo von Helsinki befindet, verbindet die Stadtbahn ab frühestens 2026 Hakaniemi mit Wohngebieten auf der Insel Laajasalo, wo sich die Strecke in zwei Äste verzweigt (zusammen ab Hakaniemi rund 8 km), so dass hier zwei Linien verkehren werden: Hauptbahnhof – Yliskylä und Hauptbahnhof – Haakoninlahti.

part of the new line 9 from Helsinginkatu to Pasila, which was opened in 2008. In 2012, trams started to serve the redevelopment area in the former port on the island of Jätkäsaari, on the one hand from Ruoholahti to the current Saukonpaasi loop (750 m), and on the other hand from Kamppi to Länsiterminaali T1 [West Port] (1.9 km); the latter was extended by 500 m to Länsiterminaali T2 in 2017, when the connection between Huutokonttori and the Saukonpaasi loop (630 m) was also put into operation. A link between the two termini is currently under construction (2021). The first section to take trams to the Munkkisaari redevelopment area is also underway up to Eiranranta (2021). By 2022, yet another 1.2 km stretch, this time from Pasila to Ilmala for line 9, is planned to be completed; in the medium term, a second track will be laid east of Pasila on Asemapäällikönkatu, so that line 9 will no longer have to take the detour via Messukeskus [Exhibition Centre]. Between 2021 and 2024, an approximately 4 km new line will be implemented to serve the former port areas on the northeastern edge of the inner city running from Sompasaari via Kalasatama to Pasila.

At the southern end, the Kalasatama tram will connect to an ambitious light rail project – in 2026 at the earliest, a spectacular new line will run from Hakaniemi via several bridges (**Crown Bridges**), including the 1200 m Kruunuvuorensilta, and the island of Korkeasaari, where the Helsinki Zoo is located, to residential areas on the island of Laajasalo, where the route will split into two branches (together some 8 km from Hakaniemi), with trams operating from Central Station to either Yliskylä or Haakoninlahti.

Artic #418 @ Kaisaniemenkatu Kajsaniemigatan

Valmet #121 @ Länsiterminaali Västra terminalen T1

Valmet #101 @ Hattulantie Hattulavägen

Das neben der Westverlängerung der Metro derzeit wichtigste Verkehrsprojekt im Großraum Helsinki ist „**Raide-Jokeri**", eine 25 km lange tangentiale Halbringlinie mit 34 Haltestellen, welche die bisherige Buslinie 550 ersetzen wird. Diese Stadtbahnstrecke beginnt im Westen in Espoo an der Metro-Station Keilaniemi und endet im Osten an der Metro-Station Itäkeskus. Abschnittsweise verfügte der Bus über eine eigene Trasse, die nun für die Stadtbahn umgebaut wird (inkl. Ausbau von zwei Brücken). An drei Stationen (Oulunkylä, Huopalahti und Leppävaara) wird es eine Umsteigemöglichkeit zu den radialen S-Bahn-Linien geben. Im Bereich Huopalahti war bereits die Bustrasse auf ca. 350 m abgedeckelt, dazu kommt nun ein rund 400 m langer Tunnel unter dem Berg Patterimäki auf halber Strecke zwischen Huopalahti und Leppävaara. In Espoo werden für die Stadtbahn je eine Brücke über die Autobahn 1 (Turunväylä) sowie über den Ring 1 (Kehä I) errichtet. Die Bauarbeiten begannen 2019 auf der gesamten Strecke, die Inbetriebnahme soll Mitte 2024 erfolgen. Vorerst wird es keine Verbindung zum städtischen Tram-Netz geben, dennoch entschied man sich zwecks Kompatibilität für Meterspur und nur 2,40 m breite Fahrzeuge, jedoch in einer längeren Version als bisher. Für später ist eine Neu-

Besides the Metro's western extension, the most important transport project in the Helsinki region is 'Raide-Jokeri', a 25 km tangential semi-circular line with 34 stops which will replace the current 550 bus. This light rail line begins in the west in Espoo at the Keilaniemi Metro station and ends in the east at the Itäkeskus Metro station. Along some sections, the bus used to have its own dedicated busway, but it is now being rebuilt for light rail operation (including the reconstruction of two bridges). At three stations (Oulunkylä, Huopalahti and Leppävaara), interchange will be provided to the radial suburban rail lines. While in the Huopalahti area, the bus route was already covered for some 350 m, a 400 m tunnel is being built under Patterimäki hill, about halfway between Huopalahti and Leppävaara. In Espoo, two dedicated bridges are being erected for the light rail line, one over motorway no. 1 (Turunväylä) and another over ring road no. 1 (Kehä I). Construction work on the entire route began in 2019, and the opening is scheduled for mid-2024. For the time being, there will be no connection to the urban tram network, but for compatibility's sake, Raide-Jokeri will also feature metre gauge and vehicles just 2.40 m wide, although in a longer version than on the

Raitiotie > Fahrzeuge | *Rolling Stock* (600 V DC***)						
Nummer *Number*	Anzahl *Quantity*	Hersteller *Manufacturer*	Typ *Class*	Länge *Length*	Breite *Width*	Ausgeliefert *Delivered*
113-122	10	Valmet/Strömberg	MLNRV I* =>	33.1 m	2.30 m	1973-1975
71-112	42	Valmet/Strömberg	MLNRV II** =>	33.1 m	2.30 m	1983-1987
403-472	70	Škoda Transtech	Artic =>	27.6 m	2.40 m	2015-2019
601-629	29	Škoda Transtech	Artic XL*** <=>	34.5 m	2.40 m	*2021-2023*

* 2013: ergänzt mit Niederflur-Mittelteil | *low-floor centre section added*
** 2006-2011: ergänzt mit Niederflur-Mittelteil | *low-floor centre section added*
*** 2018 für die Jokeri-Stadtbahn (750 V) bestellt, 23 weitere sollen für die Laajasalo-Linie folgen
- ordered in 2018 for Jokeri light rail line (750 V), 23 trams to follow for Laajasalo line

Artic #416 @ Sörnäinen Sörnäs

baustrecke entlang der Huopalahdentie bis Vihdintie und weiter nach Norden Richtung Pohjois-Haaga geplant. Der Betriebshof wird westlich des Metro-Depots in Roihupelto angesiedelt. [Weitere Infos unter *raidejokeri.info*]

Derzeit verkehren auf dem Tram-Netz von Helsinki noch zahlreiche hochflurige Fahrzeuge aus den 1970er und 1980er Jahren, die vor einigen Jahren ein Niederflur-Mittelteil bekamen. Die 40 zwischen 1998 und 2003 von Adtranz (später Bombardier) gelieferten Niederflurfahrzeuge vom Typ „Variotram" (Tw 201-240) wurden hingegen aufgrund anhaltender technischer Probleme Ende 2018 aus dem Verkehr gezogen.

2010 wurden bei der finnischen Firma Transtech Oy, einem Nachfolger von Valmet Oy und heute Teil von Škoda, neue Niederflurbahnen bestellt. Die beiden 2013 gelieferten Prototypen (Tw 401 und 402) wurden 2018/19 an die Schöneicher-Rüdersdorfer Straßenbahn (SRS) abgegeben.

Ein kleines Straßenbahnmuseum ist im Kulturzentrum Korjaamo neben dem Depot in Töölö zu finden.

urban network. In a later stage, a new route is planned along Huopalahdentie to Vihdintie and further north towards Pohjois-Haaga. The depot will be located west of the Metro depot in Roihupelto. [More at raidejokeri.info]

On the Helsinki tram system, numerous high-floor vehicles built in the 1970s and 1980s are still in service. Some years ago, they were extended with a low-floor middle section. The 40 low-floor vehicles (nos. 201-240) belonging to the 'Variotram' family which were delivered by Adtranz (later Bombardier) between 1998 and 2003, however, were withdrawn from service in late 2018 due to persistent technical problems.

In 2010, the Finnish company Transtech Oy, a successor of Valmet Oy and now part of the Škoda holding, was awarded a contract to produce new low-floor trams. The two prototypes (nos. 401 & 402) delivered in 2013 were transferred to the Schöneicher-Rüdersdorfer Straßenbahn in Germany in 2018/19.

In Helsinki, a small tram museum can be found in the Korjaamo Cultural Factory next to the depot in Töölö.

Variotram #226 @ Lasipalatsi Glaspalatset (2018)

Tram Museum Töölö

M300 @ Sörnäinen Sörnäs > **Kalasatama** Fiskehamnen

Metro

Der Betrieb der Metro von Helsinki begann am 1. Juni 1982 zwischen Hakaniemi und Itäkeskus [Ostzentrum], doch anfangs fuhr sie nur in der Hauptverkehrszeit. Ab August 1982 verkehrten die orangefarbenen Züge dann regelmäßig und ganztags zwischen Rautatientori [Eisenbahnplatz] und Itäkeskus. Die russische Breitspur von 1524 mm der Staatsbahn VR wurde auch für die Metro übernommen (hier 1522 mm!). Die Stromzufuhr mit 750 V Gleichstrom erfolgt über eine seitliche Stromschiene. Die Strecke wurde im Laufe der folgenden 16 Jahre in mehreren Stufen erweitert: 1983 bis Kamppi, 1986 bis Kontula, 1989 bis Mellunmäki und 1993 bis Ruoholahti, bevor schließlich 1998 der Ast nach Vuosaari hinzukam. Die Stationen Sörnäinen (1984), Helsingin yliopisto (vormals Kaisaniemi, 1995) und Kalasatama (2007) wurden erst später eröffnet, womit das Netz eine Gesamtlänge von 21,1 km mit 17 Stationen erreicht hatte. Die Strecke durch das Stadtzentrum liegt in einer durchschnittlichen Tiefe von 25 m und wurde größtenteils durch den felsigen Untergrund gesprengt.

Metro

Helsinki's Metro began operating between Hakaniemi and Itäkeskus [Eastern Centre] on 1 June 1982, with service initially limited to rush hour. In August 1982, the orange trains started running regularly all day between Rautatientori [Railway Square] and Itäkeskus. The Russian broad gauge of 1524 mm, used by the state railway VR, was also adopted for the Metro (here 1522 mm, though!). The 750 V dc power is supplied via a third rail. The line was extended in several stages over the following 16 years: in 1983 to Kamppi, in 1986 to Kontula, in 1989 to Mellunmäki, in 1993 to Ruoholahti, and finally 1998, with a new branch to Vuosaari. Some stations were opened later, namely: Sörnäinen (1984), Helsingin yliopisto (formerly Kaisaniemi, 1995) and Kalasatama (2007) bringing the network's total length to 21.1 km with 17 stations. The route through the city centre lies at an average depth of 25 m and was largely blasted through bedrock. The six underground stations on this 4.9 km section were also built using mining techniques.

Metro > Fahrzeuge | *Rolling Stock* (750 V DC)

Nummer *Number*	Anzahl *Quantity*	Hersteller *Manufacturer*	Typ *Class*	Länge *Length*	Breite *Width*	Ausgeliefert *Delivered*
101-184	42 (x2)*	Valmet/Strömberg	M100	44.2 m	3.2 m	1977-1984
201-224	12 (x2)*	Bombardier	M200**	44.3 m	3.2 m	2000-2001
301-320 (A-D)	20 (x4)***	CAF	M300**	88.2 m	3.2 m	2015-2017 (2022)

* Doppeltriebwagen (DT) | *married pairs (2-car sets)*   ** mit Übergang zwischen den Wagen | *with gangways between cars*
*** 4-Wagen-Einheiten (+5 im Feb. 2020 bestellt) | *4-car sets (+5 ordered in Feb 2020)*

M100 @ Kamppi Kampen

M200 @ Kamppi Kampen

Auch die sechs unterirdischen Bahnhöfe auf diesem 4,9 km langen Abschnitt wurden bergmännisch errichtet. Der östliche Abschnitt liegt vorwiegend oberirdisch, wovon etwa 2,5 km auf Brücken und Viadukten verlaufen. Die Stationen Herttoniemi und Itäkeskus wurden überbaut, während sich der U-Bahnhof Puotila unterirdisch auf einem in offener Bauweise errichteten Tunnelabschnitt befindet.

Der Bau der lange geplanten Westverlängerung, der sog. *Länsimetro* [West-Metro], begann schließlich 2009, die Inbetriebnahme fand mit etwas Verspätung am 18. November 2017 statt. Die 13,9 km lange Strecke verläuft gänzlich unterirdisch, größtenteils durch die Nachbarstadt Espoo, und umfasst acht U-Bahnhöfe. Gleichzeitig sollte auf dem gesamten Netz der fahrerlose Betrieb eingeführt werden. Aufgrund anhaltender Probleme mit dem von Siemens gelieferten Betriebssystem und der Nachrüstung der älteren Züge entschied man sich 2015 jedoch, den konventionellen Betrieb beizubehalten, auch wenn die neuen Stationen im Hinblick auf eine dichtere Zugfolge nur für 4-Wagen-Züge ausgelegt waren, während früher auf der Oststrecke 6-Wagen-Züge (132,6 m) eingesetzt wurden. Mit einer Breite von 3,2 m gehören die Metro-Züge von Helsinki allerdings zu den breitesten weltweit.

In einer zweiten Phase wird die Länsimetro derzeit ebenfalls völlig unterirdisch von Matinkylä bis Kivenlahti (7 km; 2023) erweitert. Zu diesem Projekt gehört auch ein unterirdisches Metro-Depot in Sammalvuori. [Mehr Info unter *www.lansimetro.fi*]

Langfristig ist eine Ostverlängerung durch bislang weitgehend unbebautes Gebiet von Mellunmäki bis Majvik (10 km), gegebenenfalls sogar weiter bis Söderkulla (7 km) vorgesehen.

The eastern portion is mostly above ground, with some 2.5 km on bridges and viaducts. Herttoniemi and Itäkeskus stations, which actually lay in a trench, were covered and built over, while the underground station Puotila lies in a tunnel section built by cut-and-cover.

The construction of the long-planned western extension, the so-called 'Länsimetro' [West Metro], finally began in 2009, and after a slight delay, it opened on 18 November 2017. The entire 13.9 km route with its eight stations lies underground, and runs mainly through the neighbouring city of Espoo. In conjunction with the western extension, the entire system was to be converted to driverless operation, but due to persistent problems with the operating system supplied by Siemens and the inevitable retrofitting of the older trains, the decision was taken in 2015 to keep the conventional operation, even if the new stations had only been designed for 4-car trains in view of denser headways, while 6-car trains (132.6 m) had previously been used on the eastern line. With a width of 3.2 m, however, Helsinki's metro trains are among the widest in the world.

In the second stage, the Länsimetro is currently being extended from Matinkylä to Kivenlahti (7 km; 2023). This project includes a new underground metro depot in Sammalvuori. [More info at www.lansimetro.fi]

Later, an eastern extension from Mellunmäki to Majvik (10 km), mostly through undeveloped areas, is also envisaged. Long-term plans even include an extension to Söderkulla (7 km).

M Helsingin yliopisto Helsingfors universitet *University of Helsinki*

Vormals | formerly **Kaisaniemi**

M300 @ Siilitie Igelkottsvägen

Tapiola Hagalund

Lauttasaari Drumsö

Urheilupuisto Idrottsparken

Niittykumpu Ängskulla

113

Stadler FLIRT Sm5 @ Vehkala Veckal

Lähijuna – Nahverkehrszüge

Neben Metro und Tram wird die Hauptstadtregion von Helsinki durch zwei vom Hauptbahnhof ausgehende Bahnstrecken sowie die Ringlinie über den Flughafen erschlossen. Nach einer Ausschreibung wurde der Betrieb im Mai 2020 bis mindestens 2030 an die finnische Staatsbahn VR vergeben, welche somit weiterhin rund um Helsinki einen S-Bahn-Betrieb mit metro-ähnlichem Verkehr anbietet. Auf den Hauptbahnstrecken Richtung Nordosten (*Stammbahn* nach Kerava/Riihimäki) und Richtung Westen (*Küstenbahn* nach Espoo/Karis) findet ein für Außenstehende etwas kompliziert erscheinender Betrieb statt, zumal manche *Linien* nur tagsüber (z.B. A alle 20 Min., K alle 10 Min.), andere dafür nur abends und früh morgens (z.B. L oder T) verkehren. Bis Leppävaara (in Zukunft bis Kauklahti) und bis Kerava stehen eigene S-Bahn-Gleise zur Verfügung; Linien, die weiter in die Region fahren, benutzen im inneren Bereich die Fernbahngleise. Der Flughafen ist alle 10 Minuten durch die Linie I über Tikkurila quasi linksrum (46 Min.) angeschlossen, aber ebenfalls alle 10 Minuten durch die Linie P rechtsrum über Martinlaakso (51 Min.). Anders als in Kopenhagen (*S-tog*) oder Stockholm (*Pendeltåg*) gibt es in Helsinki keine besondere Bezeichnung für die Vorortzüge, sie sind als *Lähijuna* [Nahverkehrszüge] jedoch vollständig in das Tarifsystem des Verkehrsverbunds HSL integriert.

Der elektrische Vorortverkehr begann 1969 auf der Küstenbahn bis Kirkkonummi (38 km) und wurde nach und nach auf die anderen Strecken ausgeweitet. Der 7,5 km lange Ast nach Martinlaakso wurde erst 1975 errichtet und 1991 bis Vantaankoski verlängert. Zwischen Hauptbahnhof und Pasila liegen durchgehend 10 Gleise. Als *Kehärata* [Ringbahn] wurde zwischen 2009 und 2015 eine Verbindung von der Martinlaakso-Linie über den Flughafen zur Stammbahn bei Tikkurila errichtet. Ca. 8 km der 18 km langen Neubaustrecke verlaufen unterirdisch.

Im Stadtzentrum ist seit Langem eine unterirdische Schleife (*Pisararata*; 7,8 km) mit den Bahnhöfen Töölö, Keskusta [Zentrum] und Hakaniemi geplant, wodurch die westlichen auf die nordöstlichen Linien durchgebunden werden könnten.

Lähijuna – Local trains

Besides the Metro and the tramway, the Helsinki Capital Region is also served by two trunk railway lines plus the loop line via the airport. Following a public tender process, Finnish State Railways VR was awarded a contract in May 2020 to continue providing a metro-style service in the Helsinki region until at least 2030. The stopping patterns operated on the northeastern (the main line to Kerava/Riihimäki) and western routes (the coastal line to Espoo/Karis) are rather complicated for outsiders, especially as some 'lines' only operate during daytime service (e.g. A every 20 min or K every 10 min), while others replace them in the evenings or early mornings (e.g. L or T). Up to Leppävaara (to be extended to Kauklahti) and up to Kerava, dedicated suburban tracks are available; trains that continue out into the region, however, use the mainline tracks in the inner area. The airport can be reached from the Central Station every 10 minutes via Tikkurila using an I train (46 min, anti-clockwise), but also every 10 minutes via Martinlaakso with a P train (51 min, clockwise). Unlike in Copenhagen (S-tog) or Stockholm (Pendeltåg), there is no special branding in Helsinki for suburban trains, but as 'Lähijuna' [local trains] they are fully integrated into the HSL fare system.

Electric suburban rail service began in 1969 on the coastal route to Kirkkonummi (38 km), and was gradually extended to other routes. The 7.5 km route to Martinlaakso was newly built in 1975 and extended to Vantaankoski in 1991. A total of ten parallel tracks are in use all the way from Helsinki Central Station to Pasila. Under the project name of 'Kehärata' [circle line], an 18 km railway link (approx. 8 km underground) from the Martinlaakso line via the airport to the northeastern main line near Tikkurila was built between 2009 and 2015.

In the city centre, a 7.8 km underground loop ('Pisararata') with three stations, Töölö, Keskusta [city centre] and Hakaniemi, has long been planned. This link would allow the western and northeastern lines to be jointly operated.

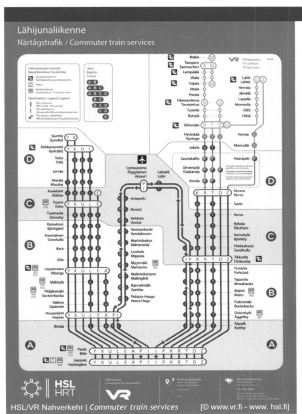

Lähijunaliikenne
Närtågstrafik / Commuter train services

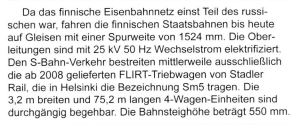

HSL/VR Nahverkehr | *Commuter train services*   [© www.vr.fi - www.hsl.fi]

Lentoasema Flygplatsen *Airport*

Sm4 – VR-Regionalzug | *VR Regional train @ Tikkurila*

Da das finnische Eisenbahnnetz einst Teil des russischen war, fahren die finnischen Staatsbahnen bis heute auf Gleisen mit einer Spurweite von 1524 mm. Die Oberleitungen sind mit 25 kV 50 Hz Wechselstrom elektrifiziert. Den S-Bahn-Verkehr bestreiten mittlerweile ausschließlich die ab 2008 gelieferten FLIRT-Triebwagen von Stadler Rail, die in Helsinki die Bezeichnung Sm5 tragen. Die 3,2 m breiten und 75,2 m langen 4-Wagen-Einheiten sind durchgängig begehbar. Die Bahnsteighöhe beträgt 550 mm.

Since the Finnish railway network was once part of the Russian network, VR trains still run on tracks with a gauge of 1524 mm. The overhead lines are electrified at 25 kV 50 Hz ac. All suburban services are now exclusively operated with FLIRT trains from Stadler Rail, which have been delivered since 2008 and are classified in Helsinki as 'Sm5'. The 4-car units are 3.2 m wide and 75.2 m long, and have gangways between the carriages. The platform height is 550 mm above the top of the rail.

Stadler FLIRT Sm5 @ Tikkurila Dickursby

TALLINN: CAF Urbos #510 @ Pärnu maantee (Vineeri)   (Foto Robert Schrempf)

DAS BALTIKUM – Einleitung

Die drei baltischen Republiken Estland, Lettland und
Litauen sind keineswegs als einheitliches Gebilde zu
sehen, wie es oft den Anschein haben mag. Was sie eint,
ist vielmehr ein gemeinsames Schicksal im Laufe ihrer
Geschichte, die vor allem durch die Zugehörigkeit zum
russischen Zarenreich bis 1918, eine kurze Eigenständig-
keit zwischen den beiden Weltkriegen und schließlich die
Eingliederung in die Sowjetunion geprägt wurde. Mit dem
Zerfall der Sowjetunion erlangten alle drei Staaten 1991
wieder ihre vollständige Unabhängigkeit und traten 2004
der EU bei.

Trotz oder aufgrund dieser Abhängigkeit von Russland
ist bis heute eine starke Orientierung nach Osten zu
beobachten, so führen z.B. auch 30 Jahre nach der
Loslösung sämtliche internationale Zugverbindungen nur
nach Russland bzw. Weißrussland (als russisches Erbe
haben fast alle Bahnstrecken des Baltikums auch russische
Spurweite von 1520 mm). Die Verbundenheit mit Russland
mag auch an dem vor allem in den größeren Städten
hohen Anteil russischsprachiger Bevölkerung liegen (auch
wenn Russisch in keinem Land des Baltikums als offizielle
Sprache anerkannt wird). Seit Langem ist der Bau der sog.
„Rail Baltica" geplant, einer normalspurigen Nord-Süd-
Bahnverbindung (Tallinn – Riga – Kaunas – Warschau),
die die baltischen Staaten miteinander und an Mitteleuropa
anschließen soll, jedoch kommt das Projekt nur langsam
in Fahrt. In Estland ist außerdem eine starke Orientierung
Richtung Finnland spürbar, schließlich sind die Sprachen
der beiden Länder miteinander verwandt (und mit sonst

THE BALTIC STATES – Introduction

*The three Baltic Republics of Estonia, Latvia and
Lithuania should not be considered a homogeneous
region, although they sometimes appear to be. What they
have in common is their shared history, which was mainly
determined by their affiliation with the Russian Empire
until 1918, a brief independence between the two world
wars, and finally, their incorporation into the Soviet
Union. With the collapse of the Soviet Union, all three
countries regained full independence in 1991 and joined
the E.U. in 2004.*

*Despite, but perhaps also because of their previous
dependence on Russia, the Baltic states are still very
much orientated towards the east. For example, still
today, 30 years after independence, international train
connections only exist between Baltic and Russian/
Belorusian cities (as a heritage from Russia, almost all the
railways in the Baltic states have the Russian 1520 mm
gauge). The bonds with Russia also persist due to a
significant Russian speaking population, especially in the
larger cities (although Russian is no longer recognised
as an official language in any of the Baltic countries).
For a long time, the construction of the so-called "Rail
Baltica" has been planned, a standard-gauge north-south
rail link (Tallinn – Riga – Kaunas – Warsaw) to connect
the Baltic states with each other and Central Europe,
but the project is progressing very slowly. In Estonia, a
strong inclination towards Finland is noticeable, which is
not surprising as the languages of the two countries are
related (and different from every other one in the world).*

kaum einer anderen der Welt). Auch Lettisch und Litauisch bilden ein sonst isoliertes linguistisches Geschwisterpaar, weshalb neben dem heute doch weit verbreiteten Englisch auch Russisch weiterhin als *Lingua franca* dient.

Eine Anreise aus Deutschland ins Baltikum ist per Bahn zwar möglich, aber eher umständlich, auch wenn die Entfernung ab Berlin z.B. nach Vilnius nur 820 km Luftlinie und auf der Straße laut Google-Routenplaner knapp 1000 km beträgt, nach Riga sind es über Kaunas bei Vermeidung des Königsberger Gebiets 1220 km (Luftlinie 850 km) und nach Tallinn 1530 km (Luftlinie 1000 km).

Grenzüberschreitender Bahnverkehr mit Personenzügen zwischen den drei Baltenrepubliken existiert derzeit praktisch nicht (abgesehen von einer Verbindung zwischen Riga und Tallinn mit Umsteigen an der Grenze). Das wird sich frühestens 2026/27 mit Vollendung des Rail-Baltica-Projekts ändern.

Auch der Straßenbahnverkehr weist noch viele russische Merkmale auf. Die Gleisanlagen sind mancherorts noch in einem schlechten Zustand, auch wenn überall eine Erneuerung im Gange ist. Andererseits stellte man in den meisten Städten sehr früh auf ein modernes elektronisches Ticketsystem um, wobei man glücklicherweise nach westeuropäischem Vorbild auf eine verbesserte Integration achtete. So sind fast überall Tageskarten für alle Verkehrsmittel (außer Staatsbahnen und mancherorts auch Minibusse) erhältlich. Die Fahrpreise liegen dabei noch weit unter westeuropäischem Niveau. Der Ausbau-Boom, den man derzeit in Skandinavien beobachten kann, ist bislang nicht ins Baltikum übergeschwappt, vor allem in Riga, der größten Stadt der Region, herrscht seit Langem Stillstand, selbst die Erneuerung des Fahrzeugparks geht dort im Bereich Straßenbahn kaum voran, während Daugavpils die Beziehungen zu Russland nutzte, um neue Fahrzeuge anzuschaffen. In Tallinn brachten die spanischen CAF-Straßenbahnen eine Teilerneuerung und erst kürzlich erreichte ein neuer Wagen Liepaja, dieses Mal aus Kroatien. Für Liebhaber der klassischen Tatra-Wagen bleibt das Baltikum deshalb noch längere Zeit ein attraktives Reiseziel.

LIEPĀJA: Končar #250 – Testfahrt in Zagreb | *test run in Zagreb*

(Foto Toma Bacic)

DAUGAVPILS: 71-631 #009 @ Cietokšņa iela – Gelenkwagen aus Russland | *articulated tram from Russia*

(Foto Wolfgang Wellige)

Also, Latvian and Lithuanian constitute an otherwise isolated linguistic family, which is why besides the now widespread English, Russian continues to be an important 'lingua franca' in the region.

A journey by train from the U.K. to the Baltic states is possible, but requires many hours of travel with numerous changes of trains (London > Brussels > Cologne > Berlin > Warsaw > ...). The distance from Berlin to Vilnius, for example, is only 820 km as the crow flies, and according to Google, some 1000 km on the road; to Riga via Kaunas, by avoiding the Kaliningrad region, it is 1220 km (850 km direct) and to Tallinn 1530 km (1000 km direct).

Currently, cross-border passenger rail traffic between the three Baltic states hardly exists (except for a connection between Riga and Tallinn, which requires a transfer at the border). This situation will change around 2026/27 at the earliest, when the Rail Baltica project is expected to be completed.

The present tram systems also still feature many Russian characteristics. In some places, the tracks continue in a poor state, even though a renewal process is taking place in every city. At the same time, most cities started to implement a modern electronic ticketing system rather early, and fortunately with improved fare integration following Western European standards. Thus, day passes for all means of transport (except state railways, and in some places also minibuses) are available in almost every city, while fares are still far below Western European price levels. The urban rail expansion boom visible in the Scandinavian countries has not yet reached the Baltic states, though. Most notably Riga, the largest city in the region, has seen a standstill for many years, with hardly any progress even with the tram fleet renewal. Daugavpils, however, took advantage of its good relationship with Russia to acquire new vehicles. In Tallinn, the Spanish CAF trams brought a partial fleet modernisation, while only recently, the first new car arrived in Liepaja, this time from Croatia. For admirers of the classic Tatra trams, the Baltic states will thus continue to be an attractive destination for some time to come.

Urbos #520 @ Hobujaama > Viru   (Foto Robert Schrempf)

TALLINN

Die estnische Hauptstadt Tallinn (auf deutsch einst auch bekannt als *Reval*) liegt am Südufer des Finnischen Meerbusens, dem östlichen Teil der Ostsee, nur 82 km südlich von Helsinki. Eine Fahrt mit der Fähre dauert nicht einmal zwei Stunden. Mit internationalen Zügen erreicht man Tallinn nur von St. Petersburg aus, von Riga kommend muss man hingegen im Grenzort Valga umsteigen. Neben dem Nahverkehr rund um die Hauptstadt (siehe S. 123) hat auch der Personenfernverkehr per Bahn in Estland in den letzten Jahren zugenommen: Die größeren Städte erreicht man mehrmals täglich, z.B. Narva (5x), Tartu (8x), Rakvere (6x) oder Valga (4x); nach Pärnu wird man hingegen per Bahn erst wieder mit Rail Baltica kommen.

Seit 2013 ist der Nahverkehr in Tallinn gratis, jedoch nur für Einheimische. Für alle anderen ist eine in Kiosken erhältliche elektronische Smartcard (*Ühiskaart* - 2 €) nötig, um darauf eine Tageskarte (Bus, Obus, Tram) für 4,50 € zu laden, für 3 Tage sind 7,50 € und für 5 Tage 9 € fällig.

Tramm – Straßenbahn

Die *Tramm* von Tallinn wurde 1888 mit Pferdewagen und einer auch in Osteuropa seltenen Spurweite von 1067 mm (Kapspur) eröffnet. 1915 kam eine breitspurige Dampf-straßenbahn vom Stadtzentrum zu den Schiffswerften in Kopli hinzu, die zwar 1931 auf Kapspur umgespurt, jedoch bis Anfang der 1950er Jahre mit Benzolwagen betrieben wurde. Das übrige städtische Netz wurde ab 1925 elektrifiziert. In den letzten Jahrzehnten gab es kaum nennenswerte Erweiterungen. Nach einer Modernisierung der Äste nach Ülemiste, Tondi und Kopli wurde in zwei

The Estonian capital Tallinn is located just 82 km south of Helsinki on the southern shore of the Gulf of Finland, the eastern part of the Baltic Sea. The ferry between the two ports takes less than two hours. On international trains, Tallinn can only be reached from St. Petersburg, but coming from Riga, a transfer is required at the border town of Valga. Besides the regional traffic around the capital (see page 123), long-distance passenger rail transport in Estonia has regained some ground in recent years, and the country's larger cities can be reached several times a day, for example Narva (5x), Tartu (8x), Rakvere (6x) and Valga (4x). Pärnu, however, will only be linked by trains again when Rail Baltica opens.

Since 2013, public transport in Tallinn has been free, but only for local residents. For everybody else, an electronic smartcard (Ühiskaart - €2) is available, with a day ticket (bus, trolleybus, tram) costing just €4.50, while a 3-day ticket is sold for €7.50 and a 5-day ticket for €9.00.

Tramm – Tramway

Tallinn's 'Tramm' was opened in 1888 with horse-drawn carriages on 1067 mm tracks (Cape gauge), a gauge rarely found in Eastern Europe. In 1915, a broad-gauge steam tramway from the city centre to the shipyards in Kopli was added. This line was regauged to 1067 mm in 1931, but was then operated with benzene cars until the early 1950s. The electrification of the rest of the urban network began in 1925. In recent decades, there have hardly been any significant extensions. After the

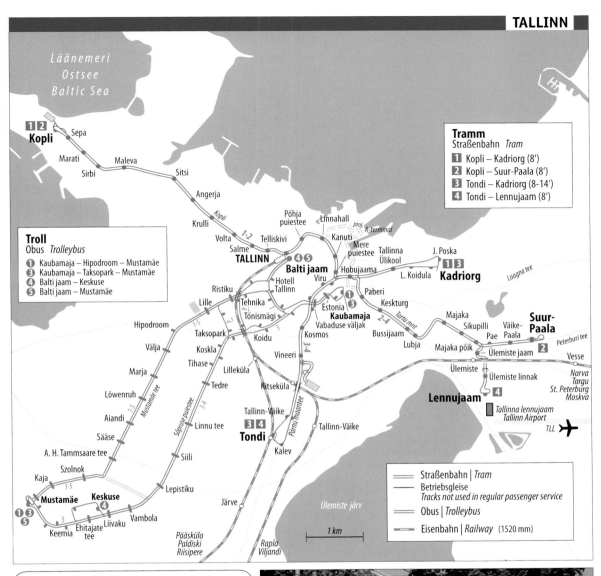

Läänemeri
Ostsee
Baltic Sea

1 2
Kopli

Tramm
Straßenbahn *Tram*
1 Kopli – Kadriorg (8')
2 Kopli – Suur-Paala (8')
3 Tondi – Kadriorg (8-14')
4 Tondi – Lennujaam (8')

Troll
Obus *Trolleybus*
1 Kaubamaja – Hipodroom – Mustamäe
3 Kaubamaja – Taksopark – Mustamäe
4 Balti jaam – Keskuse
5 Balti jaam – Mustamäe

TALLINN

Balti jaam **4 5**

Kadriorg **1 3**

Suur-Paala **2**

Kaubamaja

Lennujaam **4**

Tallinna lennujaam
Tallinn Airport
TLL ✈

Tondi **3 4**

Mustamäe **1 3 5**
Keskuse **4**

──── Straßenbahn | *Tram*
──── Betriebsgleise
    Tracks not used in regular passenger service
──── Obus | *Trolleybus*
──── Eisenbahn | *Railway* (1520 mm)

1 km

TALLINN (Eesti | Estland | Estonia)

440 000 (159 km²)

~ 500 000

Tram – 1925; Trolleybus – 1965

1067 mm

Tram – 17.2 km; Trolleybus ~ 16 km

Tram – 4; Trolleybus – 4

TLT (Tallinna Linnatranspordi AS)
www.tlt.ee

Fahrpläne | *Timetables*
transport.tallinn.ee

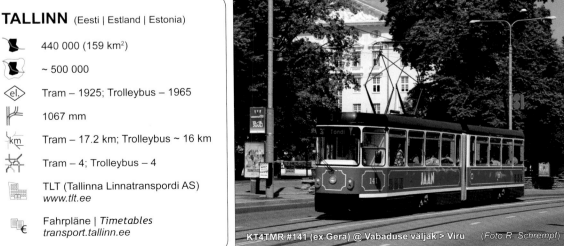

KT4TMR #141 (ex Gera) @ Vabaduse väljak > Viru   *(Foto R. Schrempf)*

119

KT6NF #96 @ Linnahall > Põhja puiesteé   *(Foto Robert Schrempf)*

Stufen ein rund 1 km langer Ast eröffnet: am 19. Oktober 2015 bis zu einer provisorischen Schleife am Bahnhof Ülemiste, dem zukünftigen Endpunkt von Rail Baltica, und schließlich am 1. September 2017 mit einem Tunnel unter den Bahnanlagen bis zum stadtnahen Flughafen. Von einst geplanten Neubaustrecken in die Vororte Lasnamäe im Osten (Schnellstraßenbahntrasse im Mittelstreifen der Laagna tee weitgehend vorbereitet) und Mustamäe im Süden ist heute wenig zu hören. Stattdessen wurde Anfang 2020 eine innerstädtische Verbindung zur Erschließung der Hafengebiete angekündigt.

Der Fahrzeugpark der Straßenbahn besteht derzeit aus Tatra KT4-Wagen von ČKD, von denen die meisten aus Cottbus, Frankfurt (Oder), Gera und zuletzt vor allem aus Erfurt übernommen wurden. Dazu kommen einige ursprünglich als KT4SU gelieferte Tatra-Wagen, die später mit einem zusätzlichen Niederflurmittelteil zu KT6NF wurden. Ab 2014 ergänzten moderne Fahrzeuge vom Typ Urbos AXL von CAF die Flotte.

modernisation of the branches to Ülemiste, Tondi and Kopli, an approximately 1 km branch opened in two stages: on 19 October 2015 to a temporary loop at Ülemiste railway station, the future terminus of Rail Baltica, and on 1 September 2017 via a new tunnel under the railway tracks to the airport. The once planned new routes to the suburbs of Lasnamäe in the east (the right-of-way for a rapid tram line was prepared in the median of Laagna tee a long time ago) and Mustamäe in the south have not been pursued. Instead, an inner-city route to serve the port area was announced in early 2020.

The current tram fleet consists of Tatra KT4 vehicles manufactured by ČKD, many of which were acquired from the eastern German cities of Cottbus, Frankfurt (Oder), Gera, and, mainly and most recently, Erfurt. Some of the Tatra trams originally classified as KT4SU were rebuilt with a low-floor middle section and became type KT6NF. From 2014, CAF of Spain delivered modern low-floor trams of class Urbos AXL to increase the fleet.

Tramm > Fahrzeuge | *Rolling Stock* (600 V DC)							
Nummer *Number*	Anzahl *Quantity*	Hersteller *Manufacturer*	Typ *Class*	Länge *Length*	Breite *Width*	Ausgeliefert *Delivered*	
147...182	27	ČKD	Tatra KT4D =>	19.0 m	2.20 m	1981-1990	
104	1	ČKD	Tatra KT4SU =>	19.0 m	2.20 m	1986	
136...168*	6	ČKD	Tatra KT4 TMR* =>	19.0 m	2.20 m	1981-1990	
96...148**	12	ČKD	Tatra KT6NF** =>	26.5 m	2.20 m	1985-1990	
501-520	20	CAF	Urbos AXL =>	30.8 m	2.30 m	2014-2016	

*2017/18 im Retro-Stil modernisiert | *modernised in vintage style in 2017/18*: 136, 138, 140, 141, 142, 168
** 2001-2005 ergänzt mit Niederflur-Mittelteil | *low-floor centre section added in 2001-2005*: 96-99, 102-103, 109-110, 114, 123, 131, 148

Solaris Trollino 18 #436 @ Estonia (National Opera) *(Foto Robert Schrempf)*

Obus

Neben der Straßenbahn betreibt der seit 2012 vereinte städtische Verkehrsbetrieb *Tallinna Linnatranspordi AS* auch ein Obusnetz (*Troll*), das jedoch in den letzten Jahren mit Entfernung des Fahrdrahts auf den Strecken nach Õismäe und Kopli erheblich geschrumpft ist. Es verblieben nur noch die beiden Strecken vom Stadtzentrum nach Mustamäe im Südwesten. 1965 waren in Tallinn erstmals Obusse von der Staatsoper Estonia zum Hipodroom gefahren. Zum Einsatz kommen heute moderne Trollino-Busse von Solaris.

Trolleybus

In addition to the tramway, urban transport operator 'Tallinna Linnatranspordi AS' (unified in 2012) also operates a shrinking trolleybus network (Troll), with the overhead wires having been removed from the routes to Õismäe and Kopli in recent years, leaving just two routes which run from the city centre to the southwestern suburb of Mustamäe. In 1965, the first trolleybus in Tallinn started running from the National Opera Estonia to Hipodroom. The system is operated with modern Trollino buses from Solaris.

KT4D #152 (ex Erfurt) @ Salme > Volta *(Foto R. Schrempf)*

KT4SU #117 @ Keskturg > Paberi (2013)

KT4D #174 (ex Erfurt) @ Balti jaam   (Foto Robert Schrempf)

KT4 TMR #142 @ Hobujaama > Viru   (Foto Robert Schrempf)

Urbos #512 @ Tondi > Tallinn-Väike (Foto Robert Schrempf)

Eisenbahnnahverkehr

Auf einem 133 km langen elektrifizierten Netz betreibt die staatliche Gesellschaft *Elron* östlich und westlich von Tallinn Vorortzüge ohne Taktfahrplan. Das beste Angebot findet man auf der Südweststrecke bis Pääsküla, wo zwei- bis dreimal stündlich ein Zug verkehrt. Im Vorortverkehr werden seit 2012 elektrische FLIRT-Triebzüge von Stadler Rail eingesetzt. Das Netz hat die russische Spurweite von 1520 mm.

Regional Rail Service

On a 133 km electrified network, the state-owned company 'Elron' operates suburban trains east and west of Tallinn without a regular schedule. The best timetable is on the southwestern route to Pääsküla, where there are 2-3 trains an hour. Since 2012, suburban services have been provided by FLIRT EMUs from Stadler Rail. The rail network has the Russian track gauge of 1520 mm.

(*www.elron.ee*)

Stadler Flirt #2404 & #1324 @ Tallinn Balti jaam (Foto Robert Schrempf)

Škoda ForCity 15T 57036 @ Krišjāņa Barona iela (Bērnu pasaule)

RĪGA

Die Hauptstadt Lettlands liegt etwa in der geographischen Mitte des Landes, kurz vor der Mündung des Flusses Düna (Daugava) in die Rigaer Bucht.

Der Personenfernverkehr per Bahn ist in Lettland im EU-Vergleich eher unterentwickelt (nach Liepaja 2 Mal pro Woche; nach Daugavpils immerhin 3-4 Mal pro Tag) und internationale Nachtzüge fahren mehr oder weniger häufig von Riga nur nach Minsk und Kiew sowie nach Moskau und St. Petersburg. Etwas besser sieht es beim Vorortverkehr rund um Riga aus (siehe Seite 132).

Für den städtischen Nahverkehr von *Rīgas satiksme* (RS) besorgen sich Besucher am besten an Automaten, in Kiosken oder im RS-Kundenzentrum ein gelbes E-Ticket (e-talons) und laden es mit einer 24-Stunden-Karte für Tram, Trolleybus und Bus für 5,00 € auf; eine 3-Tage-Karte kostet 10 € und eine 5-Tage-Karte 15 €.

Tramvajs – Straßenbahn

In Riga fuhr 1882 erstmals eine Pferdebahn. Das in den folgenden Jahren entstandene Netz wurde ab 1901 elektrifiziert, wobei die ersten elektrischen Straßenbahnen auf der heutigen Brīvības iela verkehrten. Die Eröffnung der letzten Neubaustrecke liegt lange zurück, es war 1984 der 4,3 km lange Abzweig nach Imanta. In den letzten Jahren wurde das Bestandsnetz modernisiert und nach und nach für den Einsatz von Niederflurwagen fit gemacht. Derzeit ist im Norden der Stadt eine 3,6 km lange Spange zur Erschließung eines Stadtentwicklungsgebiets entlang der Skanstes iela geplant, doch ist die Finanzierung bislang ungesichert.

The capital of Latvia is located roughly in the geographical centre of the country, close to where the Daugava River flows into the Gulf of Riga.

Compared to other E.U. countries, long-distance passenger rail transport is rather underdeveloped in Latvia (twice a week to Liepaja, but 3-4 times a day to Daugavpils). Infrequent international night trains only run from Riga to Minsk and Kyiv as well as to Moscow and St. Petersburg. The situation is somewhat better for regional rail traffic around Riga (see page 132).

For urban transport provided by 'Rīgas satiksme' (RS), visitors can get a yellow electronic smartcard (e-talons) and load it with a 24-hour pass for €5, a 3-day pass for €10 or a 5-day pass for €15; these tickets are valid on trams, trolleybuses and buses and are available from vending machines, kiosks and the RS customer centre.

Tramvajs – Tramway

Horse-drawn tramways began operating in Riga in 1882. The network, which grew in the following years, was electrified in 1901, with the first electric trams running on what is now Brīvības iela. Riga's last new tram route opened many years ago – the 4.3 km branch to Imanta in 1984. In recent years, the city has been modernising the existing network to allow the use of new low-floor vehicles. At present, a 3.6 km cross-link is planned in the north of the city to serve a redevelopment area emerging along Skanstes iela, but the required funding is still lacking.

ČKD Tatra T3MR #35294 @ Maskavas iela (Daugavpils iela) *(Foto Christopher Hecht)*

Die Taktfrequenz der einzelnen Linien richtet sich stark nach der Tageszeit und ist von Linie zu Linie sehr unterschiedlich. Von einem Taktfahrplan kann nicht die Rede sein.

In den 1980er Jahren, als man erwartete, dass Riga langsam Millionenstadt wird, gab es weit fortgeschrittene Planungen für den Bau eines Metro-Netzes mit drei Linien. Die erste Linie sollte von Imanta im Westen über den Bahnhof Zasulauks und dann tief unter dem Daugava-Fluss das Stadtzentrum erreichen und weiter über den Hauptbahnhof nach Nordosten verlaufen. Der östliche Endpunkt war in Jugla vorgesehen. Der Baubeginn für den ersten Abschnitt stand 1990 kurz bevor, als die Sowjetunion auseinanderfiel und in den folgenden Jahren die Einwohnerzahl der Stadt erheblich zurückging.

Auch 30 Jahre nach der Unabhängigkeit Lettlands und 16 Jahre nach dem Beitritt zur EU verkehren auf dem Straßenbahnnetz von Riga noch mehrheitlich ältere Tatra-Fahrzeuge mit Stangenstromabnehmern und allesamt ohne Niederflureinstieg. Es stehen bislang lediglich 20 Niederflurbahnen vom Typ ForCity Alfa von Škoda im Einsatz, eine zweite 2016 vereinbarte Bestellung über weitere 15 kurze und 5 lange Fahrzeuge wurde bislang nur teilweise ausgeliefert, doch auch drei Jahre später waren diese neuen Wagen noch nicht im Fahrgasteinsatz.

The frequency of individual lines is highly dependent on the time of day, and differs from line to line; clear and regular headways cannot be identified.

In the 1980s, when Riga's population was expected to reach the one-million mark, there were advanced plans to build a metro system with three lines. The first line was to run from Imanta in the west via Zasulauks railway station before reaching the city centre in a tunnel deep under the Daugava River; via the main railway station, trains would have headed northeast to eventually terminate at Jugla. The construction of the first section was about to start in 1990 when the Soviet Union disintegrated, leading to a decrease in population over the following years.

30 years after Latvia's independence and 16 years after joining the E.U., Riga's tram fleet is still dominated by older Tatra trams which use a trolley pole for power collection and do not allow easy low-level entry. A mere 20 low-floor trams, all of which are ForCity Alfa trams from Škoda, have so far been put into service. In 2016, a second batch was ordered including 15 short and 5 long trams of the same type, but only a few were delivered and 3 years later, they have not yet entered regular passenger service.

RĪGA (Latvija | Lettland | Latvia)

 700 000 (307 km²)

 850 000

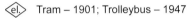 Tram – 1901; Trolleybus – 1947

 1524 mm

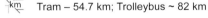 Tram – 54.7 km; Trolleybus ~ 82 km

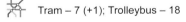 Tram – 7 (+1); Trolleybus – 18

 RS (Rīgas satiksme)
www.rigassatiksme.lv

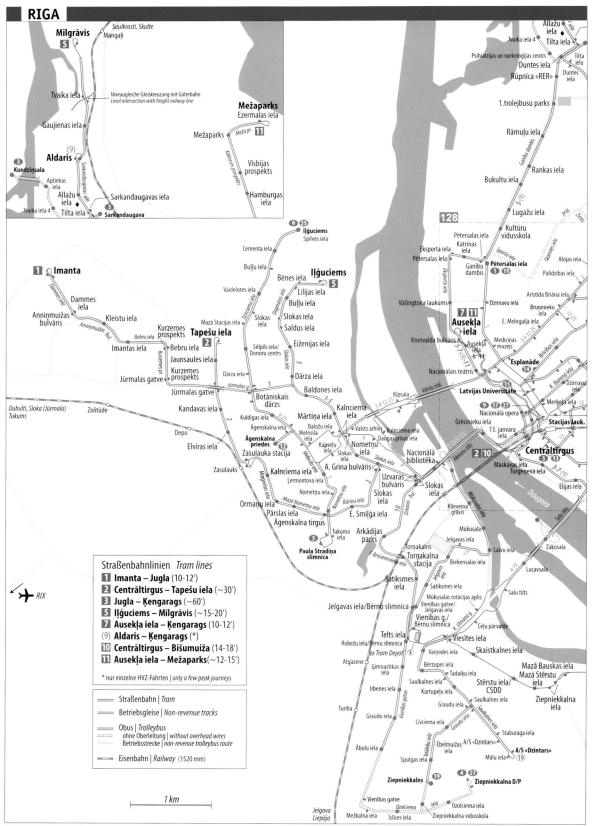

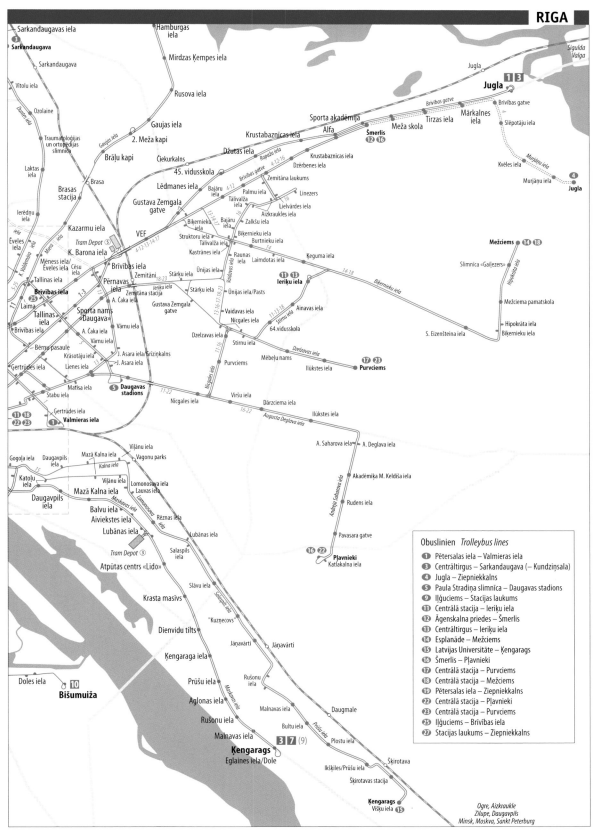

Sarkandaugavas iela
Sarkandaugava
Sarkandaugava
Hamburgas iela
Mirdzas Ķempes iela
Vītolu iela
Ozolaine
Rusova iela
Jugla
Jugla
Brīvības gatve
Brīvības gatve
Slēpotāju iela
Traumatoloģijas un ortopēdijas slimnīca
Gaujas iela
Sporta akadēmija
Meža skola
Tirzas iela
Mārkalnes iela
2. Meža kapi
Krustabaznīcas iela
Alfa
Šmerlis
Brāļu kapi
Čiekurkalns
Džutas iela
Ropažu iela
Krustabaznīcas iela
Murjāņu iela
Laktas iela
Brasa
45. vidusskola
Brīvības gatve
Dzērbenes iela
Kvēles iela
Murjāņu iela
Jugla
Brasas stacija
Lēdmanes iela
Bajāru iela
Palmu iela
Zemitāna laukums
Linezers
Ierēdņu iela
Gustava Zemgala gatve
Bajāru iela
Tālivalža iela
Lielvārdes iela
Ēveles iela
Kazarmu iela
Bikernieku iela
Struktoru iela
Aizkraukles iela
Mežciems
VEF
Tālivalža iela
Bikernieku iela
Tram Depot
K. Barona iela
Kastrānes iela
Burtnieku iela
Slimnica «Gaiļezers»
Mēness iela/Ēveles iela
Cēsu iela
Brīvības iela
Raunas iela
Laimdotas iela
Ķeguma iela
Tallinas iela
Zemitāni
Stārku iela
Ūnijas iela
Mežciema pamatskola
Brīvības iela
Pērnavas iela
Zemitāna stacija
Ieriķu iela
Stārku iela
Ūnijas iela/Pasts
Hipokrāta iela
Laima
A. Čaka iela
Stārķu iela
Ainavas iela
Bikernieku iela
S. Eizenšteina iela
Tallinas iela
Sporta nams «Daugava»
Gustava Zemgala gatve
Vaidavas iela
Nīcgales iela
Stīrņu iela
64. vidusskola
Brīvības iela
Vārnu iela
Bērnu pasaule
A. Čaka iela
Vārnu iela
Dzelzavas iela
Stirnu iela
Mēbeļu nams
Purvciems
Krāsotāju iela
J. Asara iela/Grīziņkalns
Purvciems
Dzelzavas iela
Ilūkstes iela
Ģertrūdes iela
Lienes iela
J. Asara iela
Matīsa iela
Daugavas stadions
Virsu iela
Stabu iela
Nīcgales iela
Dārzciema iela
Ģertrūdes iela
Augusta Deglava iela
Ilūkstes iela
Valmieras iela
A. Saharova iela
A. Deglava iela
Vīlānu iela
Akadēmiķa M. Keldiša iela
Gogoļa iela
Daugavpils iela
Mazā Kalna iela
Vagonu parks
Kalna iela
Katoļu iela
Vīlānu iela
Rudens iela
Lomonosova iela
Lauvas iela
Daugavpils iela
Mazā Kalna iela
Pavasara gatve
Balvu iela
Aiviekstes iela
Rēznas iela
Lubānas iela
Lubānas iela
Tram Depot
Pļavnieki
Katlakalna iela
Salaspils iela
Atpūtas centrs «Lido»
Slāvu iela
Krasta masīvs
"Kuzņecovs"
Dienvidu tilts
Jāņavārti
Jāņavārti
Doles iela
Ķengaraga iela
Rušonu iela
Bišumuiža
Prūšu iela
Aglonas iela
Malnavas iela
Daugmale
Rušonu iela
Bultu iela
Malnavas iela
Plostu iela
Ķengarags
Eglaines iela/Dole
Ikšķiles/Prūšu iela
Šķirotava
Šķirotavas stacija
Ķengarags
Višķu iela

Obuslinien Trolleybus lines
1 Pētersalas iela – Valmieras iela
3 Centrāltirgus – Sarkandaugava (– Kundziņsala)
4 Jugla – Ziepniekkalns
5 Paula Stradiņa slimnīca – Daugavas stadions
9 Iļģuciems – Stacijas laukums
11 Centrālā stacija – Ieriķu iela
12 Ágenskalna priedes – Šmerlis
13 Centrāltirgus – Ieriķu iela
14 Esplanāde – Mežciems
15 Latvijas Universitāte – Ķengarags
16 Šmerlis – Pļavnieki
17 Centrālā stacija – Purvciems
18 Centrālā stacija – Mežciems
19 Pētersalas iela – Ziepniekkalns
22 Centrālā stacija – Pļavnieki
23 Centrālā stacija – Purvciems
25 Iļģuciems – Brīvības iela
27 Stacijas laukums – Ziepniekkalns

Ogre, Aizkraukle
Zilupe, Daugavpils
Minsk, Moskva, Sankt Peterburg

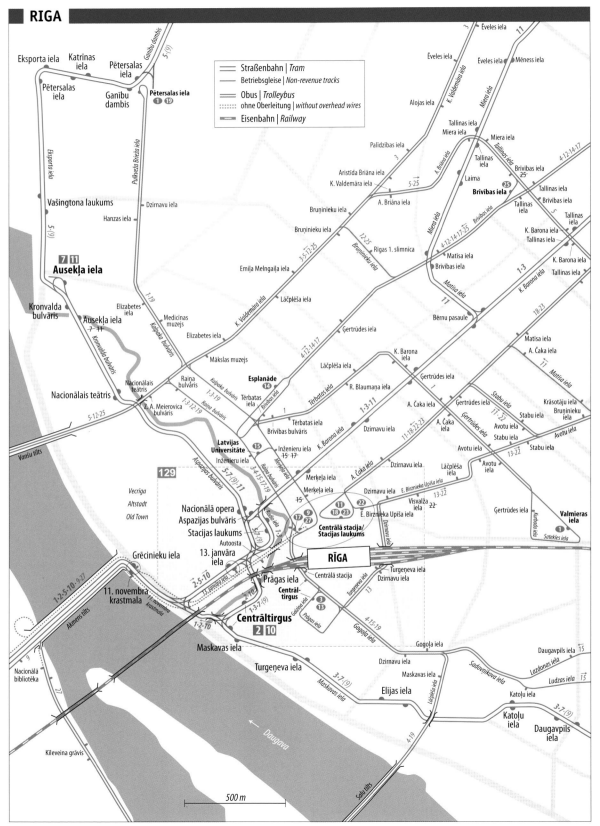

RIGA

———	Straßenbahn | *Tram*
——	Betriebsgleise | *Non-revenue tracks*
===	Obus | *Trolleybus*
·····	ohne Oberleitung | *without overhead wires*
▰▰	Eisenbahn | *Railway*

Eksporta iela
Katrīnas iela
Pētersalas iela
Pētersalas iela
Ganību dambis
Pētersalas iela ❶ ⑲
Ganību dambis
5·(9)

Eksporta iela
Vašingtona laukums
Hanzas iela
Dzirnavu iela
5·(9)
Pulkveža Brieža iela

Ēveles iela 3
Ēveles iela
Ēveles iela
Mēness iela
Alojas iela
Tallinas iela
Miera iela
Miera iela
11
K. Valdemāra iela
Mēness iela
Miera iela

Palīdzības iela
Aristīda Briāna iela
K. Valdemāra iela
A. Briāna iela
3
A. Briāna iela
5·25
Tallinas iela
Tallinas iela
Laima
Brīvības iela ㉕
Brīvības iela
25ʳ
Brīvības iela
4·12·14·17
Tallinas iela
Tallinas iela
Tallinas iela
5

❼ ⑪
Auseķļa iela

Kronvalda bulvāris
Auseķļa iela
❼ ⑪

Bruņinieku iela
Bruņinieku iela
12·25
Rīgas 1. slimnica
3·5·12·25
Bruņinieku iela
4·12·14·17·25
Matīsa iela
Brīvības iela
K. Barona iela
Tallinas iela
1·3
K. Barona iela
Tallinas iela

Elizabetes iela
Medicīnas muzejs
Emīļa Melngaiļa iela
Lāčplēša iela
Ģertrūdes iela
Bērnu pasaule
11
18·23
K. Barona iela
Matīsa iela

Kronvalda bulvāris
Elizabetes iela
K. Valdemāra iela
4·12·14·17
Lāčplēša iela
K. Barona iela
Ģertrūdes iela
Matīsa iela
A. Čaka iela

Nacionālais teātris
Raiņa bulvāris
Mākslas muzejs
Raiņa bulvāris
Tērbatas iela
Esplanāde ⑭
R. Blaumaņa iela
Ģertrūdes iela
Stabu iela
Krāsotāju iela
Bruņinieku iela
1·19
Kalpaka bulvāris
1·3·19
Tērbatas iela
1·3·11
A. Čaka iela
Stabu iela

Nacionālais teātris
Z. A. Meierovica bulvāris
13·12·19
Tērbatas iela
Brīvības bulvāris
Dzirnavu iela
11·18·22·23
A. Čaka iela
Stabu iela
Avotu iela

5·12·25
Vanšu tilts

Latvijas Universitāte ⑮
Inženieru iela
Merķeļa iela
A. Čaka iela
Avotu iela
13·22
Stabu iela
Avotu iela

Vecrīga
Altstadt
Old Town
129

Nacionālā opera
Aspazijas bulvāris
Stacijas laukums
Inženieru iela
15·17
Merķeļa iela
Merķeļa iela
15
Dzirnavu iela
E. Birznieka Upīša iela
13·22
Visvalža iela
22
Ģertrūdes iela
Valmieras iela ❶

❾ ⑪ ㉒
⑰ ⑱ ㉓
㉗
Centrālā stacija/ Stacijas laukums

Grēcinieku iela
13. janvāra iela
Autoosta
1·2·5·10·9·27
Akmens tilts
2·5·10

RĪGA
Centrālā stacija
Turgeņeva iela
Dzirnavu iela
13

11. novembra krastmala
Prāgas iela
Centrāltirgus
❸ ⑬
4·15·19
2·10
1·3·7·(9)

Centrāltirgus ❷ ⑩

Maskavas iela
Turgeņeva iela
Elijas iela
3·7·(9)
Maskavas iela
Gogoļa iela
Dzirnavu iela

Nacionālā bibliotēka
9
27

Daugavpils iela 15
Lazdonas iela
Ludzas iela 15
Katoļu iela
3·7·(9)
Katoļu iela
Daugavpils iela

Ķīleveina grāvis

Daugava

500 m

ČKD Tatra T3A #30002 @ Akmens tilts (Grēcinieku iela > Nacionālā bibliotēka)   (*Foto Christopher Hecht*)

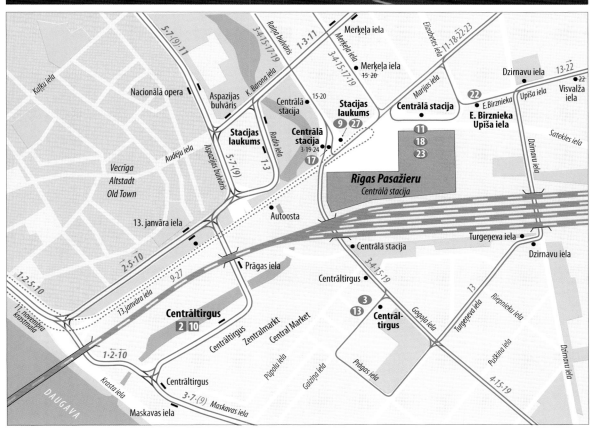

Škoda ForCity 15T 57186 @ Alfa

T3A #51211 @ K. Barona iela / Raiņa bulvāris (2013)

T3A #30798 @ Alexandra Grīna bul. *(Foto Christopher Hecht)*

Tramvajs > Fahrzeuge | *Rolling Stock* (600 V DC)

Nummer *Number*	Anzahl *Quantity*	Hersteller *Manufacturer*	Typ *Class*	Länge *Length*	Breite *Width*	Ausgeliefert *Delivered*
30002...31871	~65	ČKD	Tatra T3A (ex T3SU) =>	14.0 m	2.50 m	1976-1987
50574...51906	~38	ČKD	Tatra T3A (ex T3SU) =>	14.0 m	2.50 m	1976-1987
32036...32321	10	ČKD	Tatra T6B5SU =>	15.3 m	2.50 m	1988-1990
35010-35304	30	ČKD	Tatra T3MR =>	15.3 m	2.50 m	1988-1990
57016-57201	20	Škoda	15T ForCity Alfa =>	31.4 m	2.46 m	2010-2011
58011-58066	6	Škoda	15T1 ForCity Alfa =>	41.0 m	2.46 m	2012
57506-57560	6* (+9)	Škoda	15T2 ForCity Alfa =>	31.4 m	2.46 m	2017-2018
58501	1* (+4)	Škoda	15T2A ForCity Alfa =>	41.0 m	2.46 m	2018

* 2020 noch nicht im Einsatz | *not yet in service in 2020*

Škoda/Solaris 27Tr #27134 @ Ķīpsala   (Foto Christopher Hecht)

Obus

Seit 1947 verkehren in Riga neben den elektrischen Straßenbahnen auch Obusse. Das Netz ist heute einein-halb Mal so groß wie das der Tram, wobei manche Äste von mehreren Linien bedient werden, wenn auch nicht so exzessiv wie etwa in Vilnius. Die Bedienhäufigkeit der einzelnen Linien ist wie bei der Straßenbahn sehr auf die Nachfrage abgestimmt und ändert sich deshalb je nach Tageszeit erheblich, außerdem gibt es große Unter-schiede zwischen den einzelnen Linien. Am häufigsten verkehren die ObL 3, 15, 17, 19, 22, 23 und 25 (in der HVZ alle 3-5 Min.), eher länger wartet man auf die ObL 1, 5, 9, und 13 (teils nur alle 30 Min.), alle anderen Linien liegen irgendwo dazwischen.

Wie vielerorts heute üblich, erfolgten die letzten Streckenerweiterungen ohne Oberleitung und durch Ein-satz von Hybridfahrzeugen, zuletzt Anfang 2020 in Jugla im Nordosten der Stadt für die ObL 4.

Anders als bei der Straßenbahn wurde der Obusfuhr-park in den letzten Jahren konsequent erneuert, so dass in Riga seit 2016 nur noch Niederflurbusse unterwegs sind:
- 49 Solaris/Ganz Trollino 18 (2001-2007)
- 150 Škoda/Irisbus 24Tr (2006-2009; 90 mit Diesel-hilfsmotor)
- 125 Škoda/Solaris 27Tr (2014-2020) mit Dieselhilfs-motor
- 10 Solaris Trollino 18 mit Wasserstoffgeneratoren als Hilfsantrieb (2018)

Trolleybus

Since 1947, a trolleybus network has coexisted with the electric tram system in Riga. The network is now one and a half times larger than that of the tram, with some branches being served by multiple lines, although not as excessively as in Vilnius. Like on the tram system, the operating frequency of each line is adapted to passenger demand, and therefore varies considerably depending on the time of day. There are also significant differences between the lines. The trolleybus lines most often served are lines 3, 15, 17, 19, 22, 23 and 25 (every 3-5 minutes during peak times), while a longer wait is required for lines 1, 5, 9, and 13 (at times only every 30 minutes); the other lines lie somewhere in between.

As is common now in many cities, the trolleybus network has been expanded in recent years without the installation of overhead wires, hybrid buses being used instead; the last such extension occured in early 2020 for line 4 to Jugla in the northeast of the city.

Unlike Riga's tram, the city's trolleybus fleet has been renewed completely, leaving only low-floor vehicles since 2016:
- *49 Solaris/Ganz Trollino 18 (2001-2007)*
- *150 Škoda/Irisbus 24Tr (2006-2009; 90 with a diesel auxiliary engine)*
- *125 Škoda/Solaris 27Tr (2014-2020) with a diesel auxiliary engine*
- *10 Solaris Trollino 18 with an additional hydrogen engine (2018)*

Škoda ForCity 15T1 58033 @
Miera iela / Tallinnas iela

(Foto Christopher Hecht)

Eisenbahnnahverkehr

In und um Riga betreibt die staatliche Personenverkehrs-
gesellschaft *Pasažieru vilciens* [Personenzug] einen regen
elektrischen Vorortverkehr auf vier Strecken, wobei allerdings kein regelmäßiger Takt angeboten wird und auch
die Ausstattung der Stationen keinem modernen S-Bahn-
Standard entspricht. Alle Züge fahren vom Hauptbahnhof Rīga pasažieru ab, Richtung Westen bis Dubulti (in
Jūrmala) 34 Mal täglich, viele davon weiter bis Sloka bzw.
Tukums; nach Süden bis Jelgava 24x; nach Südosten auf
der Hauptstrecke nach Daugavpils 32x bis Ogre, viele
davon weiter bis Aizkraukle; nach Nordosten bis Sigulda
13x (nur zwei Züge erreichen den Grenzbahnhof Valga in
Estland); nach Norden 14x bis Saulkrasti und 10x weiter
bis Skulte. Zum Einsatz kommen dabei weiterhin von der
Elektritschka in Russland bekannte, jedoch seinerzeit
in Riga bei RVR (*Rīgas Vagonbūves Rūpnīca*) für die
gesamte Sowjetunion produzierte Triebwagenzüge vom
Typ ER2, ER2T sowie modernisierte ER2M. 2019 wurden
jedoch bei Škoda Vagonka 32 einstöckige Elektrotrieb-
züge zur Auslieferung 2022/23 bestellt.

Regional Rail Service

The national railway company 'Pasažieru vilciens' [pas-
senger train] operates a suburban electric train service
on four routes in and around Riga. There is, however,
no regular headway, and the standard of the stations
does not correspond to a modern S-Bahn or RER-style
service either. All trains depart from Rīga pasažieru
station, heading in the following directions: west to
Dubulti (Jūrmala) 34 times a day, many of which continue to Sloka and Tukums; south to Jelgava 24 times
a day; southeast on the Daugavpils route 32 times to
Ogre, with some trains continuing to Aizkraukle; northeast to Sigulda 13 times (only two trains reach the border station of Valga in Estonia); north to Saulkrasti 14
times and on to Skulte 10 times a day. The trains still
used on these lines — EMUs of class ER2, ER2T and the
modernised ER2M — are known from the 'elektrichkas'
in Russia, which in the old days were produced in Riga
at RVR (Rīgas Vagonbūves Rūpnīca) for the entire Soviet
Union. In 2019, however, 32 single-deck EMUs were
ordered from Škoda Vagonka for delivery in 2022/23.

RVR ER2T-711805R @ Majori (Jūrmala)

RVR ER2T-7117-03R @ Rīga pasažieru

Tatra KT4SU #233 @ Mirdzas Ķempes iela / Ganību iela (2013)

LIEPĀJA

Die lettische Stadt Liepāja (deutsch auch *Libau*) liegt im Kurland (lett. *Kurzeme*) im Westen des Landes direkt an der Ostsee, 220 km von Riga entfernt. Eine Zugverbindung zwischen den beiden Städten gibt es nur zweimal pro Woche.

Für Busse und Straßenbahn ist 2020 eine Tageskarte (*dienas biļete*) für 2,50 € erhältlich, eine Einzelfahrt kostet 0,70 € (beim Fahrer 1 €). Tickets bekommt man in den Kundenzentren, im Tourist Office oder in Kiosken.

Die elektrische **Straßenbahn** der kleinen Hafenstadt, die damals Teil des russischen Zarenreichs war, wurde 1899 eröffnet und besteht heute nur aus einer einzigen Linie, auch wenn bis 1972 ein zweiter nördlicher Ast zum Militärhafen am Karosta-Kanal existierte. Als dieser Ast stillgelegt wurde, kam stattdessen eine südliche Verlängerung von der Altstadt zum Zentralfriedhof hinzu. Danach blieb das Netz 41 Jahre lang unverändert, bis schließlich am 29. Mai 2013 die 1,6 km lange Neubaustrecke ins Wohngebiet Ezerkrasts II in Betrieb genommen werden konnte. Die Tram fährt meist auf eigenem Gleiskörper, auch wenn dieser oft nicht klar von der Fahrbahn abgetrennt ist. An einigen Haltestellen wird dennoch von der Straße aus eingestiegen.

Der heutige Fahrzeugpark besteht aus 16 Tatra KT4-Wagen, von denen die meisten von ostdeutschen Betrieben stammen. Der Stangenstromabnehmer wurde hier bereits 1961 von einem Pantographen abgelöst. Im November 2020 wurde die erste von 12 Niederflurbahnen vom kroatischen Hersteller KONČAR angeliefert.

The Latvian city of Liepāja is located in Courland ('Kurzeme' in Latvian) in the west of the country on the Baltic Coast, some 220 km from Riga. Passenger trains only operate between the two cities twice a week.

For buses and trams, a day pass (dienas biļete) is available for €2.50, while a single ticket costs €0.70 (or €1.00 when bought from the driver). Tickets are sold in customer centres, the tourist office and in kiosks.

This small port town's electric **tram system** was opened in 1899 when Liepāja was part of the Russian Empire, and although it consists today of just a single line, until 1972, there was a second northern branch that led to the Karosta Canal in the military port area. When this branch was shut down, a southern extension from the old town to the cemetery was added. After that, the route remained unchanged for 41 years until 29 May 2013, when a 1.6 km extension to the residential district of Ezerkrasts II was finally put into operation. The tram operates mostly on a dedicated right-of-way, although often it is not clearly separated from the roadway. At some stops, trams are boarded from street level.

The current fleet consists of 16 Tatra KT4 vehicles, most of which were acquired from eastern German cities. In Liepāja, the trolley pole was replaced by a pantograph in as early as 1961. In November 2020, the first of 12 low-floor trams arrived from Croatian manufacturer KONČAR.

Tatra KT4SU #234 @ Klaipēdas iela / Tukuma iela (2018)   (*Foto Christopher Hecht*)

Tramvajs > Fahrzeuge | *Rolling Stock* (600 V DC)

Nummer *Number*	Anzahl *Quantity*	Hersteller *Manufacturer*	Typ *Class*	Länge *Length*	Breite *Width*	Ausgeliefert *Delivered*
229, 231, 233-235	5	ČKD	Tatra KT4SU =>	19.0 m	2.30 m	1985-1988
236-241, 243-247	11	ČKD	Tatra KT4D* =>	19.0 m	2.30 m	(1979-1990) 2000-2005
250-261	1/12	KONČAR	TMK 2200 =>	21.0 m	2.30 m	2020-2022

* 236-238 ex Cottbus, 239 ex Gera, 240-247 ex Erfurt

Končar Tram #250 (25-10-2020) – in Zagreb bereit zum Transport nach Liepaja | *ready to be transported from Zagreb to Liepaja*   (*Foto Toma Bacic*)

Tatra KT4D #247 (ex Erfurt) @ Stacija

(Foto Ch. Hecht)

Tatra KT4D #239 (ex Gera) @ Kurzeme (2013)

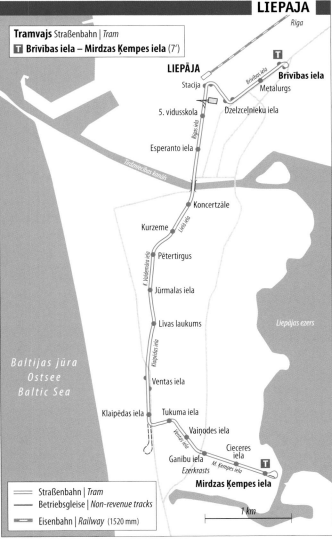

Tramvajs Straßenbahn | *Tram*

T Brīvības iela – Mirdzas Ķempes iela (7')

LIEPĀJA

Rīga

Brīvības iela

Stacija
Metalurgs
5. vidusskola
Dzelzceļnieku iela
Esperanto iela
Koncertzāle
Kurzeme
Pētertirgus
Jūrmalas iela
Līvas laukums
Ventas iela
Klaipēdas iela
Tukuma iela
Vaiņodes iela
Cieceres iela
Ganību iela
Ezerkrasts
Mirdzas Ķempes iela

Baltijas jūra
Ostsee
Baltic Sea

Liepājas ezers

Straßenbahn | *Tram*
Betriebsgleise | *Non-revenue tracks*
Eisenbahn | *Railway* (1520 mm)

1 km

LIEPĀJA (Latvija | Lettland | Latvia)

70 000 (60.4 km²)

1899

1000 mm

7.0 km

1

Liepājas Tramvajs
www.liepajas-tramvajs.lv

LST (Liepājas Sabiedriskais Transports)
www.liepajastransports.lv

Tatra KT4D #245 (ex Erfurt) @ Dzelzceļnieku iela (2013)

KTM23 #007 @ 18. novembra iela (Pilsētas poliklīnika > Baznīcu kalns)　　(Foto Wolfgang Wellige)

DAUGAVPILS

Die lettische Stadt Daugavpils (deutsch auch *Dünaburg*) liegt rund 200 km südöstlich von Riga in der Region Lettgallen (lett. *Latgale*), unweit der litauischen und weißrussischen Grenze. Beide Städte sind drei- bis viermal täglich per Bahn miteinander verbunden.

Für die Straßenbahn gibt es nur Einzelfahrscheine, die für 0,50 € beim Schaffner erhältlich sind.

Eine elektrische **Straßenbahn** bekam Lettlands zweitgrößte Stadt erst 1946, kurz nachdem die seit 1918 unabhängige Baltenrepublik als Lettische SSR in die Sowjetunion eingegliedert worden war. Die erste Strecke führte vom Bahnhof durch die Innenstadt und weiter entlang der heutigen 18. Novembra iela bis etwa zur Valkas iela (vormals Saules veikals), der Rest kam in den folgenden Jahren hinzu. Die meisten Abschnitte liegen getrennt vom Individualverkehr meist in Straßenseitenlage, wobei etwa die Hälfte des Netzes eingleisig ist. Am 5. Februar 2020 wurde der Abschnitt zwischen Brālu kapi und Stropu ezers auf eine neue 2,1 km lange Strecke umgelegt, um das Pilsētas slimnīca [Stadtkrankenhaus] besser anzuschließen.

The Latvian city of Daugavpils (also known historically as Dinaburg and Dvinsk) is located some 200 km southeast of Riga in the Latgale region, near the Lithuanian and Belarusian border. The two cities are connected by rail 3-4 times a day.

For the tram, only single-ride tickets are available, sold by a conductor for €0.50.

*An electric **tram system** was only built in Latvia's second largest city in 1946, shortly after the Baltic republic, independent since 1918, had been incorporated into the Soviet Union as the Latvian SSR. The first tram line ran from the railway station through the city centre, continuing along today's 18. Novembra iela to about Valkas iela (formerly Saules veikals), with the rest opening in the following years. Most sections are separated from road traffic and run along one side of the road, with about half the network being single-track. On 5 February 2020, the Brālu kapi — Stropu ezers section was rerouted (2.1 km) to better serve Pilsētas slimnīca [city hospital].*

DAUGAVPILS
(Latvija | Lettland | Latvia)

 82 000 (72.5 km²)

 1946

 1524 mm

 15.3 km

 3

 TU (Daugavpils Tramvaju uzņēmums)
satiksme.daugavpils.lv

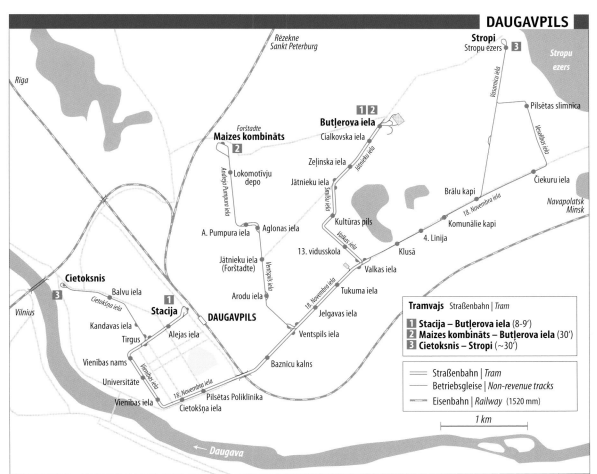

Rīga

Rēzekne
Sankt Peterburg

Stropi 3
Stropu ezers

Stropu ezers

Vilnius

Navapolatsk
Minsk

Forštadte
Maizes kombināts 2

Butļerova iela 1 2

Cialkovska iela

Zeļinska iela

Andreja Pumpura iela

Lokomotīvju depo

Jātnieku iela

Pilsētas slimnīca

Vasarnīcu iela

Veselības iela

Čiekuru iela

Brāļu kapi

A. Pumpura iela

Aglonas iela

Kultūras pils

Smilšu iela

Valkas iela

18. Novembra iela

Komunālie kapi

Jātnieku iela
(Forštadte)

13. vidusskola

Klusā

4. Līnija

Ventspils iela

Valkas iela

Cietoksnis 3

Balvu iela

Cietokšņa iela

Stacija 1

Arodu iela

Tukuma iela

DAUGAVPILS

18. Novembra iela

Jelgavas iela

Kandavas iela

Alejas iela

Tirgus

Ventspils iela

Vienības nams

Vienības iela

Baznīcu kalns

Universitāte

18. Novembra iela

Vienības iela

Cietokšņa iela

Pilsētas Poliklīnika

← **Daugava**

Tramvajs Straßenbahn | *Tram*

1 **Stacija – Butļerova iela** (8-9′)
2 **Maizes kombināts – Butļerova iela** (30′)
3 **Cietoksnis – Stropi** (~30′)

═══ Straßenbahn | *Tram*
─── Betriebsgleise | *Non-revenue tracks*
═══ Eisenbahn | *Railway* (1520 mm)

1 km

KTM31 #009 @ Valkas iela / Smilšu iela (13. Vidusskola > Kultūras pils)   *(Foto Wolfgang Wellige)*

City Star #014 @ Ventspils iela (Aglonas iela) (Foto Karl Grambergs)

Trotz in den letzten Jahren mehrfach gescheiterter Bestellungen umfasst der aktuelle Fahrzeugpark immerhin 20 Neuwagen. Die ersten wurden 2014 sehr schnell geliefert, da sie eigentlich für diverse russische Städte gebaut worden waren, womit sich der abwechslungsreiche Anstrich der Bahnen in Daugavpils erklären lässt: Die KTM23, die im mittleren Bereich einen abgesenkten Boden haben, sind in Orange/Blau u.a. auch in Moskau unterwegs, während die KTM31 (Gelenkwagen, 72% Niederflur) eigentlich für St. Petersburg bestimmt waren. Sie ergänzten KTM5-Fahrzeuge aus der Wagonfabrik Ust-Katav und die Tatra-Triebwagen, die aus Schwerin übernommen worden waren. In Daugavpils wird bis heute mit Stangenstromabnehmer gefahren. Lediglich die 2019 eingekauften „City Star", die auch bereits in zahlreichen russischen Städten im Einsatz sind, wurden mit einem Pantographen ausgerüstet. Sie sind ebenfalls im mittleren Bereich niederflurig.

Despite some cancelled orders in recent years, the current fleet includes 20 new cars; the first of which were delivered rather rapidly in 2014 as they were actually built for various Russian cities, which explains the various liveries now visible in Daugavpils: the KTM23, which have a lowered floor in the centre, can also be seen in orange and blue in Moscow, among other cities; the KTM31 cars (articulated, 72% low-floor cars) were originally intended to run in St. Petersburg. These cars complemented the KTM5 trams from Ust-Katav and the Tatra trams, which were acquired from Schwerin in Germany. The Daugavpils trams are still operated with trolley poles, except for the newest type, the 'City Star', which was delivered in 2019 and can also be seen in many Russian cities; this vehicle is equipped with a pantograph and also features a low-floor area in the centre of the tram.

Tramvajs > Fahrzeuge | *Rolling Stock* (600 V DC)						
Nummer *Number*	Anzahl *Quantity*	Hersteller *Manufacturer*	Typ *Class*	Länge *Length*	Breite *Width*	Ausgeliefert *Delivered*
070-075, 077-080	10	CKD	Tatra T3D ex-Schwerin	14.0 m	2.50 m	1973-1983
101-112	12	Ust-Kataw	KTM5 (71-605A) =>	15.1 m	2.55 m	1990-1991
001-008	8	Ust-Kataw	KTM23 (71-623) =>	16.4 m	2.50 m	2014
009-012	4	Ust-Kataw	KTM31 (71-631) =>	28.1 m	2.50 m	2014
014-021*	8	PK Transportnye Sistemy	71-911 *City Star* =>	16.4 m	2.50 m	2019

* mit Pantograph ausgerüstet | *equipped with a pantograph*

KTM5 #105 @ Vienības nams

KTM23 #002 @ 13. vidusskola   *(Foto Wolfgang Wellige)*

Tatra T3D #074 (ex Schwerin) @ Universitāte (2013)

Tatra T3D #078
(ex Schwerin)
@ Baznīcu kalns
(Foto Wolfgang Wellige)

City Star #021
(Foto Karl Grambergs)

Berkhof Premier AT18 #052 (ex Arnhem) @ Žeimenos gatvė   (Foto Christopher Hecht)

KAUNAS (Lietuva | Litauen | Lithuania)

Die mit knapp 300.000 Einwohnern zweitgrößte Stadt Litauens liegt im Zentrum des Landes, rund 90 km nordwestlich der Hauptstadt Vilnius. Beide Städte sind täglich fast stündlich per Bahn miteinander verbunden. Über Marijampolė und Šeštokai erreicht man seit 2016 auf Normalspur ohne Umsteigen Białystok in Polen, wo man Richtung Warschau umsteigen kann. Viermal täglich kommt man auch zum Grenzbahnhof Kybartai, wo Anschluss nach Kaliningrad (Königsberg) besteht.

Für Besucher, die das **Obus-Netz** von Kaunas erkunden möchten, bietet sich ein Einzelfahrschein für 1 € beim Fahrer (ohne Umsteigen) bzw. 0,70 € (mit Umsteigemöglichkeit!) mit der u.a. in Kiosken für 1,50 € erhältlichen elektronischen Smartcard (*Kauno kortelė*) – diese benötigt man auch für eine 3-Tage-Karte für 5,50 €.

In Kaunas gab es zwar von 1892 bis 1929 eine Pferdestraßenbahn, aber nie eine elektrische Tram. Der elektrisch betriebene Stadtverkehr kam schließlich erst am 31.12.1965 in Form des Obusses nach Kaunas. Heute erschließt ein dichtes Netz von 14 Linien (~ 54 km) das gesamte Stadtgebiet, wobei die wichtigsten Endpunkte jeweils direkt miteinander verbunden sind. Die Linien 9/12, 13/14 sowie 15/16 bilden dabei Linienpaare in entgegengesetzter Richtung größtenteils auf einer Ringstrecke [Fahrpläne unter *www.kvt.lt*]. Im Jahr 2004 wurden die Linien 5 und 8 zur Varnių gatvė verlängert. Zuletzt wurden 2014 Oberleitungen entlang der Parodos gatvė und K. Petrausko gatvė östlich der Innenstadt installiert.

Lithuania's second largest city has some 300,000 inhabitants and is situated in the centre of the country, some 90 km northwest of the capital Vilnius. The two cities are connected by rail almost every hour. Since 2016, some standard-gauge trains have travelled directly via Marijampolė and Šeštokai to Białystok in Poland, where a connection to Warsaw is available. Four trains a day go to the border station Kybartai, from where connecting trains run to Kaliningrad.

*For visitors who want to explore the Kaunas **trolleybus system**, a single ticket is available from the driver for €1.00 (without transfer), or for €0.70 (allowing transfer!) with an electronic smartcard (Kauno kortelė) available for example in kiosks for €1.50. This card is also required for a 3-day pass sold for €5.50.*

Although Kaunas once had a horse tramway from 1892 to 1929, there has never been an electric tram. Electrically-powered urban transport finally came to Kaunas on 31 December 1965 in the form of the trolleybus. Today, the entire city is covered by a network of 14 lines (~54 km) whose most important termini are directly connected. Lines 9/12, 13/14 and 15/16 represent line pairs which operate in opposite directions on a route which is mostly circular. The last new sections to be built were the routes of lines 5 and 8 to Varnių gatvė in 2004, and in 2014, overhead wires were installed along Parodos gatvė and K. Petrausko gatvė at the eastern side of the city centre.

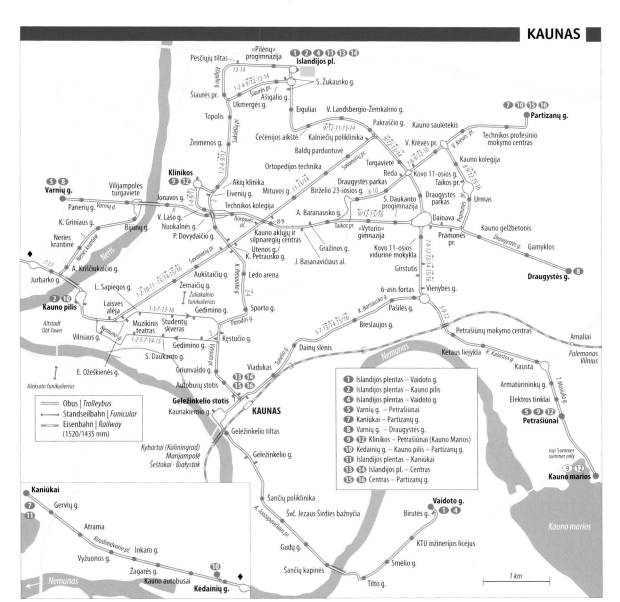

Der aktuelle Fahrzeugpark besteht aus ca. 150 Bussen, vorwiegend Niederflur-Solo-bussen (T12) von Solaris/ Cegelec aus den Jahren 2006/2007 bzw. 2019/2020. Dazu kamen 2016/2017 15 gebrauchte Gelenk-Obusse aus dem niederländischen Arnhem (Nr. 043-057). Das Obus-Netz wird von der städtischen *Kauno Autobusai* betrieben [*www.kaunoautobusai.lt*].

The current trolleybus fleet consists of approximately 150 vehicles, most of which are low-floor solo buses of type T12 from Solaris/Cegelec built in 2006/2007 and 2019/2020. In 2016/2017, 15 second-hand articulated trolleybuses (nos. 043-057) were taken over from Arnhem in the Netherlands. The trolleybus system is operated by 'Kauno Autobusai' [www.kaunoautobusai.lt].

Solaris Trollino T12 #042 @ Savanorių pr. (Laisvės alėja)

1 Islandijos plentas – Vaidoto g.
2 Islandijos plentas – Kauno pilis
4 Islandijos plentas – Vaidoto g.
5 Varnių g. – Petrašiūnai
7 Kaniūkai – Partizanų g.
8 Varnių g. – Draugystės g.
9 12 Klinikos – Petrašiūnai (Kauno Marios)
10 Kėdainių g. – Kauno pilis – Partizanų g.
11 Islandijos plentas – Kaniūkai
13 14 Islandijos pl. – Centras
15 16 Centras – Partizanų g.

Obus | *Trolleybus*
Standseilbahn | *Funicular*
Eisenbahn | *Railway*
(1520/1435 mm)

Solaris T15 #2716 @ Stotis (Bahnhof | *Railway Station*)

VILNIUS (Lietuva | Litauen | Lithuania)

Die Hauptstadt Litauens (auf deutsch auch *Wilna*; 590.000 Einw.) liegt im Südosten des Landes, nur 30 km von der weißrussischen Grenze entfernt. Mit dem ca. 90 km nordwestlich gelegenen Kaunas ist Vilnius täglich fast stündlich per Bahn verbunden, ins knapp 200 km entfernte Minsk kommt man mehrmals täglich mit der Bahn. Der Flughafen ist etwa stündlich mit Dieseltriebwagen erreichbar, nach Trakai verkehren elektrische Triebwagen bis zu neun Mal pro Tag.

Besucher besorgen sich in Vilnius am besten an Kiosken eine elektronische Smartcard Vilniečio Kortelė für 1,50 € und laden sie mit einer Tageskarte (5 €) bzw. 3- oder 5-Tage-Karte (8/12 €) auf [siehe *www.vilniustransport.lt*].

In Vilnius fuhr von 1893 bis 1916 eine schmalspurige Pferdestraßenbahn, das Netz wurde aber nie elektrifiziert. Stattdessen wurden die Wagen mit einem Verbrennungsmotor ausgestattet und fuhren damit von 1920 bis 1926. Der elektrische Stadtverkehr zog in Vilnius erst 1956 in Form von **Obussen** ein. Heute erschließt ein weitläufiges Netz (~ 57 km) fast das gesamte Stadtgebiet, die Altstadt wird allerdings nur an der Westseite tangiert. Der Takt der insgesamt 18 Linien ist je nach Linie sehr unterschiedlich und tageszeitabhängig, von 1-3 Mal pro Stunde (Linien 3, 14, 15, 18, 21) bis hin zu alle paar Minuten während der Hauptverkehrszeit (Linien 2, 7, 16, 17).

Auch wenn in den letzten Jahren zahlreiche neue Obusse geliefert wurden, ist der aktuelle Fahrzeugpark weiterhin etwa zur Hälfte hochflurig: Dazu gehören ca. 160 Busse vom Typ 14Tr und 15Tr von Škoda aus den 1980er und 1990er Jahren. 2004-2006 tauchten die ersten Niederflur-Solobusse vom Typ T15 AC von Solaris/Cegelec auf, außerdem seit 2012 zwei Fahrzeuge litauischer

The capital of Lithuania (590,000 inh.) is located in the southeast of the country, just 30 km from the border with Belarus. Kaunas, some 90 km northwest, is linked to Vilnius by train about every hour. Minsk, only 200 km away, can be reached by train several times a day. The airport is served roughly every hour by DMUs, while electric trains operate to Trakai up to nine times a day.

Visitors to Vilnius can best enjoy the city's transport system with a day pass after acquiring an electronic smartcard called 'Vilniečio Kortelė', which is available from kiosks for €1.50. A one-day pass is €5, 3 days cost €8, and 5 days €12 [see www.vilniustransport.lt].

*From 1893 to 1916, Vilnius had a narrow-gauge horse tramway, but the network was never electrified. Instead, the cars were equipped with fuel engines and operated in that way from 1920 to 1926. Electric transport only arrived in Vilnius in 1956 in the form of **trolleybuses**. Today, an extensive network (~ 57 km) serves almost the entire city, although the Old Town is only skirted on its western side. Headways on the 18 lines vary significantly depending on the line and time of the day, from a bus 1-3 times an hour (lines 3, 14, 15, 18, 21) to a bus every few minutes during peak hours (lines 2, 7, 16, 17).*

Although numerous new vehicles have been purchased in recent years, almost 50% of Vilnius' trolleybus fleet is still made up of high-floor buses; among them some 160 Škoda 14Tr and 15Tr vehicles from the 1980s and 1990s. The first low-floor solo buses of type T15 AC from Solaris/ Cegelec were introduced in 2004-2006, and since 2012, there have also been two vehicles of type MAZ 203T Amber Vilnis 12 AC, manufactured in Lithuania. With a total of 75 vehicles, Solaris added a significant number of

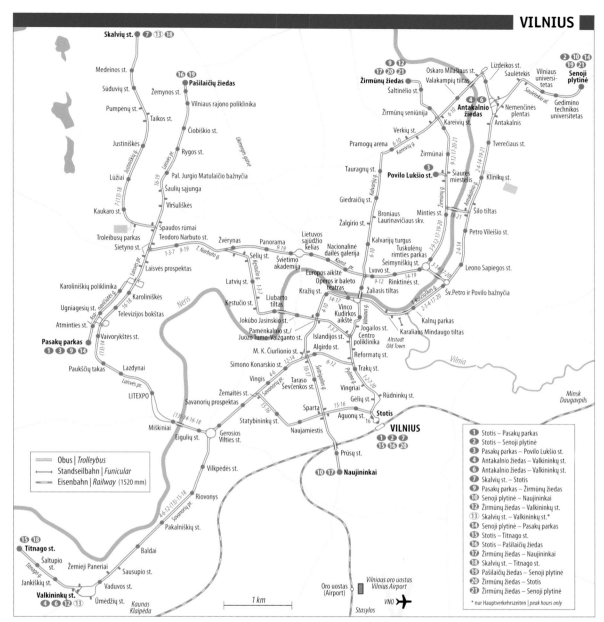

Eigenproduktion vom Typ MAZ 203T Amber Vilnis 12 AC. Mit 75 Stück lieferte Solaris 2018-2019 eine größere Anzahl vom Typ Trollino IV 12, weitere Fahrzeuge sind ausgeschrieben.

Die zögerliche Neubeschaffung von Obussen mag auch daran liegen, dass man in Vilnius seit Langem über den Bau einer Stadtbahn oder gar Metro diskutiert. Eine erste, ca. 10 km lange Stadtbahn-Strecke soll vom Bahnhof dem Fahrweg der Obusstammstrecke durch die Innenstadt nach Norden entlang der Kalvarijų gatvė bis Tauragnų st. folgen und dann weiter in nördlicher Richtung Santariškės (Uniklinikum) erreichen. Eine zweite Linie entlang der Ukmergės gatvė soll die Großsiedlungen im Nordwesten erschließen, die dritte Linie würde etwa der Obuslinie 16 folgen.

its Trollino IV 12 in 2018-2019, with more new trolleybuses currently being tendered.

The rather late acquisition of new trolleybuses may also be due to the fact that in Vilnius the construction of a light rail system or even a metro has long been under discussion: the first 10 km light rail route would run north along the existing trolleybus corridor from the railway station through the city centre, and then along Kalvarijų gatvė to the Tauragnų stop, from where it would continue due north to reach Santariškės (University Hospital). A second line is planned along Ukmergės gatvė to serve the large residential districts in the northwest, while a third line would basically follow trolleybus line 16.

VVT (Vilniaus viešasis transportas) – www.vilniausviesasistransportas.lt